T0208361

LIFE LIVED INSIDE OUT

A Memoir

Bette Logan

iUniverse, Inc.
New York   Bloomington

LIFE LIVED INSIDE OUT
A Memoir

Author photo by Lenore Juan.

iUniverse books may be ordered through booksellers or by contacting:

iUniverse
1663 Liberty Drive
Bloomington, IN 47403
www.iuniverse.com
1-800-Authors (1-800-288-4677)

Because of the dynamic nature of the Internet, any Web addresses or links contained in this book may have changed since publication and may no longer be valid.

ISBN: 978-1-4502-0124-7 (sc)
ISBN: 978-1-4502-0125-4 (ebk)

Printed in the United States of America

iUniverse rev. date: 04/30/2010

For my grandchildren
Kirsten Readman and Jason Readman
Your doors will open. Be ready.

And for my children
Cheryl, Pam, Bill, Brenda and Belinda
In the hope that things become clearer, more understandable.

ACKNOWLEDGMENTS

Joan Read served as listener, sounding board and confidante from the time this memoir was a vague idea. As the writing progressed, her readings of various sections and opinions regarding content and matters of style were invaluable. I don't know how I could have completed the work without her constant presence and support.

When I had confused autobiography with memoir, Karen Connolly not only straightened me out, but encouraged me. Through Karen I was led to Kelly Dignan as editor. Kelly's sharp eye for organization and continuity helped shaped the story into its present, improved, form. I am so grateful to both.

To Joanne Drummond, Janice Paquette and June Pennie, I express my eternal friendship. They've lived this story with me twice now and are still friends. All three assisted in the retrieval of hazy memories, Joanne served as first reader, and both Joanne and Janice helped with proofreading. Their help is deeply appreciated.

I am indebted and thankful to the following people for help with proofreading of various sections of the manuscript: Lyn Adamson, Lesley Clarke, Ghislain Deridder, Kirsten Romaine Jones, Annik Vivier and Molly Walsh. Any remaining errors are mine.

To David Evans, who read the finished manuscript and helped in practical ways concerning the actual submission of the text to the publisher, I extend a grateful expression of appreciation. His help at that critical time, when I was suffering the terror of the project actually coming into being, was not only functionally supportive, but provided much-needed reassurance.

Budding Interest

(August 1975—December 1976)

A PERFECT SUMMER AFTERNOON, warm and sunny, scheduled activities have geared down, and quietness has settled over the park after the days of buzz and bustle. A secret smugness is niggling inside, satisfaction at having come right down to the finish line without a blow up.

August 5, 1975. Civic Holiday. Pam, her friend Pat, Brenda, Belinda and I have come to my mother's cottage on Lake Couchiching for the holiday regatta, an annual event of land and water races, games, prizes, and a Saturday night dance. The most important weekend of the summer at Scarlet Park and the children look forward to it each year, just as I did when I was their age. The girls are to stay with their grandmother for the week.

For me, a fun-filled holiday weekend, it has not been. More of an endurance test. Three long days of Applied Psychology. Friday evening, all day Saturday, Sunday, right up to past noon Monday, and my diversionary tactics (changing the subject, finding work to do, going to an event) have succeeded. We've made it through without a Scene. My mother is big on Scenes. No meeting with either my brother or me is complete without one.

We're eating tuna sandwiches and potato chips outside, under the shade trees, all except Brenda who is in bed with a sore throat and fever. I'm actually feeling content, enjoying the sandwiches—they taste summery—and thinking of the nice quiet, restful week to come, the house to myself, time my own. I'm also gloriously unaware that at this very moment, back in North Bay, my future is taking shape. Events are in progress, a trajectory is being carved that will, in time, converge with my own path. I sip my lemonade.

My mother is holding forth with her ideas on the "place of women," and I'm holding my tongue. Her idea is that women should not work outside the home if they have a husband to support them. I think she's secretly jealous because when she married she was forced, as was the custom of the day, to give up a fulfilling job and potential career as a graphic artist. She has the right to feel cheated; I just wish she could be honest about it.

"Take Mrs. Johnson in the brown cottage over there," my mother says, turning to Pat, picking, as usual, the defenceless outsider, the one who can be counted on not to contradict. "She's married to a bank manager and she works. A woman like that"—she throws it in Pat's face—"takes a job away from a young person like you."

"That's a bunch of crap!"

It's out! Oh, God, it's out, and it didn't even pass by my brain. And with it flies a whole weekend of peace.

"I know what you are!" my mother lashes back. "You're one of those women's libbers, that's what you are!" This comes out so fast it must have been right there at the surface, boiling, ready. "I know about women's libbers!"

she cuts. It's a weapon. "And I know what Ms stands for, too!" She's gaining strength, coming to full force. "Loose woman, that's what it stands for. Loose woman! And that's what *you* are. Aren't you?"

I don't answer. I get up, go into the cottage and start cleaning up the kitchen. But she's right behind me, screaming out all the things she knows are wrong with women's lib, with women's libbers, and with this women's libber in particular.

"Stop," I tell her, my voice lowering. "Just stop now." But she won't. On and on she goes.

"Just . . . quit . . . now." I enunciate it slowly and quietly, resolved to avoid a scene, but I'm in the midst of one anyway. This is definitely a Scene.

My mother is yelling—to the neighbours, to the whole park, the whole world maybe—issuing a declaration of my deficiencies, of which there are many. Belinda is crying; she's only five. Brenda is moaning; she's sick and doesn't need this. Finally I shout on top of it all, "Shut up! Just shut up now!"

But she's not about to shut up.

"Why do you come here anyway?" It's the bait, the demand for participation. This is what she wants, what she thrives on, but I'm determined not to take it. I don't answer.

"You have a nerve coming here," she accuses, "foisting your children off on me like this!" That stops me cold, thrusts me into a different state: unemotional and detached. There's no arguing, no fighting, no reasoning after a statement like that. It's a knockout blow.

"Get out of here! Get out and take your children with you!" she commands. "Pack up and go home!"

I can't believe she would go this far, even though I know she once did the same thing to my brother and his family. I go to Brenda's room to check her fever. Mom rushes in, yanks open a drawer and starts pulling out Brenda's clothes. Belinda is sobbing that she wants to go home. "Me, too," croaks Brenda. She's really quite sick. They came here looking forward to spending time at the cottage, playing with their friends from other years. "Yes," I tell them, "we'll pack."

I go out and tell Pam the situation, but Pam, as usual, lets Grandma's behaviour roll off her back. "We'll stay," she says, and off she and Pat go to the beach to find their friends.

I pack up our things with Belinda's help; my mother doesn't say another word. Total silence. Is she sorry? Does she realize what she's done? I will never know. What I do know is it will be a long time before I subject myself to this behaviour again.

Brenda lies down in the back seat of the car and we set out for North Bay. When we pull onto the highway I turn on the radio and learn there are roadblocks throughout the area because Donald Kelly has escaped from the North Bay jail.

I KNEW THE NAME, of course; everyone in North Bay knew the name. It had been the subject of gossip and speculation ever since the murders of Carol and Jack MacWilliams back in 1969. Everyone "knew" Kelly had done it, but there appeared to be no evidence to prove it. Eventually, however, six years later, in the spring of 1975, Kelly, Jim Lavin and Ian Rose were all arrested in different locations in Canada and brought back to North Bay to stand trial.

Intrigue and mystery had surrounded the case from the beginning, and gossip reached fever pitch when the courthouse was broken into and evidence stolen. Shortly after that, Kelly, on a visit with his mother in an area adjacent to the side door of the jail, seized his moment during a delivery of groceries. He bolted for the open door, ran out to the parking lot where he grabbed from a parked truck a rifle that had apparently been previously planted, raced down the driveway and out onto the busy Trout Lake Road where he commandeered an approaching car. The manhunt was on.

When we got home from the cottage, my friend Paula phoned and suggested that she keep the children while I went to work, an offer I readily accepted as Brenda was only 11; I wouldn't have left them alone in any event, but I certainly couldn't with a desperado on the loose.

North Bay was a more-or-less sleepy town of about 51,000 people, and this was excitement. More than excitement, it was panic, near-hysteria: an "armed and dangerous" criminal, accused of murder, at large in our midst. Radio and television news flashed constantly, warning us of the danger; a fearful citizenry began locking its doors.

Wednesday the news came out that the car Kelly started out in had become stuck in a gravel pit and over the course of the next twenty-four hours he had accumulated captives: first, one young man; two more several hours later; then three more people in a car (out looking for the latter two). The seven had spent the night together, stopping for a time at the home of one of the captives, driving around, and finally had descended on a family at their lakeside cottage. By noon he had left the group tied up, a total, by then, of ten detainees. All those people, all that time, and no one harmed. I did have to ask myself: How dangerous can he be? Nevertheless, Brenda and Belinda continued to go to Paula's house until Pam came back.

From the start, the story was compelling. Helicopters circled over residential areas; several times when I drove out of the city I was stopped at gunpoint by police at roadblocks and required to get out and open the trunk.

Hundreds of police officers were brought in from all over Ontario. "Wanted" posters, with photo, were distributed: Reward $5,000; white male; age 37; height 5'10"; black hair (greying); brown eyes; Subject considered extremely dangerous.

The photo must have been the mug shot because it was the only one ever published, yet it was not the full-on frontal image one expects. He's turned slightly to the side and his gaze, difficult to read, goes to the left. It's a serene expression and he seems on the verge of a smile, which is odd given the circumstances of the picture-taking. The face presents an intriguing mixture of strength (high cheek bones, strong jaw line, lean musculature) and softness (the eyes and mouth).

Eight days later news, still at a pitch, was heightened yet again when it was revealed that the previous day from early morning until midnight he had held another eleven people captive at a campsite about 100 km away. The Nugget featured a fuzzy photo taken by the campers of Kelly, now with a scruffy beard, crouched beside the campfire, rifle across his knees. When he left that group he took the car of one of the campers, drove into the city and abandoned it on Seventh Avenue, the street behind ours. Suspicion that he was hiding in a nearby house prompted the OPP to call out their newly-created Tactics and Rescue Unit, popularly called the "SWAT team," on its very first operation, which caused an excited crowd to gather on our street corner in anticipation.

No news for another week but the manhunt continued in all its intensity; false sightings occurred in various locations, including Calgary. Then we heard that an elderly man and his grandson had been taken captive west of North Bay and had driven the fugitive over to the Sudbury area. So far, a total of twenty-three people had been taken and not one had been hurt. Media coverage with its "armed and extremely dangerous" image was relentless, but North Bayites were starting to get a bit light-hearted about it. The local radio station played "Has Anybody Here Seen Kelly?" frequently—it was a bit of a laugh—but the police were worried he was becoming a folk hero and put a stop to it.

Eventually, after twenty-eight days, news flashed that Kelly had been captured in a shootout at an isolated cabin on the Wanapitei River near Skead. And that was that. Story finished. Or should have been.

Escape stories had always captured my imagination. From early days I gobbled up any such story, no matter whether escape from prison, prisoner of war camp, or concentration camp. They all appealed, made the heart beat. Not only the escape but the chase as well, for the pursuers must have the same skills as the pursued: ability to plan and do advance reconnoitring, secretiveness and inventiveness, stealth and bravado, logical thinking, exactness of timing.

In the 50's, Toronto (where I lived) was scene of one of Canada's biggest escape stories when the Boyd gang escaped from the Don Jail. I followed every detail of the hunt and capture.

And so the Kelly escape stayed in my mind. I wondered about the timing. Did he know the grocery delivery would take place at that particular moment? Did he arrange for his mother's visit to be co-incident? Who planted the gun in the truck? How did the captives react? What did they talk about in those long hours? How did he survive, alone in the bush? Why didn't he get out of the area? There were endless questions to be answered. And then there was the underlying contrast between the police action—helicopters, door-to-door searches, SWAT team—and the almost-idyllic photo (except for the rifle) of a guy beside a campfire. More and more I felt this was an intriguing story—a book.

SEVEN MONTHS AFTER THE CAPTURE, Kelly was convicted on the murder charges and given a life sentence with eligibility for parole in ten years. His case had been severed from that of Rose and Lavin as it was thought his notoriety could adversely affect their trial. An order had also been made for a change of venue to Toronto where it was believed unbiased jurors were more likely to be found. In reality, publicity had been intense all over Ontario and even nationally. It was while eavesdropping on passengers lined up behind me at the Vancouver airport for a flight to San Francisco that I learned of the capture.

Shortly after his conviction, Kelly was returned to North Bay for a preliminary hearing into the twenty-eight charges with respect to the jailbreak and ensuing events, which included charges of forcible confinement, kidnapping, armed robbery, possession of a weapon dangerous to the public peace, and prison breach. At the time I was working for the Ministry of Community and Social Services as a Parental Support Worker, the functions of which were performed mostly outside the office, in clients' homes and at Family Court. As such I had no set office hours. So, taking advantage of my freedom, to satisfy curiosity, I attended part of the first day's hearing.

The defendant is led into the prisoner's box like a dog, on a two-foot-long leather leash, his left wrist attached to that of a police officer. He's a drab figure in jeans and a grey-blue shirt, dark hair grey-streaked and in need of both a wash and a cut. Good-looking enough, but expressionless, flat. His right arm is in a cast. In all, seeing him in the flesh is anti-climactic.

Evidence is presented about the jailbreak itself. Not so interesting. Assuming the captives will testify the next day, I adjourn myself after an hour and go back to work. The second day, in no time, ordinary courtroom procedures transform themselves into riveting real-life theatre, and I'm compelled to return session after session. Action, drama, suspense, even flashes of humour emerge as the "actors" deliver their lines and the central character, enigmatic throughout, watches from the side.

The first captive, it turns out, was, at the time of his capture, a police cadet, a fact he judiciously kept to himself. I look at Kelly for his reaction to this news. None. A young woman relates how she quizzed him about how much time he had spent in prison, how he had gotten into a life of crime, why he had escaped. Another, in mid-testimony, turns directly to Kelly in the prisoner's box and blurts out, "I don't know what you were thinking, but I was. . . ." before the judge can stop her. Kelly lowers his head and blushes. The man who owned the cottage where ten people were left tied up is cranky, vitriolic, glares venomously at the prisoner each time he refers to him. A theme has developed, a portrait of how individuals, according to their varying personalities and characters, react differently to the same situation. It has all the drama of a theatrical production, a drama even more compelling than I had guessed.

Few are in attendance, so my note-taking is probably what gets his attention. Exchange of glances at various points of evidence start taking place, a silent commentary on points that are surprising or shocking or make a statement of one sort or another, an optic conversation transmitted with never a change of expression on either side, never a frown, never a smile, never a face turned into a question mark.

OPP Officer Giannini takes the stand and describes searching along the Wanapitei River with Officer Ray Carson and his police dog, Cloud II. Cloud was a well-known animal hero who had won the Purina Animal Hall of Fame award for bravery and had appeared on the popular television show, Front Page Challenge. The officer describes how they came across a guy standing on the porch of a cabin.

The denouement. I look over at Kelly. How does he feel about this part? No clues in his face.

Giannini's testimony is deliberate, clear and exact.

"Do you work here?" he says Carson asked the guy.

"Yes, but is it ever a nice day to go fishing."

"Kelly!" Carson yelled, let the dog go and fired. Kelly grabbed his 30-30 by the barrel and jumped over a washstand at the far end of the porch, falling over it in the attempt.

"Shoot the bastard!" yelled Carson. With that Giannini ran forward, firing three times with his sawed-off 12-gauge semi-automatic shotgun, aiming at "the biggest part of the body—between the shoulder blades," as he stated.

The eye contact becomes more frequent and more intense.

Kelly was rolling down the hill, the dog hanging on to him, numerous shots hailing on them. Within seconds Cloud was down, Giannini specifies, and Kelly had disappeared into the bush at the bottom of the hill. I send my message: *They buried that dog as a hero, in a flag-draped coffin, with a twenty-four-person honour guard, and everyone thinks you shot it.*

The two officers retreated to the front of the cabin where they attempted, but failed, to raise assistance by radio; they then climbed to the top of a ridge a half-mile away, where they were successful. Ten minutes later they heard three shots but ignored them.

Three shots. I transmit my understanding: *the conventional distress signal in wilderness survival. They were going to let you die.*

You see, he answers, *you see what happened. That's their version of a shoot-out.* Thus emerged the second theme of the play: information propagated by the media is suspect. Beware.

Everything I saw and heard in the testimony convinced me this was a story that had to be told. The idea of writing it engulfed me, but what had I ever written beyond letters and university essays? Even if those efforts were often praised, how did I deign to imagine *I*—ordinary *me*—could do something of this magnitude?

Still, the idea had grabbed me and wouldn't let go. And so, a week after the preliminary hearing, on an afternoon labouring under the oppressive skies of a brooding storm, the kind of day that normally sinks me into inertia and despair, I inexplicably gained the courage to pick up the phone and call Donald Kelly's mother. In my naivety I assumed it wouldn't be possible for the general public to contact him directly, nor did I think an approach to write a book would be favourably received by the authorities, so I had decided to ask his mother to contact him for me. I called, she invited me over, and the next thing I knew my name was on his visiting list and the two of us were on our way to Millhaven Maximum Security Penitentiary near Kingston.

MYRTLE IS READY and waiting when I buzz her apartment at 6:30 a.m. She's excited, talkative, cheerful. I'm not ready for chatter so early in the morning; I need a coffee. When I ask her if she wants one, she says as a Seventh-day Adventist she abstains from stimulants. I pull into Tim Horton's thinking maybe I'd better get a double; it's going to be a long trip.

Myrtle is probably early-sixties, white-haired, with a stocky build and twinkly eyes. In the first hundred kilometers I learn some of the complexities of her life: how frightened she was that her son would be killed in the manhunt, how difficult it was living with all the publicity; she seems to be close to her other son who lives out west but comes to see her periodically; she has a daughter and grandchildren in Sudbury but doesn't see them often enough, it's expensive to go there, and they're so busy they rarely have time to come to North Bay; she lost a sixteen year-old daughter in a car crash. Her good-humour is a wonder; I would be incapable of a smile if I had to bear her load. Yet she has a hearty laugh, and is full of energy and enthusiasm.

The trip takes us eastward, roughly following the route of the Ottawa River through the familiar hills and rocks of the Canadian Shield to Pembroke. There I pull into a shopping centre for a rest stop and to buy shampoo. Myrtle says she's not supposed to buy anything on the Sabbath but she buys a pair of pantyhose, some Kleenex and two chocolate bars, one for each of us. From there we head south into rolling farmlands. The conversation is agreeable but my part requires considerably more listening than talking. Six hours is a long time. I make a note that my next car must have a radio.

Each hour becomes progressively more anxious than the previous. Doubts, nervousness, flagging self-confidence descend on me. What will I say? Can I present myself as capable? By the time we reach the stark flatness of Highway 401, limestone-lined and unfamiliar, the full impact of what I'm doing leaps up and seizes me. My stomach goes into full revolt and calls for a stop at the nearest gas station.

Back on the road, we turn south—hesitantly, reluctantly—to Lake Ontario and follow the shoreline west until we come to a billboard-sized sign. The driveway is lined with greenery and flowers; it curves and enters a clearing in another world. A dismal, sprawling building squats behind high link fences draped with rolls of barbed wire, gun towers looming at intervals. I don't know how I can do this. I don't *want* to do this. We pull into Visitors' Parking, lock the doors in compliance with the warning sign, and then it's a long, woozy walk to the guard's post at the gate.

Reality goes in and out of focus. The officer's lips are moving, but his voice is not connected, it surges intermittently from some other place, from a pit or a tunnel somewhere.

"Who . . . see?"

I don't want to see anybody, I want to go home, are the words I want my parched mouth to produce, but I've lost all sense of autonomy; I'm in a machine, clutched in its gears. Time extends. Things come back into focus, and I realize I must have indeed uttered the words he wanted to hear, my trembling hands must have given over the required ID, because we've locked our purses in a locker and the gate is sliding open before us in command.

We step in, it slides shut behind us, and we're trapped between the fences in a little area cordoned off from the guard dogs that are circling, eyeing us more with boredom than suspicion I think, although I wouldn't want to test the theory. Myrtle seems unfazed, but she has undoubtedly done this a few times in her life. I look at her in awe and pity. Being the mother of Donald

Kelly can't be easy. The thought reverses itself, stands on its head, but I banish it. We're between the fences a long time, controlled by unseen but watching eyes. I'm shaking, sweating, gasping for breath, feeling faint. Then, just as I think I can't take any more, the gate slides open, the machine grabs me again and pulls me up to the entrance, numb.

We're in the waiting room, which is just inside the door. "If he doesn't want to see me," I tell Myrtle, "that's all right. I'm happy to just bring you here." We sit in silence for five or ten or twenty minutes until the officer tells us we can go in. "Don't worry about me. I'm fine here," I assure her, and send her in alone. Maybe he doesn't want to see me anyway. He probably has a dozen people who want to write a book, all of them more qualified than me.

I've convinced myself I'm off the hook. I'm doing something good here: his mother has no other opportunity to come to see him. Yes, it would be just fine if I didn't see him at all, if I just did this good deed and went home. I'm starting to feel almost relaxed in the unwelcoming waiting room with its dingy, faded Institutional Green walls, a framed copy of the Visiting Rules their only adornment. Every surface—chairs, walls, floor—is hard, harsh. I'm busy analyzing the psychology of all this when the visit officer calls me over to his window and tells me to go in. The door buzzes. I do what a buzzing door tells me to do, I open it. It's heavy, crashes behind me, echoes. I enter a bleak space.

Overwhelming drabness. A big cement-walled area, windowless and smelling of dust and sweat. Inside this space, in a glassed-in room within a room, are the prisoners who sit at carrels, facing their visitors. Guards watch through a windowed office at one end. The first person I see is Kelly, and he's looking at me. Our eyes meet. He's at the third window, but there are no visitors at the first two. I have the sensation of walking slowly, for a long time. His face gives not the slightest hint of reaction, nor does mine, but something is happening with the eyes: a connection, palpable, reassuring. Time and space expand. I walk and walk, even though it's a short distance—not more than four meters. I have time to breathe, time to feel the calm settling within. It's all strangely familiar, unexpectedly comfortable. I walk the invisible thread, eyes engaged the while, and sit down beside Myrtle, at ease; I know I will be understood.

"I tried to find out who you were," he says without preamble, "but couldn't. I asked Mike Boland to find out for me."

"Well, he should have known," I tell him. "I've been to see him a couple of times." Because Boland was the lawyer I had consulted when my husband sold our house in Trout Creek and I got nothing. "But he sees a lot of clients."

"He said he asked a couple of people, but they didn't know."

"Well, the cops knew. They asked who I was, what I was doing."

He's lost weight since the court appearance, I think, and has a sallow, sun-deprived complexion. He's wearing a dark green shirt—prison regulation—over a white T-shirt, and green pants. His hair is slicked back on one side and hanging down almost over the eye on the other side in an out-of-date style that gives him a faintly sinister appearance. He still has the cast on his arm.

"What's wrong with your arm?"

"They shattered it when they shot me down."

"But that was almost a year ago."

"Yeah, but they had to put a pin and a plate in. There's a piece of bone this big missing," and he curls his thumb and index finger together to indicate the size of a large marble. "It's nearly time to take it off."

"Are you right-handed?"

"No, left."

"Well, that's lucky." Interesting, too, I think. File that for future reference: left-handed, right-brained. Creative? Widened range of abilities? Sensitive?

We spoke through a metal grille below the glass. The conversation rolled along just as if it were a continuation from another time. And in a sense, it was. We talked about the captives; he gave me his perceptions of them and how they handled the situation. I gave him my impressions from court. He asked me general questions, about my job, my family, asked how old I was. "Thirty-nine," I told him. "And how long have you been thirty-nine?" he shot back—a too-fast retort that brought on the first laughter.

There were only a few visits in progress. More laughter could be heard from a couple of spaces to my left, but across the way, on the other side of the prisoners' room, a woman was crying. Two small children ran around shrieking. It was difficult to hear at times; he was very soft-spoken.

He told me about the group he had gathered on the first day and how they had sat outside the Thompson cottage for a few hours, waiting for daylight. Even though there were men's clothes on the clothesline he decided he *had* to leave them there, regardless, and make his getaway; it was almost twenty-four hours since the escape.

"We start down the hill, me behind the group, and here comes Old Man Thompson. I tell Charlene to tell him who I am and what's happening. Before she can finish, he starts shouting at me, 'I don't give a goddamn if you *are* Donald Kelly, get the hell out of here,' stuff like that, and starts toward me. I'm backing up, the gun's pointed at him now, and he keeps coming at me, yelling, 'Get off my property! I don't want any of your kind around here!'

"I tell Charlene to calm him down, tell him what I want, but he doesn't stop. I thought he was going to have a heart attack on the spot, or a stroke—he's overweight, you know.

"So I tell Charlene to tie his hands behind his back until he calms down, and we go down to the cottage. I ask Mrs. Thompson for a sandwich, she turns and asks the others if they want something—she was trying to be the hostess—but every time she opened her mouth, he snapped at her: 'Why don't you be quiet? Don't say anything.' The way he treated her and the young girls, that Old Man Thompson sure was some misogynist."

"Misogynist!" I blurt unabashedly, "I don't know *anyone* who knows that word!"

MYRTLE AND I FOUND an excellent place to stay overnight in Kingston, a small apartment normally rented to university students, cheap because it was off-season. We bought some food in a supermarket and had a nice supper and were early to bed. She, on her side of the room, in her twin bed, drifted off immediately while I found sleep difficult. The conversation replayed in my head. So easy. Enjoyable, actually. Relaxed. So relaxed I forgot to portray myself as an author, if not experienced, at least capable, and resolved to do better in the morning.

Very near the start of the second visit, Kelly said he had two questions to ask. He stretched himself up to full height, took a drag on his cigarette, and paused. He could be good-looking. The geography is there. Good features. Give him some sunshine, a decent haircut, regular clothes, take the burden off his back, and he would certainly be good-looking. The eyes are distinctive— dark brown, deep.

"What do you think about the murder conviction?"

"With what I know right now," I start without a pause, even though I have no idea what's going to come out; I don't want him to see he's caught me off guard. "And I only know what I've read in the newspapers, and that's probably not the whole story." I'm gathering myself, for I have to say it, whether he likes it or not. "With what I know now, if I were on the jury. . . ." I look him straight in the eye, "I would vote Guilty." He studies the cigarette for a few seconds, gives a barely perceptible nod of the head, and says nothing.

"As I see it," I add, "that doesn't change a hair on your head, does it? You're still the same person whether you did or didn't."

No change in expression, no comment. A long pause.

"And what about Cloud?" he asks, "What do you think about the dog?"

There was no question in my mind about that.

"Well, that was clear in the OPP's evidence, wasn't it? They shot their own dog; there's no dispute about that."

"It bothers me more that they say I shot the dog than the people."

"Well, that's because you know the police know you didn't shoot the dog, but they probably believe you shot the people. If you had shot the dog—or shot at the police—you can be sure there would have been a few more charges on top of the twenty-eight you got."

He told me the whole story of the capture. Said he knew the cabin from years past, friends of his owned it. He hoped they didn't take too much flack for it. He tried the door, he said, and looked around for a key with no luck. He was just standing there, chuckling over a joke sign tacked beside the door, something about no maid service, when he heard footsteps. It was too late to do anything except act casual.

"At first I thought I could pull it off, my hat half-covered my face. But then Carson yells, 'Kelly!' I turn to grab my rifle and his first shot gets me here." He indicates a spot on his back, near the shoulder. "I jump over the washstand and they get me again here and here," and he taps the places in the back and the back of the arm. "Cloud has me by the sleeve; we're rolling down the bank, all tangled up together, getting peppered. He rears up, looks me right in the eye, gives a sigh, and sinks down."

At the bottom of the hill, Kelly looked up. No sign of them, so he went into the bushes to check his wounds—twelve in all, some bleeding badly, burning and sore. Then he started coughing blood.

"I know I won't last long if my lungs are shot so I fire three shots. I wait a long time but no one comes, so I go into the river to slow the bleeding. Soon three guys in a motorboat come along. I ask them to help me. They take one look at the blood and turn tail, so I decide right then that if I'm going to die, I'm going to do it in bed.

"I can't walk for pain—I'm sure my leg is broken—I have to crawl on my hands and knees—or one hand and knees, I should say, because my right arm won't hold my weight."

He struggled up the hill, turned and kicked in the bottom part of the door, squeezed through the hole, and, freezing cold, pulled off his soaking wet jacket, cut off his two shirts and rolled up in blankets on one of the beds. He was "just at a comfortable stage" when the police started shooting up the place with tear gas canisters, which were defective, as we learned in court. He had lost so much blood he needed two transfusions when they got him to the hospital in Sudbury.

He was a great talker. He liked to talk about his story, enjoyed the notoriety no doubt, but he also asked me lots of questions and we talked about some general things, things in the news. He was very much up to date in that area. Then he would realize his mother was being neglected and made a point of including her. He had brought a long list of things he wanted her to do for him. He held the paper up against the glass (prisoners were not allowed to pass things through the office to their visitors) and I copied it. That took quite a while. He and his mother talked while I wrote. He asked her if she had seen or heard from this person or that, how his sister was, how her children were doing in school.

We talked about North Bay, he asked me where else I'd lived, told me about living in Vancouver. There was never a break in the conversation, never a moment's awkwardness. He mentioned several times that he was in bad mental shape due to the Super-Maximum conditions, even worse at present because he was in "the hole"—due to what infraction he didn't say. The "bad mental shape" was not apparent to me; he was sharp, witty and full of good humour. The short of it was, as I told Pam on my return, I liked him.

AUGUST 12, 1976. I'VE WAITED four days since the meeting, not to appear too anxious.

In the top right hand corner of the page I write, almost confidently, the information he asked me to send: my address.

Now what? In this circumstance do I use the word "Dear?" Dear seems unduly intimate, but what else is there? Dear, it is.

"Dear Don," I write, and only then, seeing the reality of those words, their concreteness on the page, do I realize that the Don is more of an issue than the Dear. Donald stays at a safe distance, he's in the newspapers, on TV, is the object of coffee break gossip. Donald is someone who is "crazy as a coot and would just as soon shoot you as laugh at you," as a police officer was quoted in The Globe and Mail as saying. Go from Donald to Don and you have crossed a line. Well, there it is.

"It was nice meeting you on the weekend," I start. Nice? I have the nerve to think I can write a book, and I can't come up with a better word than "nice?" Well, what *is* the word, then? "Terrifying" comes to mind, but I can't say that. Move on. ". . . and I'm sure your mother was glad to see you."

What next? I'm still at "terrifying." I don't know how I got up the nerve. The closer we got to Kingston, the more I wanted to turn around and forget the whole thing. And maybe I would have if Myrtle hadn't been with me. "Our trip home went well. It took about eight hours because we stopped in Pembroke for lunch and a little shopping. I was glad for the company *even if she did talk my ear off, I think but don't write,* and being able to share on accommodation helped with expenses. On the whole it was a good trip, although I was quite tired going back to work on Monday."

Is that enough? I need something else before getting to the point.

"I wonder what my co-workers would say if they knew what I was up to over the weekend. When they asked, I said, 'Oh, not much.' "

Now to the point. How should I put it? Why didn't I press it when I was there? I never push when I should. "I hope everything is OK with you and I will look forward to hearing from you." Ambiguous, to be sure, but he'll know what it means: Are you willing to collaborate on the book, or not? Let me know.

"Yours truly," I write, and sign my name in full, formally.

Dear Don,

I received your letter yesterday and I'm taking a Civil Service lunch to answer it.

Where on King St. do I live, you ask. Well, we're in the first block east of Cassells St., in the same block you left that car on Seventh Ave. Is that why you're asking? I suspect it is. The funny thing is, that night I couldn't sleep, which is very unusual for me. I was up and down the whole night. And what a lot of excitement there was on the street the next day with all the SWAT squad activity.

Yes, I recopied the list for your mother, to make it legible, and I'll call her to see if she's heard from your friend.

The weather's been wonderful, so every afternoon I get home from work right at 4:30—or even before. We pack up a picnic and go down to Champlain Park on Lake Nipissing to swim, relax and watch the sunset. One of the things I like so much about North Bay is the ready access to the outdoors, especially the lakes—although I do find Trout Lake a bit too cold for swimming.

Yes, it's true what you say, a lot can be told about a person by the eyes. *I wonder what you saw in mine. Wonder, but don't write.*

I agree we need to talk more before proceeding, so I'll try to come to see you again soon. I have things planned for the next two weekends, so it will have to be after that. I'll let you know.

◆   ◆   ◆   ◆

My laugh muscles are still sore! All the way home I tried to stop smiling and give my cheek muscles a rest, but I couldn't help myself, the conversation just kept rolling back, and there I was—smiling again. There wasn't much said that was sensible, was there? I would never have thought it possible that so much laughter could happen in such a depressing environment. It was only later, by the way, that I caught your joke (when I told you I am an upstanding citizen).

"But not up standing all the time," you answered so fast. Ha! I'm a bit dense sometimes.

Now, to speak of business. I think the first thing to do is to write a publisher to see if they would be interested. I don't know why they wouldn't be, unless they think the story is no longer topical, but there's no point in going to a lot of work without knowing. I regret not having started sooner.

I'm disappointed that they don't allow tape recorders in the visit room. That makes things much more difficult. Maybe I should learn shorthand. It's something that has always fascinated me, like a puzzle or secret code.

We talked about reality and perceptions. "What is, *is*." People *are* what they *are*—even if others prefer to see them differently. That got me thinking about something Van Gogh said:

> If I'm no good now, I won't be later either; but if I *am* later,
> then I am now too. For corn is corn, though city-dwellers
> may at first think it's grass.

I'm very much taken by Van Gogh and see him as a kind of saviour or mentor. I do like his painting, yes, but it's his words, his ideas, that I find sublime. I found him at the lowest time of my life, when I didn't see how I could go on. By "finding" him, I mean I found his letters. They're published—hundreds of them—to his brother and several artist-friends. For me, Van Gogh's writing, as an artistic expression of Self, exceeds even that which he accomplished in his paintings. And isn't it odd that this person—considered to have been mentally ill by most—is the one who brought me back to mental health? (Well, *I* think I'm healthy. ☺) We did get into the subject of sanity, and we'll have to get back to it next time.

◆   ◆   ◆   ◆

I received your letter, and thanks. So, now that you're out of the hole and back in your cell, you're able to listen to the radio again. Yes, I listen to As It Happens quite often, but I didn't hear the article you mention. The way you tell it, it sounds hilarious.

I've been to the Nugget and got all the past issues from August last year, have read them carefully, and am starting to formulate a line of approach. Also, yesterday I bought a book on learning shorthand. I've scanned the first few lessons, and it looks like fun—intriguing, mysterious, like learning to write Chinese or Arabic.

I'm writing from Parry Sound. I come here to the Family Court once a month (go to Bracebridge once a month also). It's always a nice drive, relaxing, with beautiful scenery. I look through payment histories in the court office to see who is in arrears in their child support payments (cases where the wives and children are being supported by Family Benefits). On the way here I stopped to see two people. The first was a father who is two years behind. Earlier I had verified his financial circumstances and, based on that, we made an agreement on the amount he will start to pay. Now I have to talk with his estranged wife to see if she agrees. If so, we'll make an application to reduce the order, in which case both he and I will appear before the court. Sometimes the man gets a lawyer, in which case the lawyer and I bargain before going to court. The other person I saw was a "deserted" mother. I put that in quotes because they're not all truly deserted. In fact, most aren't; most are separated, but "separated" doesn't qualify for Family Benefits. I had to find out what she knows about her husband's whereabouts. She gave me a couple of leads, so now I'll try to locate him. So you see my job is part-detective, part counsellor and part adjunct of the court. I'm what is called a Parental Support Worker. It's an experimental program, newly created, and there are only twenty-three of us in the province.

I enjoy the going out of town overnight part. It's a time to be alone and eat meals I don't have to cook or pay for. The motel where I stay here in Parry Sound has a swimming pool, so I enjoy that in the evening. In Bracebridge what I appreciate is the dining room of the hotel, which overlooks a wooded hill and a rushing river. So soothing.

I called your mother and she said she hasn't heard from anyone. She'll call me when she does. She's doing fine.

I'm working ahead on the shorthand. Also thinking it might be worthwhile to go to Toronto to research all the news articles from The Star and The Globe before getting started.

◆   ◆   ◆   ◆

Just to let you know I got yours, and that I heard about the riot there. There seems to be an "epidemic of prison riots" all across Canada. First B.C. Pen and Laval on the same day, and now Millhaven. What's going on? I know so little of prisons. I'm thinking these uprisings must have been co-ordinated by design. But how do they do it? Smoke signals?

At first I was worried about you, but then I realized the disturbance was in the population and you wouldn't be involved, being in the so-called Special Handling Unit. Don't you love these euphemisms? It was probably named purposely to make people think you get special treatment—"special" as in "pampered," that is, rather than "special" as in "deprived" Let's call it what it is: Super-Maximum.

The word usage reminds me of a book I read a couple of years ago, *When in Doubt, Mumble.* I saw the author interviewed on TV and he was so humorous I had to read the book. His objective was to show how bureaucrats talk but don't say anything. Working in the bureaucracy, I see a lot of this coming from the upper levels, but I must say the administrator and supervisors in my office are down-to-earth, caring types who use ordinary language. What's more worrisome to me is the worker bees (my level) who have been there too long, have become cynical and apathetic. I look at them and wonder: Will this happen to me? It's easy to see that to some extent it's inevitable for any person who stays too long. Let's hope I don't stay that long. The Civil Service it too comfortable for its own good.

I went to the doctor about my cough but the medicine he gave me isn't working. Have to go back. It's getting worse instead of better.

I haven't read any of the books you talk about. I know Isaac Asimov is so popular, but I don't know why I can't get interested in science fiction. Lack of imagination, maybe? A book I think you would like is *The Loneliness of the Long Distance Runner*. Have you read it?

◆   ◆   ◆   ◆

I received yours, but I can't comment on everything now. This will have to be short; I have a lot of things to do. I've started a list of questions I want to ask you when I go to see you next time. Also, I've been working on the shorthand and am enjoying it—it's fun, really. I get so into it that I stay up half the night working on it, and then I'm too tired at work the next day. I'm sure that's not helping my cough any either. I've taped the first few dictations since I don't have a "dictator." (Get it? ☺) I'm actually getting most of the exercises right, but so far I'm only up to "the boat is on the bay"—said slowly, at that. I don't think I'll be taking any notes from you for a while; it will take some time to become proficient.

Meanwhile, my cough goes on and on. To hear me you'd think I was dying of T.B., but I had an X-ray and there's nothing in the lungs, so the doctor's now sending me to a heart specialist.

As I said, this is a short one this time. Just to let you know that I am working ahead.

◆   ◆   ◆   ◆

So, how are things in Toronto? Are you enjoying your "Jails of Ontario Tour?" (Said facetiously, I hope you realize.) I expect it will be easier for you there at the Don Jail than at Millhaven. Do you have any indication yet whether or not you'll be called as a witness?

Well, I can see what a planner you are. That meeting at the North Bay courthouse the other day went like clockwork—just as you planned. And I didn't even need to cheat on time from work. I had photocopying I could legitimately do there, and the time factor worked like clockwork. *I'm thinking, but not writing, about how you would have no concept of how foreign the experi-*

ence was for me, talking to a guy in handcuffs, surrounded by five cops. A strange meeting it was, too—not a word of conversation other than the instructions for the letter. I thought you didn't look well: grey complexion disappearing into a grey suit. I didn't like the moustache either. But I have the feeling a little "planning" went into that; in case you have the opportunity to "go missing," should they be looking for a guy with a moustache or a clean-shaven one? Am I right?

I was surprised they let you pass the papers, but I guess they must have verified the contents first. I sent the original to the chairman of the Sub-Committee, Mark MacGuigan, M.P., as you asked, and copies to everyone on the list. Naturally, I read the letter—kept a copy for myself as a matter of fact. Eight pages of small writing; that's a lot of commentary. Your points were well-stated and really made me think. I must say it's difficult to learn conditions in our prisons are as you describe—not that I thought they were perfect by any means. I was impressed with the fact that it's the mental games, abuses of power and psychological torment that have more weight than physical conditions in your outline. Given this description, I can see why the penitentiaries have been bursting into revolt recently. I wasn't aware of the House of Commons Sub-Committee on Penitentiaries, but I'll keep my eye open to learn what they're doing, what their mandate is.

I heard you did a plea bargain when you were here and got eight years on the escape charges. Not bad, considering you were eligible for eleven life sentences plus 85 years. Did that make the trip worthwhile? ☺

Thinking of where you are, at the Don Jail, reminds me of when I used to go past there on the way to high school football games at Broadview Stadium. It held some kind of mystique for me, the mystery of wondering where I was going to end up—Mercer Reformatory, my mother told me so many times, if I kept on behaving so badly, even though, really, I never did anything so bad—at least not that she found out about.

Reminds me, too, of the Boyd gang who escaped from the Don—twice. That was in the same era—the 50's. I was a newspaper-reader from an early age, always fascinated by stories of human drama: fires, feats of bravery, demonstrations of excellence, mysterious disappearances, murders. The Evelyn Dick case, for example. She killed her husband and dismembered his body. My friends and I thought we were tremendously clever (at nine years old) repeating a joke in which at trial the judge supposedly said to her: "You cut off his arms, you cut off his legs, how could you Mrs. Dick?" Weren't we the daring little devils?

I hope this gets to you OK.

◆   ◆   ◆   ◆

Just thought I'd send a fast one to you there at the Don because I expect most of your correspondents will still be writing to you at Millhaven and you won't get much mail.

I saw in the paper that Rose and Lavin's trial has started, so I'll be interested to see if you get called as a witness or not.

The cough continues. It's bad. I've had to take time off work. Have a prescription medicine that has me sleeping all the time. I've been to the heart guy and the respiratory guy. Neither could see anything wrong. Now I have to go to an ear, nose, throat doctor. Meanwhile, all this time lost and so little done. I'm sorry. I feel badly about that. The only thing I've managed to do is compose a list of questions to ask you.

Write if you're able.

◆   ◆   ◆   ◆

My God, Don, what you've been enduring there at the Don Jail! I can't believe it! To think we do such things to people in Canada! Your lawyer made publicity in today's Globe and Mail about the conditions they've been holding you under. "No caged animal could possibly be treated worse," he said. No clothes, no shower, no exercise, held in isolation in the death cell, wakened every fifteen minutes. What are they trying to do? I'm appalled. To think of the reverence and honour that was bestowed on a dead dog and this is the way humans are treated in this country. I'm ashamed to be a taxpayer and know that things like this are being done in my name—with my money. It sure puts everything you wrote to the Sub-Committee in perspective. Greenspan called it "cruel and unusual punishment, a contravention of the Charter of Rights." Here I was thinking you would be having an easier time with it being a provincial jail rather than a penitentiary. Shows how much I know.

I'm not even sure you're getting your mail there, so will write another letter to Millhaven and send the news clipping with it.

◆   ◆   ◆   ◆

I do hope that things have improved for you since Eddie Greenspan and the chaplain intervened on your behalf. I've been thinking of you. Here's another Van Gogh quote I like:

> Sometimes it is so bitingly cold in winter that one says: It is too cold; what do I care if summer will follow, the evil is far greater than the good. But finally there comes an end to the bitter frost, and on a certain morning the wind has changed direction and we have a thaw. Comparing the state of the

weather to our state of mind and circumstances—like the
weather subject to changes and variety—I still have hope for
a change for the better.

I hope by now you have had changes for the better, and that eventually your
appeal will bring even better changes.

You may think it strange that I use another's words instead of my own.
I guess I'm a bit "evangelistic" about Van Gogh. He was such a help to me
that I hope he can help others as well. I guess I identify with him because I
suffered so for not being understood, yet he fought on and remained true to
his own values and beliefs in spite of everything—poverty, sickness, rejection,
ridicule.

So, what is VG saying here that I couldn't say in my own words? I can
say "I hope things will improve"—which I did—but do those paltry words
have the intensity of feeling, the weight of despair, the light of hope I want
to convey? I had a boyfriend who used to say if I couldn't explain something
in my own words that meant I didn't understand it. But he was intellectual.
There's a different kind of understanding, I think, one that doesn't necessarily
go through the brain but is taken in with the breath, inhaled into the lungs,
and ends up pulsing through the body. A visceral comprehension. For me,
Van Gogh's words have that effect. Leonard Cohen's also. Do you know his
music?

Hope this doesn't make your head ache.

◆ ◆ ◆ ◆

As you can see, I have the typewriter now. And I thank you for sharing in the
cost. That helps a lot. Now I can write a long letter—if you can excuse all the
typos. A little practice is all I need. Never typed before.

I have your two letters but I think you won't have received the last one
I sent to the Don Jail. I hope they will forward it. I'm amazed that you
can laugh at "Toronto and its nudist colony," as you put it. I don't know
how you're able to maintain a sense of humour, enduring all that; I know I
certainly wouldn't be able to. At least you were able to see Greenspan. So, he's
sure you'll win your appeal—especially if Rose and Lavin get acquitted. Well,
they did—yesterday. I assume you've heard. *Something's wrong here. Either two
guilty guys got off, or one innocent one got convicted; it's physically impossible for
one person to abduct two people from their apartment, one of them a big man,
drive them out to the countryside and shoot them.* That must have made you
hopeful. It's so difficult to hope but not hope too much. I'm sure you know
that only too well. When does your appeal come up?

Glad you like the VG quotation. You're right: there's not much comment one can make in just a few words; as you say, "one would either have to talk for hours, or just nod and agree." It seems to me that some ideas need to be left on a mystical plane anyway; to apply other words to them can distort—even destroy—their meaning.

It's good to see you got a confirmation from the House of Commons Sub-Committee that they received your letter. That will be interesting when they come to interview you in February.

Well, you knew you'd get me going by sending me this *horrible* Andy Capp cartoon, didn't you? I don't happen to think he's funny!!! What's funny about a freeloading, carousing, lazy, lay-about who sponges off his wife and treats her badly besides? You're lucky you're behind that window, that's all I can say! Now you know why you're there—for protection from me! Ha!

So, you got angry about being called androgynous. Well, I certainly didn't mean physically if that's what you were thinking. *No, definitely not physically, I'm prompted to write, but resist.* I meant the ability to think on both sides of the barrier, not chauvinistic. At least that's how I've found you in the conversations we've had so far. It was intended as a compliment, not an insult. I find there are not very men in our age bracket who show freedom from sexist thought. However, I may revise that statement now that I've received this cartoon. ☺

When did I blush? I don't remember. But you blush, too. When I saw you blush in court I said to myself, "A guy who blushes can't be all bad." What do you think of that?

No, you'll never be one of society's vegetables, as you say here. I'd like to see the poem you talk about—*The Men That Don't Fit In*. Who wrote it? I'll send you *The Loneliness of the Long Distance Runner*. It's only about fifty pages so I'll send them a few pages at a time. I'll wait till you've read the whole thing before saying anything.

Now, here's good news! I went to the ear, nose, throat guy and it was a miracle—instant cure! More than two months coughing, a week off work, how many trips to doctors—including three specialists—and it's nothing more than a postnasal drip. Shouldn't my own doctor have been able to see that in the first place? After only a few days' treatment, it's almost gone. So, now that I'm better, I plan to come to see you next weekend to start working on the story—finally. I hope you aren't exasperated with the delay.

◆   ◆   ◆   ◆

I got back OK. The piece of cardboard in front of the radiator, as you suggested, worked wonders. It was much warmer on the way home. Haven't taken the car in to the garage yet. More money. . . .

How am I ever going to get this thing written if you don't co-operate? ☺ Four hours of visiting and we got to three of my seventeen questions! I'll send them to you like you said. After the Saturday visit I gave myself a "talking-to" about applying myself and getting some work done, but then Sunday morning came and there we were—back at it—discussing, laughing, arguing on every topic *but*. . . . There certainly seems to be no shortage of things to talk—and laugh—about, which I find surprising, given the differences in our backgrounds and experience, to say nothing of the miserable conditions. It's nice to talk with someone who reads a lot and has opinions. *June says I'm smitten, but that's ridiculous; I'm more of a realist than that. Who in their right mind would fall for a guy on a ten-year minimum sentence, which could, in fact, be life? No, you're in there, and I'm out here, and that's the way it is. I'll write the book, and if I enjoy the interviews along the way, well, that's a bonus. Still, I know June is right in one way: there's no doubt in my mind that if you weren't in there I would be wanting to spend some time with you. Who do I have better conversations with? Laugh more with? Besides that, you're definitely not hard on the eyes. All the same, I know it wouldn't last, would just be a fling. Too many differences.*

I liked our conversation about *One Flew Over the Cuckoo's Nest*. Too bad you didn't see the movie. Most often the book is better than the movie, but in this case the movie was better. I hope you get the opportunity to see it some day. It won almost all the Academy Awards for '75 and Jack Nicholson was amazing as R.P. McMurphy—you'd have thought he was the real person.

What is sanity? It seems if you don't fit into the conventional, you're not sane. Fit the box and die, that's what they want. Some time I'll tell you my personal experience on that subject. Meanwhile, my friend VG says:

> The doctors tell us that not only Moses, Christ, Luther and others were mad, but also Franz Hals, Rembrandt and Delacroix. One might ask these doctors: Where, then, are the sane people?

You probably don't realize how nervous I am when I go there. As soon as I drive into the grounds my entire body goes into revolt—the whole "fight or flight" response. But then, as soon as the visit actually starts and we get talking, I relax and forget where I am. The result is this: going in, my stomach aches from nervousness; coming out, it aches from laughing. Can't win.

I've decided to start with Mr. Dupuis. There's no need to write in chronological order because each segment (the escape, each captive-taking episode, the time alone in the bush, the capture) is a story on its own, not dependent on any other part. After hearing your observations on each captive, I'm most taken by Etienne Dupuis—"Pop" as you call him—as an interesting character.

I've bought all the Lands and Forests maps for all the places you were. That should make explaining to me easier.

I got the $100 from your mother toward the typewriter so, thanks again. And can you see that the typing is improving already? The speed certainly is. So, besides being an essential for the book, it has an added advantage for you—I can write more and longer letters. Good investment, don't you think?

And by the way, your mother put my name in for a Christmas basket from her church. I feel a little embarrassed because I know I don't need it as much as some, but it's very helpful, and I appreciate it. It was thoughtful of her. I live borderline—just above welfare level, actually, when you take off the car payment, which is necessary for my job, a condition of employment. In fact, the first three years I worked for the Ministry I was clearing less than the welfare recipients we served.

Things are getting busy for Christmas. I'll make my serious start right after New Year's. Bye for now.

◆   ◆   ◆   ◆

What a day I had on December 30! After a six-hour drive, I pulled into the grounds—eager for the visit—only to be told there were none. I couldn't believe it because you had let me know there were none on New Year's Eve and New Year's Day so I sure didn't expect that. What a feeling of powerlessness. What was I to do? Storm the place? He said it's the responsibility of the prisoners to let their people know. What could I say? There was no point in staying overnight in a motel with nothing to do and no visit the next day, so back to North Bay it was—another six hours. Besides being exhausting, the whole thing was disappointing and demoralizing.

Check your notification again and if you weren't notified about the 30th I'll write a letter of complaint.

◆   ◆   ◆   ◆

The other day I ran into an old friend—sort of friend—Ron Holmberg. He's just back from Toronto where he was working on his PhD for a couple of years. He was my professor of Social Welfare the year I went to Nipissing

College (71-72), even though he's younger than me. I was three weeks late starting classes so went to each professor to find out what I had missed. The others were all helpful, but Ron thrust a book at me, said if I could read it by the next day and write 750 words in answer to a list of questions he gave me, I wouldn't have missed anything. Otherwise, I'd have missed ten percent of the year's total marks.

I didn't say a word, wouldn't give the satisfaction, but the first couple of classes I sat there telling him—by osmosis—"I'll show you, you bastard. I'll show you I don't need your lousy ten marks." Turned out, though, I liked his class. Issues of poverty, inequities in society, were subjects that were never discussed in our middle-class house (not much was discussed, come to think of it), although as a child I would devour the pleas for help for needy families in the Star Fresh Air Fund and the Santa Claus Fund with their descriptions of various hardships, living in cramped quarters, etc. To me it was mysterious. I knew there was no point in asking my mother about these things; she had a Presbyterian sense of the anointed: we lived on the right side of the tracks because we were worthy.

Ron's lectures and the readings revealed to me for the first time, as an analytical construct, society's biases against the poor, the disadvantaged, and how those biases help society function. Ultimately it was his class that influenced me to change from teaching to social work, and in the end I won the prize for highest mark in that subject. After that I worked for him, interviewing and tabulating data for a study he did on public housing. So, you never know. . . .

Anyway, I told him about writing the book and he was excited, offered to help in any way he can, perhaps proofread and edit. We met last night. I told him my focus (how different people react to the same situation) and he suggested that I use changing narrators—that is, have you tell some parts and various captives tell other parts. I like the idea.

◆   ◆   ◆   ◆

I had a reply to my letter to the publisher. They are interested. He said he hopes the writing will continue "apace."

◆   ◆   ◆   ◆

Well, I've been to see Etienne Dupuis at his home over near Field, and you were exact in your description of him—his curiosity, sparkle, and compelling way of speaking. What a guy! I was there for about two hours. He was talkative, forthcoming and friendly. He told me you ate their four lunches all by yourself (two meals each for him and his grandson). You sure must have been hungry! When he described sitting in the car sharing the tea and the cake and all the discussion you had, it sounded like you were friends on a picnic.

And fishing for butts in the ashtray, one as bad as the other for a smoke! He really has a comical way of describing things. You could have trusted him, you know. He told me how he wanted to stop at his house for cigarettes and you wouldn't let him. But he said he would have just got the cigarettes and come right back out. I taped the interview. Wish you could hear it.

He didn't want to report you to the police; if left to his own devices, he wouldn't have. But you had told him to—that was the first reason—also, they had to account for his grandson having abandoned his job as watchman on that construction site. "That was serious business, leavin' that gol-darn site," as he said several times.

Wouldn't it be wonderful to have a grandfather like him? He went to the site to pass the night with Mitch, keep him company so he wouldn't be lonely (scared?) and brought the car because it would be more comfortable to sleep in than the truck, which Mitch had driven to the job earlier.

I didn't have grandparents, did you? Well, I had them—three, and all three lived within walking distance of us. But there was no contact; my mother had fought with them all. The first time I laid eyes on my mother's father I was 17 and he was in his coffin. But I used to go on my bicycle to see my father's parents from time to time, alone, with my brother, with a friend, and sometimes with my father, but there was no communication between the families per se. No gatherings for important occasions, no birthday or Christmas gifts, nothing. There must have been a relationship at one time, though, because there are photos of my brother and me when we were quite small, wearing outfits that our grandmother had knit. Elaborate outfits with tiny stitches; I think you have to have a lot of love to go to that much work.

When I went to their home I always anticipated the fresh tea biscuits Nana would have. Two kinds—plain and raisin—kept in a pantry off the kitchen. It's unclear why I stopped going but a few years later, when I was fifteen, one fine Sunday afternoon in spring, feeling very grown-up in my first pair of high-heeled shoes, I went to see them. After expressions of surprise and delight, the first thing my grandmother said was "Does your mother know you're here?" That told me something.

I don't even remember Pappy dying. I know I didn't go to his funeral. I saw Nana once after that, at my father's funeral six years later, and the next year she was hit by a streetcar in downtown Toronto and died the following day. All that outside my experience. And me outside theirs. I don't even have a picture of her, although I do have two of me with him (I look to be about three) in our back yard, so it seems that he did come to see us at one time.

TYPING UP THE TRANSCRIPT of the interview was surrealistic. Only a few short years ago I had no idea who I was; now, here I was, researching a book and the venture was proving far richer than I could have predicted.

Mr. Dupuis had such a colourful way of expressing himself. The anecdotes he related had me in stitches. He had a long story about driving to Warren to report his experience (instead of phoning), but it turned out all the phones were out anyway. He and the local O.P.P. officer got in the cruiser to drive to the Verner detachment and even the car radio was out. At Verner they waited for police to arrive from North Bay then drove back to Warren to make his statement.

"And the reporters were already there. From Sudbury, from North Bay, from all over the world! They wanted pictures and I says, No, no pictures. But they insisted on pictures. I couldn't get out of there! I called a cop and complained, but the cop says There's nothin' we can do, we're stuck with 'em. Well, I says, *I'm* gonna do somethin', I'm gonna break their cameras! No, no, the cop says, you can't do that. By the gee, I was mad! For me, it was worse with the reporters than it was with Don Kelly. I've hated them ever since."

After typing up the interview and studying the maps, I composed a list of questions for Don. "It's a great story," I finished by telling him. "Doing it is going to be not only engaging and stimulating, but fun besides."

I took the letter to the corner mailbox. As it dropped, I pictured myself that first time, standing in that same spot four months back, dropping in that first letter, all the trepidations and doubts I then had, yet this was where it had led: the delight of delving into an intriguing story; the challenge of doing it justice; and the pleasure of meeting interesting people. To say nothing of the enjoyment of "interviewing the protagonist."

Blossoming

(January 1977—April 1979)

Hi,

So happy to receive two letters, one eight pages, the other five. And—as a bonus—being in such small writing they're worth two or three times my pages.

Now that you've confirmed that the only notification anyone in your block got for visits over New Year's was "no visits the 31st and 1st," as you originally told me, I have written to the warden to complain. I have the feeling, however, from all I've learned so far, that the complaint may be received with a sense of satisfaction rather than concern; there's not much done to encourage visits.

Funny you should mention Wilf Coffin because Mr. Dupuis talked about him, too. When the other person confessed to the killing on his deathbed they couldn't "un-hang" Coffin, could they? Yes, there's also the case of Steven Truscott, as you say. I remember you telling me about seeing him—at the old pen, I think you said—and knowing just by his look that he was innocent. "A con can tell," you said. And Caryl Chessman. I followed that case, too, at the time. But I didn't know he wrote books. Louis Riel—I know the story only in general terms—haven't really read about him. I'll try to get the book you recommend.

◆   ◆   ◆   ◆

Do you feel you're in a time warp? We have so many letters going back and forth now, we make a comment or ask a question in one letter and the response comes three letters later. Then there are the ones that arrive out of order. Maybe some letters are more interesting than others and the censors pass them around? What do you think? Really, anyone trying to follow them would be bamboozled—or think we're crazy. Ah! Maybe that's it! Maybe they're reading closely . . . making a case. . . . *How I love receiving these letters! Such fun! I've taken to coming home during the day to check the mail—can't wait till 4:30 for the newest instalment, the next laugh. Never know what topic will come up. I read them over and over. Can't believe so much life—such vitality and humour—can come from such a dead-end place.*

I had to go to the library to find that article in the Star you talk about: "Inmates treated like animals." How to change what is "cruel and unusual punishment" under the Charter into something legally acceptable: give one hour per day out of the cell, add four hours of TV every second night and—*voilà*—cruel and unusual becomes "Segregation."

"What hope for rehabilitation?" they ask. What hope, indeed? All the public thinks about is the bad guys are off the street; what they don't think about is that they're going to get out one day, and how much worse will they be by then. The head of the guards' union says they're probably going to lose control in February or March when the "do-gooders and bleeding hearts" start coming. Well, that must be the Parliamentary Sub-Committee. What more can I say?

I will never again believe what I hear or see in the media after the examples of blatant error, false innuendo and slant I've seen so far. In the case of Reader's Digest, I hadn't read that article, but luckily the issue was still on the newsstands. Well, it's a masterpiece of wording, really. If you read it again very carefully you'll see it doesn't actually *say* you shot the dog; it just gives the *impression* you did. A lot of thought went into that wording. My suspicion is that the first police spokesman who announced your capture probably said something like, "Cloud was killed in the shooting." The press interpreted it the way they wanted, the story got started, and the police never bothered to correct it. And so I'm both disappointed and disillusioned to learn that when Peter Mansbridge reads "captured in a shootout," I should hear "caught in a spray of bullets to the back." In writing your story I intend to use quotes from the media as contrast to what really happened.

> I hope and trust that I am not what many people think me
> to be just now; we shall see, some time must pass.

Bet you can guess who said that. By the way, when I send these quotations, sometimes it's for you to imagine yourself saying the same words, thinking the same thoughts; sometimes it's for me; sometimes for both. You can interpret the way you want.

Well, I'm glad to see you were only playing devil's advocate (well, partly, at least) in our argument about abortion. You did succeed in getting me going, I have to admit. I do like your full explanation, though.

◆   ◆   ◆   ◆

Yes, I realize you can't tell me everything about your thinking when I'm there because of the monitoring, and I know that must be frustrating. *Nor do I want to write much because of the censors, but I understand most of it—I think—by the hand signals, mouthing of words and the cryptic written messages you hold to the window. OK, you continue to have your "hobby" (as you call it) of trying to escape. On the one hand I rather admire the determination, the planning, the creativity. It's a romantic notion that appeals to my Dreamer self. My Practical self tells me, however, that it's a dead-end dream. In the first place, it surely is impossible, but more importantly, all it does is get you more and more time in the hole, which is self-defeating. But I can see it's what keeps you going, so what right do I have to say anything? It's who you are—the Long Distance Runner: true to yourself in what you see as a noble cause, and yet ultimately it will bring you to grief.* Besides that, there are the time limitations. Glad to see, though, that you manage to keep up with the news, are still writing many people, and have the occasional visit besides. Do your correspondents send you clippings of the articles you refer to, or do you have newspaper and magazine subscriptions?

Ah, *Papillon!* I haven't read the book but I saw the movie. It was truly amazing, both the story and the acting—heart-wrenching to watch. And, oh, the spirit! The will! Do you remember what Papillon said to his friend when the friend had lost his passion and decided to adapt? "Me, they can kill, but *you* they own." In other words, better to go out in a Blaze of Glory than to die a vegetable. I didn't realize the book was written by the actual person. What a story! Recounting it must have been excruciating. I've made a note to read it and his other book, Banco, as well. Autobiography and biography are my favourite reading.

Two years ago when I was in San Francisco I took a tour of Alcatraz. There may have been one successful escape from there, but it's uncertain. It really is "The Rock"—so barren I had a hard time to find any little piece of it to take away with me. Finally I found a tiny stone, which I still have. The tour took us through the cellblocks, and they pointed out the Birdman's and Al Capone's cells. In the isolation block I volunteered, along with two or three others, to go in a cell while they shut the solid door and turned off the light. It was black, black in there without a chink of light. But you have the opposite problem: constant light. I wonder who determines these things.

Did you get all the pages of the *Loneliness of the Long Distance Runner* yet? I don't know how many times I've read that story in the past four years, and just think—now I've met him!

I like what you say about capital punishment—except the public viewing part, although logically, you're right about that. All it does is show that those who kill are doing what society sanctions. So hypocritical. "Do what I say, not what I do."

◆   ◆   ◆   ◆

You know sometimes I get so fed up with all the trappings of middle-class life. I really don't want to own a house, for example. It's too much responsibility. I only bought it because the government had a deal for low-income first-time buyers. The mortgage and taxes are cheaper than rent. I really feel that after the kids have left home I will sell the works—house and everything in it—and buy a pup tent. This is just one more way in which I seem to be the oddball. I don't know anyone who feels like this. Everyone wants Bigger, Better and More. I want Smaller and Less—although maybe Better.

> I conclude that I know nothing, but at the same time
> I feel sure that life is such a mystery that the system of
> "conventionality" is certainly too narrow.

◆   ◆   ◆   ◆

It was a long, slow trip coming back Sunday afternoon—roads icy in places and snow-covered in others, but it was worth it because I did enjoy all the topics we covered and of course the laughs—as always. Plus I even got four of my questions answered amid all the bantering and debating. When you consider I only had fourteen this time, you can see that the success ratio has gone way up. It came to me that if our repartee had been a tennis match, it's hard to say who "won." I spent most of the trip home replaying the volleys and managed to get in a few more good shots! "I should have said" is so easy in retrospect, isn't it? *How can it be that we find so much to talk about, have such an easy rapport? So much to laugh about? I would never have predicted that such an environment—face-to-face with a window between—actually creates a setting for communication more intimate than "normal" situations. In the social world, with all its distractions—TV, movies, other people—one never talks eye-to-eye with complete absorption for hours at a time like that. Time to sink through the eyes into the soul. I enjoy going to see you more than I want to.*

Like I told you, I've given up on the shorthand, and since we can't seem to apply ourselves to the work when I'm there—which is *supposed* to be the purpose of the visit, after all—I guess getting my info will have to be done the slow way, by mail. So I'm including the questions that went unanswered on the weekend.

Well, you sure got me on your opening salvo Saturday afternoon: "What happened, Bette?"—with such a look of concern—"Were you in an accident?" There I was, checking everything, my hair, my face, my clothes, to see what was wrong. It's so funny how we do our digs in opposite ways. Have you noticed? You do the insult first (tear down the ego) and then follow up with a compliment, while I let you get all ego-inflated *then* burst the bubble.

◆   ◆   ◆   ◆

I have your letter where you talk about your depressed mood and how the visit perked you up. You say you had been waiting patiently. That reminds me of one of VG's letters where he talks of "waiting patiently with how much impatience" for his brother's letter. I don't have time to look it up right now; maybe I'll send it later.

Your answer to my sometimes feeling trapped and frustrated about the kids makes me laugh. I simply can't picture you babysitting six kids—oldest twelve or thirteen, a baby in diapers included—for a whole week! I have to chuckle, though, in your description of it. I'll bet you let the kids do everything they wanted and their parents had to train them again when they came back.

◆   ◆   ◆   ◆

Did you think I had abandoned you? I realize I'm a few letters behind, but I've been so busy. For one thing, I had to go to Bear Island this week. (Not that I'm complaining about that!) I drove to Temagami and flew from there. It's a great trip because in a little plane like that you're not high up and can see everything. I've only been there once before—in summer, by boat—so I was happy to have the chance to go in winter. It was a beautiful day, clear, cold and sunny, the kind of day when snow squeaks under your boots. It's so refreshing to be where there are no cars, and walk from house to house on a path. I love the quiet, the naturalness, the "humanness." The guy I went to see took me to the home of the grandmother of his separated (I hope!) wife to talk. I said "hope" because twice now when I've located a guy, I found he was living with his wife all the time, a sham separation in order to collect welfare. Those cases got reported to the Fraud Squad. Guess we're on different wavelengths there, eh?

◆   ◆   ◆   ◆

Last weekend I went to Toronto, to the Reference Library, and got copies from the Star and the Globe of all the articles about the manhunt. I left right after work on Friday, got to my friend Evie's house about ten o'clock, and spent most of Saturday at the library. Evie and I have been friends since Grade Seven. She has three small children and her husband doesn't seem to like to babysit, so we didn't go anywhere, just stayed home and caught up on our lives. I told her why I was in Toronto, about my project, how fascinating it is. She was interested, supportive and encouraging. I had expected her to be surprised—even shocked—that I was doing this, yet she seemed to take it all as matter-of-fact. I came home Sunday after breakfast. It was a good weekend, enjoyable and profitable.

◆   ◆   ◆   ◆

Yes, I did get your things from Personal Effects when I was there: your wallet with just a couple of business cards in it, a pair of well-used boots, a T-shirt full of bullet holes, and a crushed-up straw hat.

So, you've answered Pam's letter. She didn't say anything about it, or about a puzzle. What kind of puzzle? Did she tell you that now she's decided to be an architect's assistant rather than a surveyor? It will probably change a few more times before the final choice is made. She will do well no matter what she decides. At least she has a choice. In my time it was teacher, nurse or secretary. And then it was seen only as an insurance policy in case your husband died. My mother decided I wasn't going to be a secretary. According to her that was for "common" girls. There's no way I was going to be a nurse (too gory, no inclination) so, teacher it was. Not that I wanted to be a teacher either, but I guess I accepted it gracefully and did what was expected. In a Grade 13 Physics class I did once have a thought that passed through my head without stopping. "If I were a guy," it occurred to me, "I would go to Ryerson Technical Institute and study electronics." Electronics was a new field and I enjoyed learning how televisions work. But I wasn't a guy, so that was the end of it. No resentment. Just fact. Such was the indoctrination of the time. At least now I'm doing something that is my own choice.

Did Pam tell you about all the action around here the day they found the car you left on Seventh Ave.?

◆　　　◆　　　◆　　　◆

Well, I didn't say my ex-boyfriend was intelligent—although intelligent he was. I said he was intellectual; there's a difference. (One time when he wanted to insult me he told me he was sick of my "quasi-intellectualism." No comment, but you notice I haven't forgotten.) Anyway, glad to see you agree with me that sometimes the soul—or core—understands even if the brain can't come up with the words. That boyfriend was a lawyer, so I guess he prided himself on his logical thinking. Which reminds me of one of my favourite VG quotes:

> Who is the master, the logic or me? Is the logic there for me,
> or am I there for the logic? And is there no reason and no
> sense in my unreasonableness and lack of sense?

Don't you love it? Logic, or lack of it, gets me to sanity and lack of it. I'm sending you this interesting article on a study on sanity done by a psychiatrist. Bottom line: "Some people prefer to be crazy." I'll wait for your reaction.

◆　　　◆　　　◆　　　◆

I received the article from Time magazine you sent, and once again I'm on a tear about use of words. They say you took "hostages!!!" My God, what kind of illiterates do these publications hire? (To say nothing of the editors.) Don't they know what a hostage is? Who told them you took hostages? I want to know how this happens. I don't know why I continue to read *anything*.

And, what's this? Another Andy Capp cartoon! You really are a brat! But I do like the Hagar the Horrible one.

◆　　◆　　◆　　◆

I never did find out if you have a subscription to the Toronto Star or not. Of course, even if you do, I know enough by now to realize that wouldn't guarantee you're *actually getting it* every day. And I have no idea how much news passes through from the population, so I will tell you everything I've read about the Sub-Committee's visit to Millhaven. That way you will know for sure. I'll be anxious to hear if they talked with you and whatever else you know.

A group of four M.P.s went there for the first time last week. Apparently they spent thirteen hours interviewing management and members of the guards' union, the main subject being long-standing accusations of the existence of a group of guards ("the Millhaven Mafia") who are accused of using various intimidation tactics to gain control of the prison (just as you said) and over other guards as well. Then there's the overtime scam in which they are accused of fomenting problems in order to create a need for overtime. One guard was reported to have made $30,000 last year—more than the warden: 1,454 overtime hours on a base salary of $13,000.

Arthur Truro, Regional Director of Canadian Penitentiary Services, told the Sub-Committee that a "goon squad" does exist, while Warden Dowcett says there is a small group of guards who "oppose policy" and have "attempted to persuade" others, but he doesn't believe there is "any overlap between the union executive and a group of officers who are less responsive to a liberal program in the institution." When in doubt, mumble.

A former Commissioner of CPS is quoted as having been against the unionization of guards from the first, fearing it would result in this sort of thing. Well, he has been proven right but, as a supporter of unions, I have difficulty with the concept of any workers being prohibited from unionizing. Seems to me proper supervision would solve all the problems. Administration is where the real problem lies.

In related reading I learned that the so-called Special Handling Units were built to appease guards in the first place, as a response to their protests after the abolition of the death penalty. It also talks of the Segregation Review

Board that sends you your notice every thirty days stating you are in the SHU "for the maintenance of good order and discipline of the institution." Reminds me of *Cuckoo's Nest* where the schedule was more important than therapy. (About watching the World Series, do you remember?)

I'm thinking now of what you told me about the day Millhaven opened (prematurely) in 1971, when you were in the group transferred from the old pen after the riot and were forced to run a gauntlet of club-wielding guards. It's truly unfathomable to me that all this passes with no protest from the public, at least none that I'm aware of. When you told me that, I was thinking why would they do such a thing? Have they never heard of "kick a dog and it will bite you?" But now, in the context of this information, it becomes clear: create a problem and make more money on overtime. Simple. Yet when the general public hears of riots and disturbances they never imagine it could be the guards who are at the root of it.

Meanwhile, amidst all this, I received a letter from the warden in answer to my complaint about the non-visit of December 30. Don, he tells me all prisoners were notified that there would be no visits that day and it was their responsibility to advise their visitors. Well, since you have checked with all the guys on your block and none was advised, my conclusion is probably the notice did go out but it didn't get circulated. And guess why??? Fits in with the "goon squad" picture very nicely. I want to write him again, counter his argument, but what's the point? I don't know how you deal with these irritations on a daily basis. I would be a raging lunatic in no time.

◆   ◆   ◆   ◆

I'm finished transcribing the interview with Mr. Dupuis and here's the rest of the questions on that part. Not so many this time. I will use him to relate most of this chapter, although some will be in your words. I especially like the part where you tell about who can and cannot drive his car. "His wife will not be happy if anyone but Etienne drives, and so I learned the pecking order: his wife, not present, was still Boss Number One, then Pop was Number Two; the grandson and I were Three and Four." Which raises an interesting point. Did you notice it's always a woman in charge wherever you go? The first night and the next morning with that group of young people it was Charlene; with the campers it was Anne Marie and Kathleen; and now it's Mrs. Dupuis even if she's not there. I love it!

We'll need to talk about how we'll handle the part after he dropped you off—where you want to conceal the identity of the people you saw next.

Maybe you could start writing out where you were and what you were doing from the time you ditched the car here on Seventh Ave. to when you met Etienne. It does seem there must be a more efficient way of doing this—like doing the question-answer bit when I'm there, for example? Doesn't that sound reasonable? Yes, I know it would be much easier if we went on a camping trip to see those places—as you suggest—and I'm willing, but maybe we should at least wait until the snow is gone. ☺

You're still bugging me about the title. How many times are you going to ask? I'm not telling! *The title is HAS ANYBODY HERE (really) SEEN KELLY? I think it's delightfully ambiguous, could lead to endless sub-questions. And would we come up with a definitive answer in the end? Or are we dealing with an enigma? A chameleon? Does "anybody" include me? Have I "(really)" seen you? But the main reason I won't tell you is because I think you don't know how to be quiet about things that pertain to your notoriety, and I just plain don't want the title known by others at this time.*

◆   ◆   ◆   ◆

I knew you'd enjoy that clipping on the study of psychiatric patients, and I love the one you sent in return. I've typed it out in capital letters and tacked it up on the bulletin board over my desk. The doctor is telling the so-called mental patient to struggle with reality and the "mental case" replies: "Doc, I wrestled with reality for forty years and I'm happy to state that I finally won out over it." I love it! Should become a motto!

I set up an "office" in my bedroom: table, typewriter, file box, bulletin board for reminders. Why don't you come to my office so I can interview you? Said the spider to the fly.

◆   ◆   ◆   ◆

Last night June and I went to the Lakeview on Lakeshore Drive. So nice to go there in the evening, sit with a quiet drink in front of the fire or at the windows overlooking the frozen lake. I don't go to bars (don't like the noise), but this is like sitting in a living room. We've gone to a more bar-like place a couple of times, though, but it's small—maybe eight tables—and has live music. Last week the performer was singing James Taylor songs. I like his songs a lot; they're so "basic life." I requested "You've Got a Friend." You must know it. He tells how people can be so cold, how they'll hurt you, desert you, "take your soul if you let them." Then he gives his advice—so simple, so haunting: "Don't you let them."

I met June at a Social Psychology class when I first came to North Bay. We ran into each other around town from time to time after that, but didn't see each other socially. I knew she had gone into real estate, so in '73 when I wanted to buy a house I contacted her. Since then we've developed a close friendship. She's so natural, unpretentious and honest, and has a great sense of humour. I feel fortunate to have her as my confidante in all this—the writing *and whatever else is happening. What* is *happening? I don't know myself. Or maybe I do. . . .* She's very accepting and non-judgmental. I feel I can tell her everything.

I had to ask Pam for the puzzle—your "female puzzle"—as you call it. Well, does that mean that once I solve it I'll get the *easy* one—the "*male* puzzle?" Last night I stayed up until 3:00 a.m. (on a work night!), working furiously, drawing it again and again, trying one scheme after another, and all that got accomplished was the waste basket got filled with a lot of paper. Now tell me *truthfully*: Can this actually be done? I think there's no answer, and you're such a brat for getting me going on it.

Glad you liked the *Long Distance Runner* story. I knew you would. What I like are its contrasts: the "delinquent" who is more honest and more insightful than those who judge him. ("He's stupid and I'm not," he says, referring to the governor of the Borstal, "because I can see more into the likes of him than he can see into the likes of me.") The end is debatable, though. He made his point, yes; he lost the race, thereby embarrassing (and defeating) the governor, but look what he paid—he did more time. Was it worth it? Let's remember to put that one up for debate next time, along with all the other issues we have going.

◆   ◆   ◆   ◆

My brother was here this week for a couple of days. He had to do some work in North Bay (he's a lawyer). He brought up your name at one point. I didn't respond, figured it would have to be a long explanation and probably still wouldn't be understood. Thursday night we went to the Voyageur for a drink and even danced. A guy from work saw us there and next day told everyone at the office that I was out with "a young stud." I just let that stand, too, but what a blow to the ego since Gary is only twenty-one months younger than me!

◆   ◆   ◆   ◆

Well, now that I know your subscription to the Star has expired, I'm glad I sent you all that info about the Sub-Committee. Glad, too, to learn your friend has ordered it for you again. So, the Sub-Committee came to see you, but with guards, reporters and cameras all round, what could you say? I saw the feature on W5, but with only the food slot in a solid door, how was I to know it was you they were talking to? Well, let's hope something good comes from their investigations. The February 10 issue of the Star reports they have acknowledged the existence of "a goon squad" amongst the guards—just as you said.

◆   ◆   ◆   ◆

Now I'm feeling a little guilty where you say that in my discussion of Valentine's Day and Mothers' Day and other special days, I "hinted" for a birthday gift. I hope you're only teasing because I certainly had no such intention. That's not something I would do. Actually, come to think of it, I'm probably not subtle enough to hint.

You present me with quite a choice for a birthday gift: you, or a work of petit point. Well now, let me think. . . . A few years ago, on being faced with a choice I would write down all the pros and cons of each, and try to reach a rational, sensible conclusion. But now, as I told you before, I go by gut reaction. "Am I there for the logic, or is the logic there for me?"

So, let's see. First choice: you could send yourself C.O.D. What a proposition! You didn't even consider that I might refuse delivery, did you? Ha! What would that do to the "egotistical bastard?" (Your words, but I'm happy to adopt them.) Which reminds me, now I know why you couldn't get out of the cell that time you had a toy gun at the North Bay Jail. Your head wouldn't fit between the bars! Ha!

Seriously now, I'm picturing the Post Office delivery truck pulling up in front of my house with a large Birthday Box for me. What if I decide I do want the parcel but don't have the money to accept it? That would be a problem—to say nothing of a shame. But let's not drop the idea completely; by then the Income Tax rebate should be here. Listening to my Leonard Cohen records and sipping a brandy—as you suggest—does sound mighty appealing. As for the petit point, I do hate to appear pushy, but since you've offered, tell me more about it.

After all past joking it was a different thing to read your twelve pages where you explain your real views on the things we argued about, or I took you to task about. I do like what you say, especially your ideas on chivalry and—see—that's exactly what I meant when I said I see you as non-chauvinistic. I agree that at the base of it we really would agree on most things if we had the time to talk them out. Yes, because we never seem to complete one subject before going on to another, we run into misunderstandings, as you say. Expressing ourselves in letters is another problem. Sometimes things are meant to be joking but are taken seriously or misconstrued—like when I told you I hesitate to bring Pam to the visit because of "what she will see." You took it personally, took it to mean she will see the "bad shape" you consider yourself to be in. But I didn't mean anything like that. I meant I'm worried about her seeing how we relate, the laughing, joking, that there's a lot more going on than interviewing for a book. Kids are so restricting, see their parents as one-dimensional, think they have no lives of their own—especially mothers. I really think that if a kid were given a choice between a mother who is physically at home, preferably in the kitchen baking cookies but with a heart sinking to the floor, and a mother who is happily pursuing some line of interest outside the home, he/she would chose the former. Every time. Hands down.

As for grey, well, I've always considered grey hair and a young face to be exceptionally attractive.

◆   ◆   ◆   ◆

Here comes your laugh for the day! I wasn't laughing then, but I can now. For weeks now I've been trying to track down a woman who was obviously not living where she is on record as living. There was a ferocious dog tied up outside of the house (out in the country, near Feronia)—looks German Shepherd mixed. I knew she must be going there to feed it—at least occasionally—it looked awfully lean—so I left a note on the door for her to call me. She did, and we arranged a time for my visit. When I arrived the dog was in the house and as soon as I entered it splayed itself out on the floor in that about-to-attack posture of a wild animal, growling at me with evil in its eye. I was scared but tried not to show it because people say if a dog knows you're scared that's when it will attack. The woman told one of the kids to take it into the kitchen, which he did, and I forgot about it. We had our conversation (I think she's living downtown with a man) then I got up to leave. Just as I approached the front door, the dog went into its act again, but the kid grabbed it and held it by the collar. I had just reached the car when—oh my God!—you should have seen it! It bounded at me, snarling, teeth bared, eyes savage. I had no time to do anything more than turn my back and hunch myself against the car door to protect myself. It leapt up, took a bite at my rear, I shrieked, the kid rushed up and grabbed it by the collar and I jumped into the car. All in a flash. With me safely in the car, the kid freed it. Well! That dog lunged at the car window time and time again, wild-eyed, snarling, snapping, teeth bare, nails scraping on the window, determined to get at me. Such hatred! Why? Am I that unlovable?

From there I went home to examine the damage. Can you believe this? It bit me so hard that there was actually visible on my butt one whole row and one partial row of teeth marks. Blood was even drawn, and this through *six* layers of clothing: winter jacket, sweater, pants, blouse, pantyhose and panties. Can you imagine if it had been summertime? I hate to think.

Well, then I went to the office and told Roy what happened. He says if the skin is broken I need to go to the doctor for a tetanus shot. So I went.

"Let me see it," says the doctor.

"Only if you don't laugh," I tell him, turn around, expose the area (you're picturing this, aren't you?) and—get this—he laughed!!! What do you think of that? Bet you have no sympathy for me, do you, with me trying to catch that woman on welfare fraud. I think she trained that dog to get me.

You must wonder why I'm wearing all those clothes when I'm in a car. Well, for one reason, it's been cold lately (−20°C), but the main reason is that I have to be prepared for getting stuck in any God-forsaken place. My territory is enormous—the entire Districts of Nipissing, Parry Sound and Muskoka—bigger than some countries, and sometimes I have to go into remote areas where there's danger of getting stuck and stranded.

◆   ◆   ◆   ◆

I have your solution to the puzzle, and all I can say is you really *are* a brat—a sneaky brat, at that! OK, I admit the solution stays within the rules technically and no one said we couldn't sneak *along* a line instead of crossing over it. Guess this betrays my inability to "think outside the box," eh? Literally and figuratively.

Thanks a lot for your answers to the questions on the Mr. Dupuis part. I'll just make those few revisions and the chapter will be finished, then I'll send it to you. Thanks also for the account of the time between leaving Hamelins' car here on Seventh Ave. up to when you met Mr. Dupuis. It's very helpful. The descriptions are clear and detailed, plus I was able to find most of the route on the map. I have about half of it typed out already.

Well, the day after you abandoned the car here I was at the office when Roy came out and told us his wife had called to tell him you were cornered in a house near Fraser and King. Oh my God! I grabbed the phone! No answer! Panic! Told Roy I've got to go home and flew out of there.

Crowds, police, police vehicles everywhere. Fraser St. was blocked off and what we call the SWAT Squad was there in their grey uniforms and caps and big army boots, marching down the street military-style, bayoneted rifles held out in the cross-breast position. Quite impressive. They had a house on Fraser St. surrounded. Do you know someone in that house? It's between Sixth and Seventh Avenues. Cloud was there too, sniffing around like crazy.

I found the kids near the corner, in the first row, watching the action. I wasn't pleased and tore a strip off Pam for allowing the younger ones to be in such a dangerous place—especially a five-year-old. Nevertheless, we stayed and watched for a while.

When I write this part of the story, I'll use Pam as narrator. She wasn't scared so didn't bother to lock up when I went back to work like I told her. Not long later came a knock to the door. Unconcerned, she opened it, and found herself looking down the barrel of a shotgun! My God! Did they think you were going to answer *in person*? So there she is with four city police officers, all with guns pointing at her, one at the door, another at the foot of the porch steps directly ahead, and one on either side of the door, backs crunched against the wall. Three shotguns and a revolver! Jesus! She's only a kid!

"You seen anybody around, or seen anything strange going on?" he asked her. All she could do was utter a faint No, but even though terrorized, the thought was running through her head: "I think *this* is mighty strange."

He asked if we had a garage, so she got the key and took them out back, shaking in her shoes all the while. There was no one in the garage. ☺ On the way back she told them about the two crawl spaces under the house. They didn't bother with the first one (you could have been there and they didn't even look!) but they did look under the porch. No one there. Then they told her to keep the doors locked and went on to the next house. Well, she definitely locked the doors this time. *Now* she was truly scared.

About four o'clock it came on the radio that you were trapped in the French church down the street. I came storming home again, but it was another false alarm.

The Nugget arrived with lots of pictures of the street action that morning and news of the eleven captives at the lake the previous day, complete with a photo of you beside the campfire. I remember saying to Pam, "What's going on here? All these people he's 'taken captive' and not one harmed—and everyone worked up as if some wild animal is on the loose!" She pointed out that "not everyone" was worked up.

◆   ◆   ◆   ◆

You ask about the car keys. Yes, it was six years ago that he took them from me. That was what forced me to make my own escape—of sorts. He was trying to keep me in jail (and I don't say that because of you, I've always described it that way). Everyone says I was so "brave" to leave with five children and Belinda only twenty-one months old. I wasn't brave; it was a matter of survival—get out or die.

Actually, he wasn't really a bad guy—until the end, that is. It was more the unstimulating nature of the relationship and the little town we lived in. Really, we had nothing in common. He didn't read, for one thing. The only things we ever talked about were the children, the house, town gossip, who's playing hockey Saturday night. That kind of thing. Mind numbing.

Well then, "Why did you keep having more babies and lock yourself in like that?" a person might rightly ask. I didn't know why at the time—just did it, and wanted to—but I know why now. Since the feminist movement has come to the fore, I see it clearly. All of us girls of the 50's were brainwashed into thinking that being a wife, mother and keeping a house was the sole means of fulfillment, and we went at it with a fervour. Don't forget that after the war, when the men came home, women, who had been working outside the home, were pushed back in. One of the main ways in which the pushing was made palpable was widespread media propaganda promoting the Happy Housewife. Movies, TV, and a plethora of women's magazines that popped up at the time, fed into that image, indoctrinated us. Housewives were now Household Engineers. Professionals. But the promise was empty, the "job" didn't fulfill, so we (I say "we" because there are legions of us), with this kind of socialization behind us, concluded that if what we were doing wasn't fulfilling us, then we probably weren't doing enough, needed to try harder, or needed more of what we had. If two children didn't satisfy, well then, have another; if the house didn't satisfy, put more effort into it, redecorate, buy a bigger one. On and on. We never questioned the theory; we questioned ourselves. It's a sad, sad story when you think of all the intelligent women whose talents and abilities went to waste. The conventionality of the 50's! What a mind-crushing decade. I'm sure, from your reading, you're aware of all this.

Well, after Belinda was born I went into post-partum depression. Now this is a whole topic in itself—both what causes it and the experience of it—too much to get into here. The prevailing theory is that it's a chemical imbalance. In my case I've come to the conclusion that, yes, there was probably some kind of physiological trigger, but the underlying cause was the excruciating boredom of my life (overwork, the repetitive nature of that work, lack of mental stimulation). The proof is that the depression had been going on for almost two years, but once I made my escape it disappeared, never to be seen again. I did love having the babies, looking after them, playing with them, but after thirteen years my world had become house-sized, my vocabulary and interests child-sized.

Some time ago I mentioned that Van Gogh had helped me through a hard time. This was the time to which I was referring. Depressed, struggling to put one foot in front of the other, on anti-depressants, which have side effects of their own, seeing no hope for change, I stumbled on this passage— or it was sent to me, as I prefer to think:

You say, "Let us hope for better times." You see, that is one of the things one must be careful of, it seems to me. To hope for better times must not be a *feeling*, but an *action* in the present.

Are we getting to the keys, you must be wondering. Hold on; we're getting there. The taking of the keys was the result of the "action." VG had told me it was no good sitting around hoping for improvements, I must take *action*. So, take action I did. The first act was to register for a night course, a university credit course in Philosophy at Nipissing University College in North Bay. Then I started going to the city more often (kids with me, of course—shopping at Towers and eating in their restaurant was a big thrill, that's how hard up I was), going to see old friends (again, the children with me). Well, he didn't like any of this. Called it "running around." He wanted me in the kitchen like his mother, who seemed to have been housebound most of her life as far as I can tell.

To prevent me from "running around," he took money out of the bank account so I couldn't buy gasoline. If he left the car at home (went to work with others) he made sure the gas tank was empty so I couldn't go anywhere. I was effectively in prison.

At some point, however, I managed to teach a few days. When I got paid I put gas in the car and went to visit friends at Kearney for the day, the kids with me. It was when we got back that he took the keys. And that's when I took the definitive "action"—I left. It didn't take any thought; it was Survival. (My leaving must have been quite a scandal. I was only the second woman in the history of the town to have left her husband. But my exit, alas, was boring in comparison to hers. She left on the back of a motorcycle, with a man, *sans enfants*.)

Leaving when you have children isn't as easy as I'm making it sound. You can't do it without money, without a job, without a place to go to. Welfare was not in my background, so it never occurred to me that I could use it as a resource. But Fate—as a result of a dream—provided me with a place to stay, and that's a story I'll have to tell you another time. Various problems with the children since then perhaps make it seem leaving might not have been the best thing for them, but I'm convinced that if I had stayed it would have been even worse: they would have had a mother who was seriously depressed, ineffectual, and in and out of the psych ward. Of that, I'm sure.

What moulting time is for birds, so adversity is the difficult time for human beings. One can stay in it, in that time of moulting, but one can also come out of it renewed.

Do you find that inspirational? Reading Van Gogh's letters bolstered me, gave me courage. I felt I had a friend, a supporter, someone I could identify with, a person who understood me. Most people have a completely mistaken idea of him. It's true he lost his balance at the end, but only at the very end. Before that he was not crazy; he was seized with ideas to which he had to be true, no matter the cost.

It's interesting that his way of thinking means so much to me, and yet he and his life are so totally removed from my experience (lived in a different time and place, was a man). It's odd, too, that I like him so much because he was, in fact, often unlikeable, disagreeable. In his religious period he was quite obnoxious, and indeed obsessive over many issues. But I can relate to that—just think of me staying up half the night in order to solve a "female" puzzle.

It's wonderful to be able to express myself to you in this way, Don. I know you understand. We've lived such different lives; I don't know what accounts for the common ground.

Now, when am I going to get the writing done, if I keep on writing all these long letters? (I don't hear you complaining, though.) I *am* working on it. I've finished the Mr. Dupuis chapter—will send it soon. Also finished transcribing the notes you sent. Will start developing the Fraser St. manoeuvres next.

THAT LETTER COULD HAVE BEEN considerably longer. I sat there a long time, thinking. I wanted to tell the rest, for if *he* didn't understand, who would? But the stigma was just too great. Later. And better done in person.

Trying to recall the events was like watching a faulty video: a few clear frames flip by, for a while the pictures are indistinguishable, then a few more frames come into focus.

In the first scene I wake up in an unfamiliar bedroom with two single beds. The other bed has been slept in; I'm not alone. I get up and pull open the drapes. Apartment buildings across the street; I'm in a city. I've been kidnapped. Someone has drugged me (that's why I don't remember) and brought me here. The reasons can only be sinister. I'm very calm about this; I know I have to be smarter than them in order to get away.

My roommate comes in. She chats like I'm supposed to know her. I try to be noncommittal. She seems so innocent I decide she's probably another victim, so I take a chance and ask her where we are. Branson Memorial Hospital.

But this is definitely not a hospital room, so I know I'd better be careful in talking to her. She proceeds to tell me the hospital is in Toronto, on Finch

Avenue near Bathurst Street. But I know this is not Finch Avenue. I grew up in Toronto and in my teens lived not far from there, so I know Finch Avenue is a Concession Line out in the country, north of the city. I used to go horseback riding in that area.

I go out into the hall. A pleasant-looking man comes along with a little tray of paper cups. Says it's time to take my medication, come with him to my room so I can take it with water. I go along, I have to, until I can figure it all out and seize my moment. I go with him and take the pill, even though I dread what it might do.

When he leaves I ask my roommate who he is. A nurse, she tells me. Since he's wearing ordinary clothes, I know she's lying. Besides that, he's a man. He must be one of the captors.

The memory-screen goes blank.

The next scene is set in a small dining hall. I'm sitting on a wooden chair at a long wooden table and honey is dribbling off the slice of toast I'm eating. I've got honey all down my front and I'm hunched over, trying to corral the rest of it onto the plate. A woman is bent over beside me, her arm around my shoulders.

"It's good to eat something sweet after shock treatments," she tells me. I know nothing of shock treatments.

"Why would I have shock treatments?" I ask her.

"Because you're depressed."

"I'm depressed? I don't remember being depressed."

"It's a post-partum depression. You had a baby."

"I did?" I think hard about that and a vague memory stirs. Yes, I think I do remember having a baby. Maybe. I'm not sure.

I go back to my room, lie on the bed and think about it, and I do remember having a baby—a little girl—and I remember Bill and the children coming to get us from the hospital. Civic Hospital in North Bay. I have a picture of the nurse coming out to the car with us, pushing me in a wheelchair. She says, "Happy Landings" as she closes the car door. My eyes are brimming with tears and I can't understand why because I think I'm happy. She must think I'm crazy, it occurs to me, with a carful of children like this. Another memory surfaces. I'm sitting with—whom? It's a woman. I think she's a friend. I have the baby on my lap and we're watching a Remembrance Day service. And then I find myself in this place.

Black screen. Lines. Flipping images.

Next picture. I'm in the common area. Many people say they're patients and all the "staff" wear ordinary clothes. I know this is a monumental plot; they're all cooperating in a grand deception. One of the "staff" tells me it's time for my appointment with the psychiatrist. I know I don't have a psychiatrist, but I follow along to his office. He's a tiny man with a ramrod straight back. Elfish in appearance. Dr. Wolanski. He refers to things we talked about at our last meeting, but I know very well I've never seen this man in my life and play my cards appropriately.

This movie is very confusing, pictures indistinct, plot sketchy. I'm standing at the door to my room and two men are approaching me from the hall—"nurses." I back away slowly, imperceptibly; I don't want them to see I'm scared. They come nearer and nearer. The soundtrack has gone silent, but I know what they're saying. They're telling me to come with them, it's time for my shock treatment. Slow motion takes over. I'm inching . . . inching . . . backward into my room. They come nearer . . . and nearer . . . until I'm trapped against the closet door. I want to scream, to fight, to beg—anything—but won't allow myself. I'm smart; my moment will come. The screen clouds over and I don't see what happens next.

Next picture. I'm back in Dr. Wolanski's office and this time I have a better grip on reality. I know I'm in a hospital and I believe he's a doctor. I even tell him about last time, how I only pretended to know him. He hadn't realized; I had pulled it off nicely. He tells me my baby was born on September 18. I remember all the details of the birth, of going home, taking movies of the children holding their new sister as soon as we got there. The next thing it's November 11th. And then I'm here.

I go for a shock treatment. Get up on the table. Don't worry, they tell me, we're going to sedate you, you won't know anything. I don't like this, don't want it, but I'm in the machine. I do what I'm told.

It's late December. Where was Christmas? I've been here four weeks. I'm chair of the Patients' Committee. How did that happen? We're planning a New Year's Eve party, ordering pizza. How is it that I fit in here, but don't fit in where I live?

One day I decide to phone Bill. I go around asking everyone to make change so I can call from the pay phone in the common room. After he answers and I drop in all the coins, he asks me why I didn't just call Collect like all the other times. But for me, this is the first time I've called. It's a mystery how the brain works—or doesn't, as the case may be.

The doctor tells me I've had seven shock treatments and they aren't working. Usually they give them on the non-dominant side of the brain, so now they're going to try the dominant side. I have no idea what he's talking about, nor do I have any curiosity. They can do anything they want.

Next thing I'm told I'll soon be ready to go home, I can go out on my own—a trial run, so to speak. I go to the nearest shopping centre and buy myself a two-piece outfit, a skirt with a long top, blue, size 16 because I've gained so much weight.

It's the final "Group." The day before I'm to go home. We're in a circle and Warren asks me what I'm going to do differently when I go home. I say I don't know. "Are you going to stand up for yourself?" I don't answer. I don't know what the answer is. I don't even understand the question.

He repeats the question and still I have no answer. He gets up and stands in the centre of the circle. "Get up here," he tells me. I get up in the circle with him. "What are you going to do to stay healthy when you go home?" I'm mute. "Well, are you going to speak up for yourself?" I don't know what to say. "Look," he says, "are you going to let people push you around?" I wish I could collapse into myself, disappear. "Speak up! What are you feeling now? You've got to tell people what you think, what your needs are! Are you going to tell your husband what you need?" I have no answer.

With that he pushes me in the shoulder. I'm astounded that he would do such a thing. "Well? . . . Well?" He's getting aggressive, pushes again. And again. "Well," he repeats, "what are you going to do?" I don't understand how he can do this to me, and in front of the whole group. What am I supposed to say? What am I supposed to do? He pushes again. "Doesn't that make you angry?" he taunts. Push. . . . Push. . . . I back away. . . . Push. . . . Back away. "You let people treat you like this?"

To my own surprise, I take both hands and push him hard in the chest. I'm shocked at myself. How could I do that?

"Good!" he shouts, with a big smile. Everyone applauds and he follows up with a lecture on depression being anger turned inward and how I have to learn to let it out.

The next day Bill comes to get me, and I leave the hospital quite uncertain about both the nature of the problem and the solution to it. But they had said it's time to go home, here are your pills.

A few evenings later we go to see Pam and Billy who are staying with people somewhere in the country between Trout Creek and Powassan. I have no idea who these people are or how they were found, but the children are able to go from there to their school in Trout Creek on the school bus—Pam in Grade Four, Billy, Grade Three. It's good to see them looking well and I'm gratified that they're happy to see me. But it's more of an intellectual construct than a feeling. I feel nothing.

The following weekend Cheryl and Brenda come home. Brenda had stayed with Bill's sister and family in Powassan because her Kindergarten was there. Cheryl's Senior Public School was near Powassan (she was in Grade Seven) so she also stayed in that town, with friends of ours. I marvel how it could be that I could have such lovely children. I had—and have—no idea what they thought of their mother's disappearance. They certainly must have felt her absent presence before she even left. I'm overwhelmed, don't know where I'm going to find the strength to do all the work, prepare the meals, wash the clothes, clean the house. . . . Especially from the distance. I'm operating from some other location; I don't know where it is. If I knew, maybe I could come back.

Pam and Billy return a week later. Four beautiful children. All seemingly happy. How could I have such happy children when I'm so poorly put together myself? And why did the hospital tell me I was ready to come back when I know I'm not?

For the next month, once a week, when the children are in school, I go on the bus to Powassan—12 km to the north—to see Belinda. Walking to the bus stop is an ordeal. Everything floats far from me. I've nothing to hang on to. I'm a pea in the middle of an ocean. On the bus it's better, I'm enclosed, secure, don't have to be in control; the bus will do what it has to do without help from me. In Powassan the streets are filled with white cotton floss gone wispy. It's everywhere, and it's wrapped around me like gauze, separating me, cordoning me off. I struggle the five or six blocks to Elaine's house.

Elaine, whom I don't know—she's a friend of a friend—takes me into a bedroom. There, in a crib, lies a four-and-a half month-old baby. Smiling. Beautiful. Healthy. I know she's mine because people have told me so; I believe them because she looks like the others. But she could just as well be Elaine's—or anyone's. In March, we bring her home. I put her on the bed to change her diaper, and look her over from head to toe. She's my baby, she's six months old, and I don't know her.

I have no feeling. No energy, no enthusiasm. No curiosity, no interest. I'm not thinking enough to figure out that maybe this isn't right; maybe it's the pills. Or maybe their Electroconvulsive Therapy has wrecked me. I do what I have to do, day by day, and sleep in the afternoons, with the baby. I try to read but can't. I know the words, they're all lined up nicely on the page, but they have a way of disassembling themselves in mid-air. I practice every day and gradually, gradually, improve, although I find in reading the newspaper just how much has been eliminated from my recorded life. When reports of the upcoming Charles Manson trial start appearing, it's the first I've heard of him, his cult, and what they did the previous August. I have a vivid picture, however, of Neil Armstrong walking on the moon only nineteen days earlier. The My Lai massacre of September 5 is news to me, as are the protests to the Vietnam War that grew out of it. Woodstock and Hurricane Camille come to my awareness. Obviously, I must have known about them at the time. The Concord has had its first flight. Rocky Marciano was killed in a plane crash. A lot of things happened in my absence.

One day slides into another and when May comes and the warmer, sunnier days arrive, this, conversely, plunges me into despair. I'm devastatingly aware of the contrast between the blossoming of Nature—its hopefulness—and my hopelessness.

IN JULY, WHILE LOOKING through the bookcase, I come across my copy of Van Gogh's letters. Its wavy, discoloured pages evoke a clear image—me, accidentally dropping it in the water while camping at Wolf Lake, a memory from August still available. Underlined passages, paragraphs with stars and exclamation marks beside them, indicated I had read about half, but I needed to start again from the beginning.

I read and re-read, chewed and digested. The letters spoke to me, made sense. He spoke my language, articulated my thoughts. I had found a brother, a soulmate, someone who knew what it was to be different, to be misunderstood. I felt Vincent was an extension of me, that he was expressing *my* pain, *my* yearnings, in a way I was unable to. So beautiful, consoling, endlessly inspiring.

And thought-provoking. "How does one become mediocre?" he asked, then answered: "By complying, by heeding public opinion, by never contradicting the world." Reading that made me recognize that I had become a watered-down version of myself, was living a mediocre life, was not "contradicting the world." But what to do about it? Various letters expressed his optimism that things would improve. These entries were of no help. Everyone was telling me that things would improve, but when you're looking out from the depths, hearing that doesn't help; in fact, it makes things worse, only serves to widen the chasm between you and the "encouraging" person, who evidently doesn't understand. Then one day I hit the pivotal sentence: "Hoping for better times must not be a *feeling*, but, rather, must be an *action* in the present." I could no longer sit around lamenting my lost self, hoping for better times; I had to *do* something.

I registered in the Philosophy class—my first university course. Reading the textbook and deciphering the concepts was an ordeal for scrambled brains. Paragraphs had to be read over and over again. The Christmas exam was written with success, but over the winter and into spring—the second spring—a new consciousness was growing, leading to a different kind of despair. In spite of my best efforts to change things, to perk up my life, I had become convinced there would be no end to the abyss in which I lived. It never occurred to me that I needed to see someone other than my family doctor about my state of mind (she kept renewing the anti-depressants, changing them from time to time); I had been declared "well" the year before, and sent home. It was up to me to cope.

Completely unprepared for the March exam, having been unable to study, I read over the questions and began writing. It streamed out—I wrote and wrote—but not answers. I wrote that I was depressed, that I knew nothing was going to change unless I changed it myself, I knew the change I needed to make was to leave my husband, but with five children how was that possible, how could I look after them and work at the same time, and even if I could find a job, could I make enough money to pay rent and feed them, and where would I go. . . . Page after page of desperation. I didn't know this man, had no idea of whether or not he was a sympathetic person, he was just someone who stood before the class lecturing about Socrates and Aristotle. I had lost all sense of decorum, had no shame, no pride.

The paper came back with no grade recorded, but he must have been sympathetic because in the end he discounted it, used only the marks from the first and final exams, and I passed the course.

All this time I was reading and re-reading Van Gogh's letters. I tried many times to explain my needs to Bill. It was clear that he cared for me, that he tried in his way to listen, and sympathize. But I was beyond his comprehension. His idea of a woman was that she should be content to be in the home doing what women are meant to do, like his mother and virtually every woman he knew. I was the oddball, the square peg. Self-realization for women was a concept foreign to him, bizarre and unfathomable. Finally, when he took the car keys and I saw myself being trapped forever, I fled, not really knowing what I would do beyond the short term. "The goal will become clearer," my mentor told me, "will take shape slowly but surely, just as the rough draft turns into a sketch, and the sketch into a painting, bit by bit, until the original vague idea comes into being."

And so, in June 1971, the children and I left to spend the summer in a log cabin in an idyllic setting near Kearney, Ontario—a massive acreage of forest and lakes, owned by old friends. With me was my sketchpad and pencil, figuratively speaking.

Hi Don,

I have your two letters, which I brought with me to Bracebridge where I have extra time to answer them here at the hotel. You started the first one after the Saturday visit and finished it after the Sunday morning one. Your words of appreciation of the long drive I have, winter conditions, the fact that I have family obligations which prevent me from coming more often are, in turn, appreciated.

The drive home was fine, no problems, the road was clear all the way. *It's an odd, odd thing to leave there and re-enter the "real world." Leave the confinement, drabness, harshness, the clashing and crashing of the smallest sound. Then, abruptly—and reluctantly—I'm propelled into a spaciousness—and quietness—that's at first hard to fathom. Exit to the open fields surrounding the prison; drive along the shore of Lake Ontario, the lake and sky joined in heartbreaking expansiveness. My world, the one that's supposed to feel comfortable, yet even the car, so familiar, feels other-worldly. Everything is disjointed. Physically, I'm in a geographical location that can be pinpointed—Bath, Ontario, near Kingston—but the Me Within is encased in a giant bubble, a warm, protective covering that allows me to linger for a while in that other space, the place where I'm understood, can say what I want, can be completely Me. It's a precious feeling coming out of the visit; I'm happy, even if tinged slightly by sadness.* I never turn on the radio immediately; for the first couple of hours I replay our conversation.

Your description of the tender moment in which we ended the visit was touching. Well, "touching" is a peculiar word to use, isn't it, considering the lack of it—physical touch, that is. *Heavy with the touch of emotion, though, the tip of my index finger joined to yours, oblivious to the glass between.* It never fails to astound me that such communication can occur in that setting. *Eyes linked, saying more than words can say. Longing and satisfaction blending, sinking to the core of the being. The fingers know, the eyes know, the soul knows. They know this is a Moment.* As for me putting up with your "messy thinking" (as you say) and your "poor mental state," I'm just glad I don't have to deal with you in a "good" mental state—I wouldn't be up to it!

Tuesday night I went over to my friend Paula's place. We worked together five years ago on a committee to get a municipal day care centre set up (unsuccessfully), and after that on the committee that got the Women's Centre started. I told her about writing the book, which is ironic when you consider that the first week of the manhunt I took Brenda and Belinda to her house every morning and picked them up after work. There was a madman on the loose, remember?

Paula was astounded, obviously, and had lots of questions: what have I done so far, how will I approach the story, what are you like, what do we talk about, that kind of thing. Because she and I have a common interest in feminism, I immediately thought of the article on masculinity in Psychology Today you were telling me about. Well! She had the issue! Right there in the house! She brought it out and—oh, Don!—the picture is priceless! Just as you described, and I agree: words can't do it justice. We had quite a discussion on it; it says so much—the woman in her business attire (male suit, adopted), looking down her nose at him, her stance saying "So, what are you going to do about it?" And the poor guy—totally denuded (literally and figuratively)—can only turn his back and look over his shoulder while protecting his "masculinity." It's so clever. She has taken "everything" from him (symbolized by the suit) and left him with "nothing" (symbolized by his nudity). At first glance the message is: Women are taking over and what is a poor defenceless guy to do? That's the body language. Then I told her you had said, "But it's their facial expressions that tell all."

We agreed. That's where the subtlety of the message lies. Isn't there a little twinkle in her eye that says, "Come on now, you can handle this." And isn't there something in his face that says, "O.K., you've got me for the moment, but I'll figure this out." Was that your interpretation? Or, is this my wishful thinking? Because, as I said on Sunday, feminism is really about sharing, expanding and blending. No need for one sex or the other to be limited to just a portion of the full range of human characteristics and possibilities. (Did you notice the "androgynous ideal," they mentioned in the third paragraph?)

◆　　◆　　◆　　◆

Did you read about George Chuvalo getting his heavyweight title back after they took it away for not defending it for so long? I had a wild crush on him in high school. Had no idea what he was like in reality—just admired him from a distance. Think it was the fact that he was doing something different that intrigued me. A couple of times I contrived to go to my brother's locker, which was right next to his (they were in the same class), in the hope of running into him. One day I hit it lucky. George was there, but Gary wasn't. That gave me an excuse to talk. I asked him if he knew where Gary was because I needed to borrow his French text. Well, he didn't know, so he lent me his! (Wow! What a thrill!) Another time, I had the car for some reason. Gary and I were driving along after school when we happened upon George. We picked him up (guess whose idea?) and drove him to his training club on Lansdowne Ave. Those are the only two contacts I had, but they provided a background that has made it interesting to follow his (more or less unfortunate) career over the years. He does have the distinction of never having been knocked down, one mustn't forget. Nobody—not Floyd Patterson, not George Foreman, not Joe Frazier—not even Muhammad Ali—ever knocked him down. Imagine lasting fifteen rounds with Ali!

◆　　◆　　◆　　◆

I feel honoured that you've decided to do the petit point for me. Knowing you want it to be something I will always keep and remember you by is special to me. I'm glad, too, to see that you were already thinking of making it for me before the birthday thing came up. Otherwise, I would feel guilty.

The description intrigues me. "Persian Garden: an ancient Indian print with representations of the Lamp of Life; the Tree of Life; the Mount of Life; peacocks signifying Eternal Life, doves for Peace, and a border of animals of the Orient." The deep red, two shades of blue, gold and olive green sound rich in tone. But, to tell the truth, I'm having a hard time imagining it. Can you bring a picture of it to the visit room?

I know nothing of petit point. I've never done it. Little kid things I've done with the children don't count, but I guess that's needlepoint. I can't imagine doing something that size by counting only—i.e. no stamped pattern to follow. And over 100,000 stitches! You say you don't know how many months it will take, or what it will take to motivate you to get started. Well, I hope the motivation will come from knowing how much I look forward to receiving such a special gift. As for time, don't worry about that. It certainly is too late for this birthday. Maybe next year?

◆   ◆   ◆   ◆

Well, I have now picked myself up off the floor and recovered. Your letter describing your balancing act at the visit was so hilarious it had me gasping for air. "Flustered, inhibited, trying to juggle conversation and give equal time and attention to three women" was some task indeed. I felt the strain myself, but until I put myself in your chair (or stool, should I say—they would never give us something as comfortable as a chair, would they?) I really hadn't appreciated just how difficult it was for you. And, as you always say, it takes the first two hours to get your head in gear in any event. But this time—two hours and . . . finished.

You're not the only one who was flustered. Your opening remark had me acting like a hopelessly incompetent imbecile for the rest of the visit. I hadn't wanted that kind of remark in front of Pam (about me looking good) and didn't know what to do or say after that. I don't know what she thought. Maybe nothing. Maybe I was being overly sensitive.

And more compliments here in your letter. Poor Don, you must be having problems in perception due to being sensory-deprived. (Or is that sensually deprived?) I don't know why you thought I didn't like the beard. I like it. I think the grey in it makes you look distinguished—not old—as you seem to think.

All in all it was a very enjoyable trip—surprisingly so. Felt good to have the three generations together like that. We got along well, had good conversation (I can see where you got the chat-genes from), a good meal on the way home, and driving conditions were fine, thank goodness. Pam didn't say anything about you or the visit, but then she rarely expresses her feelings. (Maybe the mother inhibits her?)

I got the bottle of brandy on the way back. Thank you. I do appreciate the thought. You must think I'm some kind of lush with me always mentioning about going out with June and having a brandy. But we only go out about once every two weeks, and I only have one drink.

JUNE AND I GO TO the Capital Theatre to see Barbra Streisand and Kris Kristofferson in *A Star is Born*.

Kris is a rock star at the height of his "success," but he's burned out. He's had too much of everything: too many concerts in too many places, too much booze, too much cocaine, too much hero-worship, and too much money. Attractive in an unkempt sort of way, he's virile, but rough-cut and ungrammatical. His eyes are unsettling. Light blue and piercing, they emit, but don't attract, give him a remote, inaccessible look. And I wish they hadn't dyed his hair, but left it grey-streaked, like his beard.

He has the fans at his feet but disdains their worship, which he sees as undiscerning. "Am I a figment of your imagination?" he asks at the beginning of each concert, "or are you one of mine?" Now that's something to ponder; that could keep you going for days.

His lyrics tell us he knows he's taking too many chances with no net below, but he's proud of it, says he'll teach us we have to be free when we fall. "I'm the master magician who's setting you free from the lies you've been told," he sings. Tells us to bring the last straw to him; he turns straw into gold. Now that's an appealing proposition. I would like someone like that. Not him, though. It's hard to understand what the fans see in him; his singing is mechanical and he's confrontational, raucous and soulless.

In an effort to escape his managers' demands and those of the clambering fans, Kris flees in his limousine. When the driver asks him where he wants to go, he sinks back in the seat and sighs, "Back ten years." Aha! He wasn't always like this.

Half-drunk, half-stoned, Kris stumbles into a local bar where Barbra is singing. Conservatively dressed and well-groomed, Barbra's appearance and manner are the antithesis to his; she's the picture of middle-class constraint. But her song speaks of curiosity, the need to experience life more fully, learn new things. She wants Everything, wants to play the cello, play Othello, learn foreign languages. She's a good singer but her delivery is lacklustre and tentative. She doesn't know who she is.

Kris is taken with her. There's eye contact. Interest. When a fight breaks out Barbra signals to him to sneak out the back door with her where they jump into his waiting limo.

"What am I doing here?" she exclaims, only after the door is closed. "This is crazy!" She knows it's crazy, but there she is. I love it—her ability to be spontaneous, seize the moment.

"You want Everything, right?" he reminds her.

She realizes who he is but is unimpressed. "Aren't you embarrassed driving around in a thing like this?" she asks.

"God, you got incredible eyes," he tells her. They look at each other in a long unspoken moment. Ah! There's more here than we thought. Maybe I could like him after all. His eyes soften and we think maybe he *can* go back ten years, or maybe he can gain a different future.

He speaks softly. He's not the person the public thinks it knows. She's at ease. The effortlessness of conversation, the wit and laughter send signals: something is going to happen between these two—oh so very different—people.

Next day Kris takes Barbra to his concert where she sees his wildness when he gets drunk, takes a motorcycle on stage and crashes it. So, she knows. She knows.

They're out of touch for a while but later accidentally run into each other and, after protesting that it will never work, she ends up going to his mansion with him. She's not impressed; she'd get rid of it. I love her flippancy and her sense of what is important.

"Who are you?" he asks. "Where do you come from?"

Barbra plays a melody on the piano, a concerto she's been working on. He gives it lyrics, words that spring from his secret place of longing, of loss and vulnerability, words that tell how much her coming into his life means to him, how she's going to make his dreams come true. He rearranges her hair tenderly, slowly caresses her face. It's a statement. She sinks into his eyes. A long silent Moment, charged with desire and unpronounced words. The magnetism is palpable. They kiss . . . their worlds connect . . . their bodies blend. . . . I melt.

Kris presents Barbra at one of his concerts. Because of his encouragement and the happiness he brings her, she blossoms, no longer sings robotically. She becomes a star. They get married and retreat to the desert where they live in isolated bliss, in a bubble, outside the reaches of everyday life. She's ecstatic, and it looks like he has become the person he wants to be. But Real Life, we have a suspicion, is lurking around the edges.

It doesn't take long. While Barbra's star is rising, Kris's is falling. His band goes on without him, and he sinks into his old ways. It's clear that although she loves him, love is not enough.

If her efforts have failed him, he, on the other hand, has more than succeeded in his role as mentor. The irony is that his wild abandon—so self-destructive in his own case—has served as a model to her, an inspiration, which has put her on the path to Everything.

The end is ambiguous. Kris stands beside her bed admiring her as she sleeps. She wakes up, and the last words he says to her are: "I love you."

He drives recklessly across the desert, drinking beer and playing a tape of the song they wrote together . . . "being close to you made all my dreams come true. . . ." Turns the volume louder and louder. Sings along. Drives faster and faster. Crashes at 160 mph.

An accident or planned? My take is that, understanding a love so sublime could not survive, he decided to end it in a flash of ecstatic awareness. The Blaze of Glory, the bursting flash in which all is perfect. The point of Pure Light.

Barbra is devastated. In time, however, she does a memorial concert. Total silence. She starts ever so softly, tears in her eyes: "With one more look at you. . . ." It's barely a whisper. What will she do without him? For when he looks at her (the words of the song tell him), she's everything she had dreamed she'd be. . . . Her voice becomes stronger, louder, the tempo increases. She's flying, exuberant, has changed to Kris's genre. She breaks into his song: "Watch closely now. Are you watching me now?" Tells him his eyes are like fingers touching her body, When she gets to the part about flying high with no net below, we know she can do it, she won't look down, she's become the Master Magician. It's a tribute to his indomitable spirit.

I live in this movie. See it a second time. Buy the album, play it again and again, inhabit the words.

Hi,

Received your letter today. You're too beautiful. I've been working on Pam's narration of the SWAT Squad chapter and wanted to keep at it, but after reading your letter I just *had* to write you. That's what you call being "irresistible," Don. (Now that I have your ego all inflated, what shall I spring on you?)

I do enjoy hearing from you so much—just wish I could write a letter long enough to include only half the thoughts I have between visits. I "talk" with you a lot, you know. Shall I say "Thank you for being there?" (I don't mean *there*—where you are—I mean "there—in my life.") Knowing you does mean a lot to me.

> Well, what shall I say? Our inward thoughts, do they ever show outwardly? There may be a great fire in our soul and no one ever comes to warm himself beside it; passers-by see only a bit of smoke coming out the chimney, and continue on their way. Now, what must be done? Must one tend that inward fire, have faith in oneself, wait patiently yet with how much impatience for the time when someone will come and sit beside it—to stay there maybe?

It feels to me that someone has sat down.

Just as I started this letter a guy from work called and invited me over for "a sauna and a drink." I think that's a euphemism. I told him I couldn't, I have "something important to do." So, here I am with my pot of coffee, the bottle of brandy (most of it still remaining), and Leonard Cohen singing that he finally broke into the prison. Now, that's what I should do. Do you think that's a good idea? He finally broke into the prison, finally found his place in the chain. One would wonder why he'd want to. But he says even damnation is poisoned with rainbows. That's intriguing; I can relate to that. His lyrics aren't always easy to understand in a cognitive way. They're mystical, spiritual; the soul understands.

How nice to know you've made a start on the Persian Garden. And I certainly will "bare" with you (as you say) if it takes some time to complete. I love puns, although I'm no good at them myself. Your namesake in the office, Dick Kelly, is the "punniest" guy I know. He can come up with a pun for almost anything. For example, yesterday the secretary told him that Mrs. Firestone was on the line. Without missing a beat he answered, "Well, I'm too *tired* to talk to Mrs. Firestone." And there's another fellow, Bill Dyke, who is almost as good. Sometimes the two of them get into "punning duels." They bounce them back and forth like a ping-pong ball. We do have fun at work; it's a great group of people.

◆   ◆   ◆   ◆

Well, I see we even have the same book-reading habits. I also read to the neglect of everything else when I get into a good book. (If we keep on agreeing about things, what are we going to argue about? ☺) Don't tell me about any more books. When am I ever going to get my writing done? Every time you tell me about one, I need to read it right away. Do you know what's going to happen? One day you will be out of prison, you'll phone me up for a "sauna and a drink" and there I'll be—still working on the book—and I'll have to say, "Sorry, but I have something *important* to do!!!"

I'm getting anxious to see you again. This Wednesday I'm taking my car in for a tune-up, new shocks and possibly a new starter. Then, as soon as my Income Tax comes I'm going to take a week's holiday, go to Toronto for a few days, and to see you.

Don, I went to the doctor last Friday about this ongoing tiredness. Now, if I had known you were willing to make the examination, as you say here, I wouldn't have wasted my time. I can see it now—you the doctor and *you* being "just what the doctor ordered."

When you mentioned the song "Misty Blue," I couldn't believe it! That song has to be one of my all-time favourites—typifies *exactly* my favourite kind of music. Similar to Aretha Franklin's. Soul-filled, so beautiful it's painful. Gut-wrenching yearning and ecstatic satisfaction rolled into one. I was just playing my record by her. I especially like "You Make Me Feel Like A Natural Woman" and "Dr. Feelgood." Mmmm. . . . Wish you knew the words to that, "Doctor."

Isn't it interesting that almost all the singers you mention are female, and almost all the ones I like are male? Yes, I like "Una Paloma Blanca" ("No one can take my freedom away"). I hear it on the radio quite often. Done by The George Baker Selection.

◆   ◆   ◆   ◆

So, you met Chuvalo in North Bay in the 60's. I didn't know he had trained here. Where was that? I laughed at your comment that he may be in better shape than you now, but you *look* in better shape. That's for sure! He beat "Pretty Boy" Felstein last week (knock out in the ninth), but I don't think either of them was very pretty.

Thank you for the compliment: I can seduce you with no more than water. Am I right in taking that as a compliment, or does it just mean you're "easy?" Ha! Being serious for a minute, I'll tell you the best and fastest way to seduce me: seduce my mind—make me *think*. Which reminds me, did your read that little bit in Playboy about the most intelligent women being the most at ease about sex? Don't like to say too much there, but . . . ahem! And yes, I do agree that the eyes are probably the best indicator of all. Did you know they account for seventy percent of the body's sense receptors? *And I wonder again what, specifically, you saw in mine. Your first letter indicated your decision to go along with my proposal was based on a judgment of the eyes. "You can tell a lot by the eyes," you said. I'd like to know, but I'm not going to ask. It's part of the Mystery.*

Come on now, don't blame *me* for your not visiting me when you were as far as my back yard! (The way you describe the pile of lumber behind the garage and the barking dog tied to a tree on the other side of the fence, indicates you definitely were there as you did your reconnoitring before approaching your friend's house.) And there I was, waiting up *all night*, turning the bathroom light on and off to signal you, but you wouldn't accept my hospitality. I even had a place to hide you. (Under the covers! Ha!) Seriously, it's very strange that I couldn't sleep that particular night when usually there's no problem.

So, *you* cuddle *your* pillow, too. Well, tonight just remember I'm doing the same and thinking the same thoughts. Tonight, let's think of bodies, minds, trust and seduction.

Nite, Gorgeous.

THE INCOME TAX REBATE ARRIVES and I set out for Millhaven. Driving into the grounds never gets easier. The entrance procedures make me feel like a criminal, inexplicably guilty of some vague offence. Guilty until proven innocent. They check his visit list, check my ID. Outer Office phones Inner Office. I know it's a maximum security prison, but it feels like it's designed against *me*.

It's the same every time: I'm excited, eager, nervous, wonder what I'm doing here, wonder if there's such a thing as Fate, wonder if I've taken leave of my senses, wonder if he got my letter and expects me, hope he did because then I won't have to wait so long, tell myself Don't forget to say this, Don't forget that. I wonder if one day this will become normal, wonder what normal is.

The visit is great fun. Lots of laughing, lots of discussing, play-arguing. Before we even get started they make the announcement that the visit is over. I look at my watch and tell him, "But it's only an hour and twenty minutes!" I'm indignant that they should cut the visit short like that. But my watch has stopped, and it's true, two hours have flown by.

Friday morning plays the same. How can there be so much to say, so much to share? He's interested in my family, my work, my friends, anything I do. With endless time to listen to the radio, read newspapers, magazines and books, he's much more informed than I am; he brings the world to me. And no doubt I bring another dimension to him. And the laughing! When have I laughed so much? I don't know how I suddenly became so witty, but I'm quite able to hold my own in the humour department. We have joke duels, opinion duels. We challenge each other. I'm braver than ever before, a larger version of myself, full of confidence.

Two hours pass in an instant and Don says, "See, that's what they do in here. They speed up the clocks at visit time. Another one of their tricks."

"I wonder what the Guinness Book of Records has for the longest conversation ever?" I ask him. "I bet we could beat it."

"Whatever it is, by that time we'd just be getting wound up."

I have to go. But I'll be back Monday.

IN TORONTO I CHECK IN at the guesthouse a co-worker recommended and call Ivy. Ivy is one of the more interesting people I know. When she was small her family—First Nations, Ojibwa—lived in North Bay where she attended the first three grades of school. Then they moved to an island on Lake Temagami and her formal education was over. Yet with her limited schooling, supplemented by correspondence courses, she was able to teach her younger sisters and brother to read, write and do arithmetic. A person of formidable ability and resourcefulness.

Ivy is living in Toronto because she had called up her ex-husband, told him she had looked after the children on her own for a few years, and it was time for him to do it for a year. He moved into the house, and she moved to Toronto and got a job.

Ivy's sister, Betty, has told us we "just have to" go to a teacup reader whose name is "John Dear." This seer is so good you have to call ahead to see if he's there because if it's a day when he's not feeling receptive he doesn't come in. Lucky for us "the feeling is on" so Wednesday noon finds us in a seedy tearoom at the corner of Gerrard and Logan.

I'm skeptical about this, but I'm willing to go along and try something new. Not totally new: Evie and I used to go to Madame Sophia across from Eaton's College Street store to find out if our boyfriend was being true (if we had one) or who he would be (if we didn't).

John Dear is seated at a little table in a shabby back room. He picks up the cup, turns it slowly, studies it from various angles. I study the decor: stacks of cardboard boxes, a once-light-blue but now-obscure-grey curtain only partially concealing a grime-encrusted window. I don't expect much.

At length he proclaims, "You've just entered into a business arrangement."

Not very likely, I think, for business would be the last thing I would be interested in.

"And there's another person involved."

I give no reaction, don't want to send signals, want everything to come solely from him.

He turns the cup again. "There are books all around," he says. "I see many books. This business arrangement has something to do with books."

A frisson goes through me. I don't believe in this, yet out of the blue—out of tea leaves?—out of somewhere—he hits on this. I try not to change my face.

"Have you started a business?" he asks.

"No," I tell him truthfully, but then add, "not exactly" because I want to hear where that might lead.

"Well, there's a business agreement, and it has to do with books," he re-affirms. "I don't see you in the city, though. You're surrounded by trees. In a forest."

I'm thinking about how North Bay is in the middle of a forest and how can he know that? Do I look "uncitified?" I concentrate on not giving clues.

"I see a forest," he continues. "There's peace and calm in the forest—it's a kind of retreat—and yet around the edges there's a lot of action, a lot of noise and excitement." *A fugitive spends a month in the forest while the police search all around.* I'm faint, barely breathing. It's impossible for a total stranger to come up with this. Maybe they have a listening device in the outer room where we had our tea? I think that over but I know we didn't mention anything about North Bay, and we certainly didn't mention my project because up to this point I haven't even told Ivy about it.

"Do you have any questions?" he asks.

"Yes. Who is this other person?"

"A man," he says. "It's a man, and he will be a big help to you. It's someone you haven't known long. This is a new venture for you and it will be successful."

Numb, light-headed, I waft out in a fog of incredulity onto the street where Ivy and Betty are waiting, and I'm quite unable to say a word.

Ivy is housekeeper for a well-to-do lawyer, and he has agreed to let me to stay a couple of nights. It's too early in the season for the swimming pool, but we spend hours in the whirlpool and sauna, which are both indoors, chatting and giggling like teenagers, then I move on to Evie's. She's busy with her three little children who are only two, four and six years old. We distribute flyers for Neighbourhood Watch and when John comes home, we go to dinner and to see *Equus* at the Royal Alexandra Theatre.

EVIE IS SWEET, FUNNY, LIVELY and intelligent. How could I have sat across the table from her, talking so intently and intimately, enjoying her company—my dear friend since we were twelve years old—and not have seen the tragedy growing inside? How could I not have realized she had already begun her long perilous descent? Several years later, eating at The Old Spaghetti Factory behind the O'Keefe Centre before attending the ballet, she told me that in her divorce the court had given her husband custody of the children due to her alcoholism, but she had quit drinking and was working as a nurse again, living with her mother, and trying to regain the children's confidence.

"The doctor told me if I drink again I will die," she told me; such was the damage to her liver.

His prophecy came true, but not in the way he meant.

When I went to live in Toronto in 1991, enjoying Evie's company was the first thing I looked forward to. We did meet a couple of times, but then my many phone messages went unanswered. Naively, I assumed her troubles were a thing of the past, but later I learned that during this period she had reverted to her old ways, had been hospitalized, nearly died, but had continued to drink even after that. The sadness of her life came to a fiery end in 1993 when, under the influence of alcohol, alone in her apartment, a fire started and she died in the fumes.

Dear Don,

Sorry I haven't written until now, but at least I did send your birthday card, which I know you will get a kick out of. (Did I miscalculate? You *are* 29, aren't you? ☺)

It has taken me this long to recover from my whirlwind twelve-day "vacation." You can imagine how tired I was after all those trips back and forth to Bath and, finally, back home via Orillia to pick up the bicycle—2,800 km in all. But I had a piece of good luck! When I knocked on the door at his father's place, my son answered. I'm quite sure he didn't know I was coming, he looked surprised and—more importantly—pleased. And I was delighted because I hadn't seen him for three and a half years. I asked him to come to North Bay some time and he said he would, so I'm ecstatic with anticipation.

I came back to a houseful of mice. Taking dead mice out of traps is not for me, so I'm paying the young boy next door to do it.

There were two letters waiting when I got back, and then there's the one that arrived before I left, which never did get answered—a total of thirty-one wonderful pages.

What? Never been called Gorgeous before? I can't imagine why. You'll have to keep that one close to your ego.

I enjoyed the part where you tell me about the articles you've been reading about L. Cohen. So now you can relate more to the things I've been saying. Interesting that you quote in particular the statement "he is frozen in an anarchist's posture but unable to throw the bomb." Kind of describes me, I think. You say you never hear him singing on the radio. Well, it's unlikely you will—he's not actually played much—although you may hear one of his songs sung by another, especially "Suzanne" or "Bird on a Wire" where he compares his attempts to be free to a bird on a wire or a drunk in a midnight choir. Such images! I wallowed in his *Songs of Love and Hate* the entire summer of '71—the summer of my defection. His words are a tonic.

No, I don't play chess. I bought a book once, learned the basics, and taught Billy. However, he beat me every game and he was only 10, so I gave up. Nor do I play Backgammon. I've never even seen a board. But I love cribbage. Do you play?

And more of your "wise little devil," Andy Capp. I would say more like a sly little devil, myself. I've taken to checking him out daily and am definitely not impressed. But thanks for the photo of you and the totem pole you carved. Some day I'll go to see it.

Oh, Don! Six wonderful visits—even if they did cheat us of time on the last two. Eleven hours with endless things to say. Even so, I know both of us came away saying, "But I didn't say *this*! I didn't say *that*!" It's too funny to think of—twice now my watch has stopped during the visit. I must have willed it. Do you think that could be?

I'm still puzzling on the fortune teller—all the possibilities we mentioned. Body language? Ability to read personality types by appearance? ESP? I know I didn't change my facial expression. Too eerie for words.

This gets me thinking about all the things that come our way subliminally that we don't pay attention to: dreams; a dog barking in the night; a bathroom light turning on; a dropped comment. . . . What would life be if we tuned in to these things, acted on them?

There's a recurring dream I've been having for the past two or three years, which speaks to this—at least that's my analysis. I open a door in the house in which I'm living and see there are many rooms I didn't even know were there. Room after room, one after the other. I'm amazed and puzzled, walk through them, asking myself: How could it be that I've lived in this house all this time and never knew these rooms were here? It makes me wonder how much of what's around me do I fail to see in everyday life.

Next time I will tell you about the dream that changed my life.

I was sorry we didn't have time to go further in our discussion of *Equus* and the psychiatrist's dilemma. I wanted to tell you how similar the theme of this play is to that of *Clockwork Orange*, and the *Loneliness of the Long Distance Runner* to some extent: by "helping" (i.e. changing) people, are we actually harming them? (In the sense that they lose their inner mystery, their passion, the essence of their being.) Well, we said all that, but I'm still puzzling because it's also true that their anti-social aspects don't do them any good in the long run. It *is* a dilemma. Then there's the "Why?" Why is the boy like that? The parents agonize over what made him that way. Did they do something to cause it? "If you add up everything we ever did to him from the day he was born, every influence we created, you don't get the total," the mother tells the psychiatrist, "because he's himself. Every soul is itself." Just like you said once: "Because I'm me." By the way, I forgot to tell you Evie asked me to say Hello to you and give you her best wishes. Isn't that dear? There *are* such good people around.

Another thing I forgot—among the many—and I know you will be interested in this because of your admiration of Native American societies—Ivy's sister is married to Grey Owl's grandson (from his first wife, the legal one).

Don, I hope you don't think I go there for a laugh with no thought about what it means to you; it's not like that. You looked so sad when I left, it made me wonder if visits make you feel worse in the end. I go back to my life, but you go back to your cell. I tell you all the things I'm doing, all my enjoyments, and I wonder if it only makes you feel more isolated. I hope I'm not being insensitive. Please tell me if I am.

Well, it's 2:00 a.m. and I have to get up and go to work in a few hours, but at least it's Friday.

I've been taking stock. I know this is a ridiculous situation. A losing proposition, no doubt, in the long run. But is there a "long run?" There's no long run. This is a guy who is in prison on a life sentence. OK, he's eligible for parole in eight years, but at the rate he's going with his constant infractions of the rules, he'll be lucky to be out in ten or twelve (sixteen to eighteen in his estimate). But that's a moot point, for I know in my heart that there's no possibility of this thing working in real life. It would be a fling. Nothing more. Can I see him sitting beside me at the Royal Alex? Do I see myself beside him in the bars in which his social life seems to have taken place? To say nothing of the house parties where shooting guns was considered normal (which I try not to think about). No, there would be no meeting of the minds there. Still, looking at the present, the now, who do I have better conversations with? Who makes me laugh more? Who is more interested in me, what I think, what I do? I've been thinking a lot about this and realize I'm at a juncture. This is where I could put on the brakes, pull back, be "sensible." But this is what has come to me. OK, it's not a "real life" relationship, but it's mind-to-mind, heart-to-heart, soul-to-soul. Pure in form, unique and precious. Why deny it? "Am I there for the logic, or is the logic there for me?"

I come to a decision. I accept what's happening, embrace it, welcome it as a blessing. This doesn't mean I'm closed to meeting someone in my daily life. If someone comes along, there's nothing to hold me back. This is not a commitment; it's simply a recognition of reality.

Until this point I've signed off in various ways: Sincerely, Best Wishes, Strength, Courage, even Warm Thoughts. Then there was the impetuous "Nite Gorgeous" which must have signalled something. This may not be news to him, but for me it's an acknowledgment. I sign the letter

Love,

Bette

ON JUNE 7, 1977, THE HOUSE of Commons Sub-Committee on the Penitentiary System in Canada tabled its report in Parliament. The all-party committee had been set up by the House Standing Committee on Justice and Legal affairs in response to a motion by the Solicitor General following two years of violent incidents in maximum security prisons, more frequent and more violent than the total of the previous forty years.

The result of six months of private interviews with 2,000 people (prisoners, guards, wardens, doctors, Classification Officers, psychologists, psychiatrists, wives of staff, concerned citizens) and 72 formal hearings, their recommendations were forthright, hard-hitting, bold and brave:

"A crisis exists in the Canadian Penitentiary System [and it] can be met only by the immediate implementation of large-scale reforms. It is imperative that the Solicitor General act immediately on this Report as a matter of the utmost immediacy. [. . .] Prisons as they now exist, protect society only during the two or three, ten or twenty years the inmate is in there; but if the institutions are boring, oppressive and lack programs preparing the inmates for release, they come out angry, vindictive, frustrated, snarling like animals released from long confinement in a cage."

Sixty-five recommendations were put forward, all geared to the creation of a system that would function with discipline and produce results that would benefit everyone. Recommendations touched on all areas, from training of staff, to re-organization of the system as a whole, to treatment of prisoners with respect to the goals of incarceration. The final recommendation was that the Standing Committee on Justice and Legal Affairs should have a permanent reference during the rest of the present sitting of Parliament and the next in order to review implementation of the report.

The next day the handwriting was on the wall. The Solicitor General, Francis Fox, was quoted as denying that a crisis existed and he summarily rejected the final recommendation. So the report was destined to join the long list of previous unacted-upon reports lining the walls of the Department of Justice: the Archambault Report of 1938; the 1956 Fanteaux Committee of Enquiry; the 1966 Special Joint Committee of the Senate and the House of Commons on Penitentiaries; and others, including the annual reports by the Correctional Investigator. All pointed to systemic problems and suggested ways of making fundamental change; all were ignored.

Hi again,

Now I want to tell you about The Dream, but I have to give you some background first, in order to put it in context. My first friend, Judy Sanderson, who lived around the corner from us, had a cousin, Helen. When I was 8 years old and Helen was 18, she married a man who came from what we considered the wilderness—north of Huntsville. His persona fit the perception— ruddy complexion, untamed hair, rough clothes, and his speech had an unusual cadence to it. The idea of marrying him and going off to live in a log cabin without electricity, at the end of a bush road, two miles from the nearest neighbour, was to me, endlessly romantic. And mysterious.

In the next few years George built several log cabins overlooking the lake on their property, which had exclusive access to vast territories of Algonquin Park and its hunting and fishing grounds. George served as guide into the back country while Helen cooked meals and looked after the cabins. Both were hospitable hosts, so in time an informal resort developed.

When I was 16, I went to work there—my first summer job—helping Helen. In addition, from time to time, if George had more guests than he could handle, I would go on the long bumpy ride on a wagon behind the jeep, over makeshift roads, in to the secluded lakes of the park, and paddle canoe for the fishermen. I dreamed of living there, far from what I saw as the materialism of the city.

The second summer another girl was working with me and the two of us had a nasty blow-up with Helen and George, which resulted in our leaving summarily. So you can imagine how strange it was that seventeen years later, on a January morning in 1971, I awoke to a particularly vivid dream in which I had gone there.

An unusual dream it was, seen, not as myself, but in a detached state, as through the lens of a camera, a camera on a leisurely aerial trip over the route from the town of Kearney to their place, 11 km away. Ever so slowly, my eye-lens travelled over the snow-covered road with its few lonely houses, swept up higher for a panorama of brilliant white-crested hills and icy lakes, sailed up over the final long incline to circle the clearing with its log house, two log bunkhouses, the barn and the old house up on the knoll.

For weeks this dream stayed with me, hung on to me, haunted me, whispered, "Go there. Go there."

But that was preposterous. There was no way I could go there, given the way the relationship had ended. Still, it murmured, "Go there. Go there."

All January: "Go there."

Throughout February: "Go there."

Into March: "Go there . . . go there . . . go there," until it could be resisted no longer, and one crisp and sunny Sunday—a true replica of the dream day—the kids and I set out down Hwy #11 South.

Everything was the same except now there was a mobile home where the old Phoenix house had sat for years, abandoned but fully furnished. Judy and I used to sneak into it—creaky and musty as it was—examine every nook and cranny, and I would play the organ, even though there were gaping holes in every melody.

In that back country it's so quiet you can hear a car coming for ten minutes, and so Helen was watching from her window as we got out of the car. She came out to see who had arrived. Halfway down the hill she starts running, calling, "Bette! How wonderful to see you! Oh, I can't believe it!" and pulls me into a hug. That was a relief; it was going to be mighty embarrassing if I had to turn around unwelcomed. "George! George!" she calls, leading us up to the trailer, "Come see who's here!"

George comes out. "Well, by the gee!" he declares, "Betsy!" and lifts me up in a bear hug. The children are all introduced and fussed over, and after we've had a nice hot chocolate, Helen and I take them for a tour of the log house (still furnished, the moose head still pondering from the living room wall), the bunkhouses and the barn. Then we strike out across the snowy fields to see Peter Lake, still the same awe-inspiring, soul-filling view. You would love it there.

In May we visited again and then again at the beginning of June. Only this time a "getaway" was involved because by then the campaign to restrict my movements had begun. My husband was out in the back garden. I knew that in his terms this was "gallivanting," so I hadn't told him we were going. When I saw our chance I told the kids, "O.K.! Now! Run for it!" We dashed for the car (*my* "escape" story—ha!), he sees us, starts running toward us.

"Don't you dare take that car!" he yells. "I'll call the police!"

We jump in.

"Lock the doors!" I order the kids, while starting the engine and checking the rear-view mirror. He's still coming, three car lengths away now, furious, gesticulating, still threatening the police. I gun the accelerator and screech away in a spray of gravel. I don't know what the children thought of all this. They even had one of their friends with them, who must have had an impressive story to tell when she got home.

It was when we got back from that trip that my freedoms as a person ended; he took the car keys from me.

Well, besides the principle of the thing, living in a small town like that—population 410—you're a prisoner without a car, and so not long after, I went to Toronto on the bus to visit Evie and to think. Helen happened to be in Toronto at the same time, so I got a ride back with her as far as her place. I poured out my troubles, she talked it over with George, and they decided that as long as Bill didn't make trouble, the children and I could live in the log house for the summer. And so I had a place to go. More than that, when September came Helen and George moved us to North Bay, donating a truckload of old furniture and furnishings, everything we needed.

And so, that's how a dream changed my life. Or maybe I should say how responding to it did.

◆　　　◆　　　◆　　　◆

My mailbox was left empty and forlorn for two whole weeks—but then, in the past three days, an avalanche, four long ones—well worth waiting for—hours and hours of reading and re-reading, relishing, and relishing again. . . .

Did you hear the Prison Investigator tabled her report on Solitary Confinement in Parliament yesterday? In spite of the Federal Court ruling last year that solitary confinement constitutes cruel and unusual punishment, there has been no improvement in its use. "It is difficult to say anything positive about the dissociation areas of any of the Maximum institutions," she says, and especially criticizes not giving time outdoors each day as proscribed by law. Seems some institutions don't know what "open air" means; therefore, she recommends that it be defined by law as "a space without a roof between a prisoner and the sky." Mind-boggling. Drives me into fits of rage. How do you live with it?

At the same time you tell me your block is moved so they can retrofit the cells with steel-plated walls, steel bed, steel table and chair, all welded to the floor and wall. Steel sink and toilet as well. Don't tell me any more. I know this is done in the name of security, but do they never give a thought to what happens to people as human beings when they are deprived of tactile sensations? I'm sure there must be all kinds of studies on that. Even the short time I'm there I'm conscious of the effect of hard surfaces—not only the harshness of touch and the bleakness, but the jarring impact they give to every sound. Even a dropped pencil can make you jump.

In answer to my offer to send you writing paper and stamps you give me more bewildering news. Only $4.20 every canteen day for everything you need—writing paper, envelopes, stamps, pens, tobacco. . . . and you

can't use your own money. I can't believe it. This system has me in perpetual
bewilderment. It's evident that they do all they can to discourage contact with
the outside.

◆   ◆   ◆   ◆

We had a two-day In-service Training session at the Pinewood Inn this week.
The facilitator was the same fellow I had for the Field Worker training sessions
in '72 and '73 and some of the Parental Supporter Worker training two years
ago. A nice person; everyone likes him. When it was over, most of us retired
to the lounge for a social hour. About ten of us stayed on for supper and a
few more drinks. It came to me as a surprise when, very much in his cups,
he started talking about his lost love. Surprise, I say, because I had always
assumed—by his appearance and manner—that he was homosexual. Not so.
Very much not so, as you will see.

Thirteen years ago, he told us, he was engaged to a woman, loved her
intensely, but she became sick, was sick for a long time, he waited and hoped,
but in the end she died.

"Yes," he continued, the whole table his audience, "it took a long time to
get over it, and I never again met anyone I could love. . . ."

We're all caught up in the story, imaging how difficult that would be.

". . . until Bette."

Oh-my-God! Where to look? What to say? I'm squirming, wish I could
evaporate into thin air, be sucked into a drainpipe, anything. No one says a
word.

"The first time I saw Bette," he elaborates, "I knew she was someone
special, someone I could love."

Oh, shit! He's a nice guy, and I do take it as a compliment that he would
like me, but damn—what a situation to be in! You could feel the tension, the
cringing, until finally one of the Rehab guys managed with great subtlety to
turn the conversation to something else. I left as soon as I comfortably could,
and hope I don't have to take any more training sessions. Or hope, at least,
that he doesn't remember.

◆   ◆   ◆   ◆

OK, I'll bring the kids any time I need to. Glad you're easy with that.
Although we'll have to be "conservative" in our demeanour—if you know
what I mean. ☺ Haven't talked to Billy yet. I'll wait till school is out. Thanks
for your concern and advice.

Paula and I went to another of our dinner theatres at the Pinewood.
It was an excellent performance, as always. We're so lucky, in such a small

city, to have a professional company set up shop. It's successful so far, so I'm hoping they'll be able to return next year.

I'm including a new photo although I hesitate because it makes me look young and beautiful. Maybe if you look at it too much, you'll be disappointed when I appear. . . .

◆   ◆   ◆   ◆

Well, I have to admit (shamefacedly) that you've got me here: "Four females in the house and even the nerve to say 'liberated females' but they can't even empty a mouse trap. That just proves my theory that four liberated Msfits are not equal to one boy."

I'm left speechless.

Then you add insult to injury: "How many liberated females would it take to equal one *man?*"

You're lucky you're behind that glass! ☺

◆   ◆   ◆   ◆

Here I am at the motel following our wonderful visit today—first time I've had the emotional energy to write immediately after a visit. It was so good to see you after so long (or what seemed long—more than a month), but if only that glass would melt away like I know everything would melt if it weren't. . . .

You know, Don, it's more than worth driving so far just to talk to you for two hours. How far would I drive if we could do more than talk???? I know we do a lot of fantasizing about "other forms of expression" (shall I say?) but to me the conversation is still the most important. How many people do you meet in a lifetime with whom you can talk endlessly like that? Not very many. Bodies are plentiful; minds are few.

You seemed shocked that I reacted that way when you were looking all over my face like that. But people don't usually scrutinize another's face inch by inch, and it made me uncomfortable. Your explanation more than satisfied me, though, and now as I sit here and recreate it in my mind, I feel your eyes as fingers caressing my face, stroking my hair. It feels "warm and fuzzy"—as you say.

I liked the things you pointed out as possibilities with Billy, and I will think about them. I guess I've been guilty of just giving up in the face of a difficult situation instead of persevering. But, as I told you, I did have the father to contend with, who has sabotaged things for me at every turn, yet was never man enough to get his own apartment so he could have them to visit, or even live with him when they didn't want to accept my discipline or direction. Just boarded with old ladies until after a few years he finally got the place in Orillia.

We really do understand each other, and I like the way you described the ideal way of living together—it's the only way I ever could now. When I first got separated I thought that after about three years or so I would want to live with someone, but the longer I've been on my own, the less inclined I am to give up all the freedoms I have, and I certainly could never get chained again to that typical routine. I like the way Obi and I lived. When I bought my house he bought one around the corner and we saw each other almost every day, ate supper together two or three times a week, slept together two or three nights, and most other days we dropped in on each other for a coffee, a chat. We never operated as a "couple." I have to admit, though, that twice I was very disappointed when he made Christmas and New Year's plans without me; I did think our "understanding" should have included special holidays. The truth is we had no understanding, and knowing it wasn't going to be forever made me appreciate it all the more. I told you before: "I know what great is and I refuse to settle for less." Well, how could one *ever* have a traditional clinging sick relationship after that??? I can't.

Changing the subject, let's talk about my birthday gift. You asked me to figure out why you chose to give me a cactus plant. Well, is it because you're such a prickly bastard? (I ducked when I said that!) Seriously, what comes to mind is that the cactus can get along with little nourishment—can survive in an inhospitable environment. Is that it? I'll shop for it and the bottle of Drambuie closer to my birthday, but I did go into Kingston today after the visit and got the card. I'll drop it off with this letter in the morning. You can sign it and send it to me. (Bad enough I have to go shopping for my own gift and card—I sure don't want to sign it too!) You're going to split your sides when you see it.

You know, when I tell you you're beautiful I don't mean your looks (although that's included), I mean *you* are beautiful. I just wanted you to know that.

It's 11:45 now and I'd better get some rest—it's been a long day from 5:30 this morning. Sorry I missed our shower fantasy; I'll just have to have a bed fantasy instead.

See you tomorrow.

◆   ◆   ◆   ◆

I have the cactus! I chose one called Curiosity Plant. I don't know if it's called that because it's a curiosity in appearance, or because it *has* curiosity. I hope it's the latter. I have it in a good light on a ledge beside the stairway, along with some of my other treasures—stones and pine cones from B.C. and California (a trip in '75) and fossils from Manitoulin Island (given to me by my friend Sue—she found them personally). I put the little Alcatraz stone with it, and I've taken a photo of the whole arrangement to send you.

By the way, I thought of another characteristic of the cactus, which reminds me of you. It's "funny looking." ☺

Thank you again. It's so nice to be given something that has some thought behind it. I got the Drambuie (who am I to drink it with?) and the card arrived too, so now I'm all set for my birthday—the Big One. You didn't say what you thought of the card. I thought it so special to find one that illustrated your original proposal exactly. There you are, all nicely wrapped up in a box, but then—turn the page—and the idea isn't going to work: you can't breathe. Ha!

Last night I went over to see Cheryl's little apartment she's renting for the summer while she works at the Royal Bank. She and Pam worked cleaning that bank in the evenings for a few years, from the time they were very young, maybe 13 and 14 years old. She got to know the bank manager—used to babysit his children—that's how she got the job. She has a boyfriend here in North Bay, so maybe we can guess why she wants her own place????

TURNING FORTY was much more painful than I had anticipated.

June 27. A ringing alarm brings the first consciousness of the day; self-pity is the second awareness. I'm all alone. One should not be alone on her fortieth birthday, but Pam has gone to her summer job at Keewadin Lodge on Lake Temagami, and I just took Brenda and Belinda to my mother's cottage to spend the summer.

Reaching over to turn off the alarm, I notice that from the waist down I'm stiff and sore—like I've done unaccustomed exercise. Since I haven't, I'm puzzled, but don't think more about it. I lie there planning my day. Monday. Should I go to Family Court and check the records of payments, or go to the office and draft the letter I want to send to the men who are in arrears?

I start getting out of bed and a shrieking pain stabs me. I'm sitting on a knife. Or could be. What can it be? With the help of the night table, I struggle to my feet. The pain eases with standing and is better still with walking. A trip to the bathroom clarifies the matter: hemorrhoids. Lovely.

I go downstairs, make a coffee, get out my work folder, sit down at the kitchen table and bounce back off the chair. A more gingerly second attempt yields the same results. After so much time off work with the cough, there's no way I can stay home so I decide on court, where I stand while checking the files anyway, and maybe the pain will ease as the day progresses.

It doesn't.

Tuesday it's worse. I call in sick and go to see the doctor. He recommends an ointment and Sitz baths three times a day. Tuesday and Wednesday it's Sitz bath, sleep, Sitz bath, read, Sitz bath, read, then sleep some more. By Thursday there's no improvement. I'm supposed to go to see Don Friday—it's the July First holiday—but I can't. And there's no means of letting him know. Imagining him waiting and me not showing up sinks me lower. I send him a note telling him I'm sorry but I have "a painful problem." I'm too embarrassed to name it.

Monday—one week now—I call the office and tell them I'm no better, I can't come in, I'm going to the doctor again. The doctor says try a different ointment, keep on with the Sitz baths. Why can't he see how I'm suffering? I tried to tell him.

The pangs are relentless; it's torture day and night, night and day. Cheryl comes over, goes to the supermarket for me. June drops in. Sue brings soup. Paula phones. Otherwise I'm alone in this big house, wallowing in my misery. I take 222's. Lots and lots of 222's. Lots of baths. It feels better in the bath. Days are a blur, a fog of sleep and pain. Nights cannot be distinguished from days. The radio plays full time beside my bed. "When I need you, I just close my eyes and I'm with you," Leo Sayer comes to me out of the haze, singing his hit of the day. Sings about the miles and miles between us. "Honey that's a heavy load that we bear." It's heavy all right, and it has taken on proportions. "Oh, I need you." Where's Belinda? I need Belinda to cuddle. "What will I do when you get too big to cuddle in bed?" I asked her. "Well, you'll just have to get a teddy bear," she told me. I want a teddy bear. Where's my teddy bear?

Thursday I go back to the doctor, this time determined to impress on him just how bad this is. He examines me, does a little procedure, and says it should be better now, keep on with the ointment and the Sitz baths.

The office calls and tells me I've used up all my sick days for the year and now I have to use vacation days. Whatever. I can't think about that now. I have to overcome my embarrassment, write Don and tell him what's happening; he'll be worrying. I go to mail the note and at the same time go to the Liquor Store and buy a bottle of wine. Pills aren't enough. I wash the 222's down with wine, sleep . . . wake up . . . the pain's still there . . . wine . . . 222's . . . sleep . . . until I'm in a state of near-delirium. "Tonight's the night, it's gonna be all right." Oh, Rod Stewart says it's going to be all right. Concentrate on it being all right. "Ain't nobody gonna stop us now." It's not night, it's still day. I wish the kids were here. The radio is my company, my only companion. Burton Cummings comes to me, tells me to stand tall, not to fall. Is it only the songs I like that wake me up? Do I sleep through the others? Or are they sending me only songs that can help me? Music as balm. Thank you. Thank you. "Sometimes late at night. . . ." I open my eyes. Still daylight . . . "when there's nothing here except my piano. . . ." If I could go downstairs and play the piano, that would be a comfort, playing the piano is always cathartic, but I can't. Burton can play for me. "Stand tall; don't you fall." I can't stand. I'm falling. . . . The pain is interminable, resistant to 222's, impervious to wine. It seizes me around the lower trunk, squeezes, exerts the pressure of a vice, causes my head to go light. Belinda! I need a hug! I have no teddy bear! "Your love is lifting me higher than I've ever been lifted before. . . . " I forgot to answer your question: Yes, I do like Rita Coolidge, and I like that song. Do those words mean the same to you? Is that why you mention it? "I miss your laugh and I miss your smiles. . . ." Burton's back. It's dark out, night now. I'm hungry. No one to help me. Another pill, another drink. "I hope you hear this across the miles." Do you hear it? I hope you hear it. My singer says if you do, my nights won't seem as long. Timeless Love. It's living on. Does Burton sing the whole night long? He's coming at me in waves. Pleasant, excruciating waves. How can he live with the beauty of his own voice? The perfect, true, clear voice. Who talked about the pain of beauty? I think it was Jung. Burton smiles because it "feels good even missin' ya." I miss you . . . miss you. His voice has changed to a woman's. How did he do that? "I wasn't lookin' but somehow you found me. . . ." Did *you* find *me*? Or did *I* find *you*? Carly Simon. The Spy Who Loved Me. Who's sending these songs? All the ones I like, that make me feel close to you? "Do you wanna make love?" Not now. Not now. Later maybe. Later for sure. Have you been hearing that on your radio? Oh, I forgot, you're in the hole, you don't have a radio. Peter McCann. In the Top 30 this week. "Do you wanna make love? Or do you just wanna fool around?" What a laugh we had over that. I'll be you didn't think I could be so brash. But then, you're so vain, aren't you? Aren't you? *Bet you think this song is about you, don't you? Don't you?* Is that the radio, or is that my head? This night goes on and on. But then it started at five in the afternoon. Now it's The Commodores. "Know it sounds funny, but I just can't stand the pain." Not this kind of pain. Another kind. Heartache. Easy Like Sunday Morning. This one has a picture, It's deep red and marine blue and gold and olive green—all in stripes. It's the Persian Garden, but I know the petit point isn't in stripes, yet it's the Persian Garden and there's no explanation for that except that it's easy on Sunday morning, even if I don't know what day it is but it's daylight so it's tomorrow and someone's here, someone's coming at me. Ahhhhhhhhhhhh!

"Sorry," Sue says from the foot of the bed. "I didn't mean to frighten you. I called from downstairs, I could hear the radio, so I came on up."

She sees the state I'm in and takes charge. You can't go on like this, she tells me, I'm going downstairs and call your doctor. I feel only relief; someone is looking after me. She calls, tells him what I'm up to, he gets me on the line and lectures me about what I'm doing. *And what about what you're* not *doing?* I want to ask, but of course I don't. The pain is too much, I tell him, I can't stand it, it's getting worse. But it's now Friday afternoon, so he says come see him Monday. Monday, now *that's* a help.

Sue and I talk the whole thing over. If I were a man, I tell her, and I went to the doctor, explained to him time and again that I was in horrendous pain, he would take me seriously. But a woman isn't taken seriously. She agrees; we've all experienced this. So, I know what I have to do, I tell her: I have to cry. I hate to admit it, and I hate to do it, but I can see that I will have to cry. So Monday, I go into his office, tell him how bad the pain is, and let the tears roll. And it hurts—hurts in a different sense—to do this because I want to believe that a woman can be taken seriously on equal ground with a man, that she doesn't have to resort to "feminine wiles." So I cry. And he takes me seriously. He picks up the phone and talks to his colleague down the hall, a surgeon. I go down to the surgeon's office, he examines me, calls the hospital and, yes, there's a bed available. I check in that afternoon and I'm operated on the next morning.

So much for feminism.

Dear Loved One,

I miss you. I guess you know that. I've been home six days now and am finally able to sit for short periods with the aid of a rubber "doughnut." Will have to write this in just little bits at a time.

Yes, those little joke notepapers are a riot, aren't they? Glad you're enjoying them. It was lucky I had them on hand when I wasn't able to write. They're apt to the situation, as you say, but nothing could be more apt than the card you sent me. It's hysterical! I have it on the piano and every time I see it I burst into laughter. "Scuttlebutt has it that . . . (turn the page) . . . your butt has been scuttled." Ha! You always manage to come up with something special. Did the warden let you out shopping? ☺

Well, going back in time, the first two days after the operation were Utopian. I loved everyone and everyone loved me. (Easy to see how one can get addicted to Demerol.) On the third day they started gearing me down. More than two weeks later, it's still painful; in fact, two nurses told me this is the most painful operation to recover from, which was encouraging. I have a public health nurse who comes in every morning to "attend to business."

(Enough said about that.) Cheryl's been over—went to the store for me. Sue helps a lot—brought me soup yesterday. June went to the library and got me some books I've been curious about for a long time. One is on handwriting analysis, so watch out!

Just finished The Fountainhead, which you mentioned more than a year ago, and I have to say that in the end I didn't like the architect at all, although I did in the beginning. It seems to me there's a point at which individualism can go to an extreme, crosses over into selfishness, to the detriment of all. But imagining your 18-year-old self standing meekly at attention before the members of the Boyd Gang, giving the proper respect, ("obliged to discuss it intelligently," I remember you saying), brings a smile to my face. I picture myself only three years earlier, sitting on our front porch after school, waiting for the newspaper and the latest developments in the search for them. How could I—in my wildest imagination—ever have imagined that one day this link would come into being?

I, too, am "waiting patiently with how much impatience" for "one more look at you." Your letters help so much—the "warm, cuddly thoughts" (as you put it) and the encouragement. In fact, I don't know what I'd do without them, for I've turned into a weak, weepy, snivelling female. I don't know how you deal with all that time in isolation, living in your own head. Even with a radio, a TV, a telephone, books and windows, I still feel cut off from the world, and my thinking is muddled. Everything seems to be tumbling in on me. "Miles and miles in between us. That's a heavy load that we bear." It's still played frequently. "When I Need You."

Things do have their lighter moments, though. This image came to me when I was in the hospital. Picture this: a split screen—me on one side, you on the other. I'm in a hospital bed, lying on my side, in pain, laboriously scratching out a few lines to you; you (on the other side of the screen) are writing me. You're kneeling on the floor on a folded blanket, mice sniffing at your feet, using the bed as a table, sweltering in an airless, windowless cell. Isn't that a picture? It's too humorous to be heart-breaking. Or is the word pathetic? (I censored the nudity, you notice.) *So, now they've found "a whole workshop" in the steel walls of your cell, including hacksaw blades, and you're in the hole again. What can I say about that? I wish censorship didn't prevent asking how a feat like that gets accomplished. It's a mystery. I'm perpetually conflicted on this subject: it's clear, on one hand, that you're your own worst enemy, that you'll never progress though the system if you keep up like this; but in truth, overall, I'm in awe of the ingenuity and spirit it requires—and relish the sly joke on the System. The Long Distance Runner. But who lost in the end? The governor or the prisoner?*

◆   ◆   ◆   ◆

I feel badly about telling you what I've been eating—only told you because
it seemed so boring. Didn't realize you were on "punishment diet"—fifteen
days of a Dixie cup of porridge for breakfast (no sugar, no milk) with two
pieces of dry toast; supper, a Dixie cup of soup and three pieces of bread. You
don't mention lunch. I assume there is none. Who would ever believe these
conditions exist in Canada? It's like something out of Dickens.

I'm, relatively speaking, in dire straits myself. First I used up my sick
time, now my vacation time for the year is gone (some vacation!) and I have
to apply for Unemployment Insurance Sick Benefits. Who knows when that
will come through and there's a two-week period when I get nothing. Since I
live one pay cheque from disaster, and currently have no pay cheque at all and
no promise of one in the near future, what can I say? Disaster looms. Come to
think of it, it's already here. I feel I've fallen into a pit of pain and problems.
And all this time going by with no progress on the book. I feel badly about
that, but obviously I didn't plan it that way.

◆   ◆   ◆   ◆

I sent the kid who uses my garage to Canadian Tire to get new headlights in
the prospect of going to see you one day. He backed up with the passenger
door open and smashed it against the wall of the house. It still closes, but
barely.

You have your own problems, I know, but send some of your Strength.
I need it.

◆   ◆   ◆   ◆

If it weren't for bad luck I wouldn't have any. Cheryl borrowed the car Saturday
night to go out with her friends. Two hours later she was back at the door in
tears; the grille and left front fender had been smashed in a collision with a
motorcycle. No one was hurt, and the police deemed it 50-50 responsibility
due to unclear markings at a road construction site. It's still drivable, but here's
my present situation: I have no money, no prospect of money, a mortgage
payment due in three weeks, and a car that needs serious repairs. And I'm still
in pain—won't be able to sit without the doughnut for weeks yet.

◆   ◆   ◆   ◆

Well, the car is junk. Took it to the insurance adjusters and then to the garage.
Their advice was scrap it. With a new loan from the bank and insurance
money to come, I got myself a new one (new to me, that is). I did it the easy

way; I called on Bob (one of the Field Workers in the office) to help again. When I was hired at the Ministry, it was on condition of having use of a car. He had previously owned a used car lot, so he took me there to see the Pinto. I drove it around the block and bought it. That having been a success, I asked him to help me again. He took me to see a '75 Valiant. I drove it around the block and bought it. As a consumer I'm a complete failure; for me, shopping is *not* a recreational activity, and I have no interest in researching information on consumer goods.

Did you know Van Gogh signed his letters to his brother: "With a handshake in thought"? Would you like a handshake?—Or what?

◆　　◆　　◆　　◆

How wonderful to see you—finally! Four hours bursting—exploding!—with things to catch up on, and even laugh about—in spite of all the problems. When you're in the hole you always say it takes the first two hours to get your head in gear, but believe me, your thinking wants for nothing as far as I can see.

On the way back I got to analyzing the differences in first-day and second-day visits, how they begin and end. I find they're quite distinct. The first afternoon I arrive excited, full of things to tell you, nervous (I'll never get used to going through Security) and, of course, happy. I expect it's about the same for you—minus the "nervous about Security" part.

I wait at the window, heart pounding, go over my list of things to say, check out the other visits. Finally the door clangs, you enter your half of The Great Divide and give a slight nod as you cross the room. No smile. Why is that? You sit down and scan my face. In this regard, I can tell you, changes have taken place; what once made me squirm now feels good.

When they announce the end of the first visit, we give a shrug of disappointment, finish up what we were saying, and part in a light mood. "See you in the morning" are such encouraging words.

The next morning everything is easier—the entry, the wait—and this time you come in with a smile. Bet you didn't realize that. And then the conversation picks up so easily from where we left off. (Do you realize you don't do the scanning bit on the second visit?) When they call time the second day, the reaction is dramatically different: words freeze in mid-air; eyes link; fingers "touch," and we fall into the Unspoken Moment. I wonder if my face looks as sad as yours.

Does this all seem silly talk? As you know, I love to get into the minutest details of things—a "nit-picker" some say—and I guess I have too much time to think on the long drive home.

As planned, I came back via Kearney and found Billy well, happy in the bush (if perhaps a bit lonesome) and glad to see me. He likes working with George but wishes he could go guiding into Fox and Morgan Lakes like I did when I was his age. I told him about the book project. (Do you remember that at one time we started doing a book together???) He seemed a bit uncomfortable with that—embarrassed—"Why would you want to do that?"—and wasn't sure he wanted to go to see you, but when I told him Pam has been, he said, "Well, if Pam goes, I will."

Helen invited me to stay the night, an invitation I eagerly accepted because I was quite done in by that time. And it was while the four of us were eating supper that the news came on the radio that Elvis had died. You probably haven't heard that, being cut off from all media. Only 42. They say it was his heart, but one wonders. . . .

Why don't I check my watch before starting long stories when I'm there? To continue with what I was saying, after a few months in North Bay it was plain Billy was not happy. I know I'm probably to blame for a lot of it. Certainly I feel guilty for having taken him away from his father (he vented his feelings on that very clearly once), but his father didn't do his part either. From the beginning it was an amicable separation; I made a point of never saying negative things about him to the children (after all, my problems had nothing to do with them) and even invited him for Christmas the first year. For some time he came to see them nearly every week—didn't take them anywhere, just sat there in my place—until finally I told him he couldn't do that, he had to take them out. After that the visits became scarce.

So, seeing how unhappy Billy was, failing in school, and having almost no male influence in his life, I arranged to get a Big Brother for him. The Big Brother was a well-known, well-liked person in North Bay and he took him along on his regular activities nearly every Saturday and often phoned during the week. They got along famously and that did the trick. Billy came back to life, his spirits soared and he started doing well at school.

Things went along like that, very nicely, very calm, for about a year. Then tragedy struck. The Big Brother got killed in a car accident. It was shattering. Billy was only 11 at the time. I often wonder if things would have turned out differently if that hadn't happened.

Shortly after that, he blew up at me and ran to his father. The father, of course, didn't have a place of his own, as I told you, so he boarded him with someone, and then someone else, and someone else. He lived in eight or ten foster homes in the next year, then with friends for a year before Bill finally got the place in Orillia and took him to live with him. Can you imagine? Well, I guess you can; you had your own experiences, didn't you?

So, that's the story. After he left I tried to contact him a couple of times but he hung up on me and I gave up, which I guess was the wrong thing to do; at the time I thought it best not to force myself on him. But letting it go so long was probably wrong on my part. After all, I was the adult and he was the child.

Sometimes I feel guilty about having left in the first place, but I don't know what the alternative was. If I had stayed, they wouldn't have had a functioning mother, of that I'm positive. And so I left, which resulted in them basically not having a father. I often feel it would have been better if I had left them with him because I would have seen them every week, would have taken them places, done things with them, had them stay over, and in that way they would have had two parents.

◆　　◆　　◆　　◆

We got back OK. What did you think of Billy? He didn't say much, did he? Shy, or just sizing up, I'm not sure, but he seemed content with the trip on the whole. Brenda was shy at first, but it didn't take her long. She's just young enough that the environment didn't really inhibit her. Belinda, of course, is the Old Pro. She doesn't even realize it isn't normal!

So now you say the Persian Garden has the main border and most of the background finished. But that means nothing to me! I can't visualize it at all. I wish you could bring it to the visit room, but I understand how difficult it would be to take it off its frame and then attach it again. Security. Always Security.

◆　　◆　　◆　　◆

You mention about Brenda being a kid who will always look on the happy side of things. Yes, but if you had seen her five years ago you would never believe she's the same person. I used to call her the Gloom and Doom Kid because she always looked on the dark side and had the idea that if anything bad could happen, it would. I feel removing her from that environment was what made the change, but maybe it would have happened anyway.

◆　　◆　　◆　　◆

What a day this was! First, the eight o'clock news reported someone shot and killed trying to escape from Millhaven. That had me on edge the whole day. But here's the good part—I had friends to worry with. Brenda and I went to see Harry and Phyllis.

Phyllis met us at the door, I explained my mission, and she immediately gave a big welcome—coffee with a piece of cake, open chatter, no holding back. The men were at the camp, hunting (I hadn't thought about it being hunting season), so after coffee we walked out there, along the railroad track, which turns out to be five miles by the way, not three. But on such a beautiful day it was pleasant, although I admit I was a bit tired on the way back. When we got there we found Harry cheating on the hunting game, having a nap. But he welcomed us in the same vein.

Everything was exactly as you described but it's helpful to have a first-hand picture. One thing that became even clearer (even though I always believed it) was that, considering where you were standing, where the rifle was, how you turned and grabbed it by the stock with your left hand, jumped and fell over the washstand, there was no way you could possibly have got yourself organized—while falling downhill—to get off a shot. Well, it's a moot point because in their testimony the OPP never said you did, and I certainly will stress that point in the book.

From the top of the riverbank, I could see you in a circle of red water. The image is too heart-rending. I'm such a concrete writer I don't know how I can possibly write this part with the intensity it deserves. I can describe the physical aspects—you labouring up the hill on your knees and one hand, blood seeping from your back, neck, leg and arm. But how can I get into the head of someone going through this kind of exertion in order to die in bed? You're going to have to help me there. What struck me, too, was the contrast of the setting—so peaceful, calm and quiet—with what took place there. And the nostalgia (irony?) attached to it—you back at a place that had meant so much to you, like going home.

I couldn't believe that couple! You certainly were right in your description of them. I would never have believed anybody with *seventeen* kids could actually still be in love. Incredible! The way they tease each other! The sparkle in the eyes! Harry has beautiful eyes. I told him you were right when you said he was full of the old devil! And I gave them your message that you hoped they weren't hassled too much because you chose their cabin. They said they were questioned quite a bit the first few days, but not really grilled or anything. Oh, Don, I enjoyed those people so much. If they're a sample of the kind of friends you have, I have to say I'm definitely *impressed*. Brenda also liked them and enjoyed the day, and I'm sure it was fun for her to be "on the inside track" and see the place where your story ended. It was so much a part of our lives at the time.

We were all relieved—to say the least—when we got back to the house, turned on the five o'clock news and learned it wasn't you.

They told me secrets about you, by the way. (I'll never tell!) We were invited to stay for supper, and guess what we had? Moose meat pie! And came home with a huge bag of frozen blueberries plus an invitation to come back in the summer and stay at the cabin. I think that might be too sad, though; I'd be thinking all the time of what happened there.

Well, I was just so excited about it all that I had to let you know before I sleep. I've heard there are better things to do on a Saturday night than typing letters. Is that true?

With sincere good wishes and all kinds of silent conversation.

◆   ◆   ◆   ◆

Only three weeks since one was killed and three others were shot in their escape attempt, and you tell me you've hurt your foot while jumping off the fence. You worry me so. *I say that for the censors—secretly I'm actually ambivalent: a large part of me honours the idea of "going out in a Blaze of Glory"—doing it your way. But, damn, I'd rather you didn't.*

Yes, I definitely do know Buffy Ste-Marie's song "Until It's Time For You to Go." ("Yes, we're different, worlds apart, we're not the same.") *You realize that, too, don't you?* "You could have stayed outside my heart, but in you came." See, you're romantic too. (I saw you blush!) I like it by her, but I have it by Roberta Flack. And on the same album is "Do What You Gotta Do"— also appropriate. "So you just do what you gotta do, my wild sweet love . . . I had my eyes wide open from the start. . . ." Sure wish I could sing. I sing with great gusto along with the records, but on my own? Let's just say I'm not talented in that department. Although, somehow, when I was teaching Grade Seven in Powassan I led the class to a win in the Kiwanis Music Festival. It must have been *in spite* of me, rather than *because of* me.

When I was young I had an ongoing fantasy of singing before huge crowds, pouring out my soul, bringing the masses to their knees in an emotional tsunami. Or sometimes I led an orchestra. I used to act these scenes out in front of a mirror, can you believe? (Is that nutty?) The crowd would roar in approval, not a dry eye in the house. And all this in spite of the fact that I really couldn't sing at all.

I wanted to, though. One day when I was in Grade Four the music teacher came to our room and announced she was forming a choir. We stood beside our desks singing God Save the King while she went up one row and down the next, bending over each child, listening for potential, and tapping on the head the ones she judged to be musically endowed. Those who had been singled out were to present themselves in the music room after school for choir practice.

At 3:30 I rushed up the stairs, a jingle-jangle of nerves and excitement, and joined the lucky few. Excited I was about actually being in a choir, to be sure, but my quaking had another source, the fear of being discovered, for I was *not* one of those she had tapped; I was a fraud. But I did join the choir, and no one ever knew. There now, you didn't know what a phoney I am, did you?

INTERVIEWING CAPTIVES and others connected with the story was becoming something akin to a social life. Next I went to see Anne Marie and Andy, who were camping when Don came into their lives. Once again he was exact in his description. I could see why he had told me he liked Andy as soon as he saw him. There was a lot of mischief in those eyes and the laugh lines around them testified to his having laughed a lot. Anne Marie, as Don had said, was completely natural in appearance and manner, no airs, no deceptions. They were a friendly, engaging, fun-loving couple, and forthright in relating their experience.

"A lot of people wouldn't go camping that August," Anne Marie told me, "but I thought: I'll be damned if I'll let somebody like him spoil my holiday."

There were about fifteen camps set up at the time, but they, in their camper, and Anne Marie's sister with her family (husband and two children aged 10 and 12) in their tent, were the only ones present. The others came out for weekends only.

That morning, just after seven o'clock, Anne Marie and Andy went in their car to investigate fresh footprints they had noticed on the road. "No one comes around without making themselves known," Andy observed, "so it was suspicious. We did consider it could be Kelly, discussed whether or not we should go to the Ranger camp and call the OPP."

"If it's not him and we report it, we're going to look pretty silly," Anne Marie pointed out. "But if it *is* him and we *don't*, we're going to look stupid there, too."

"Ah, the hell with it," Andy decided. "The cops are in here every day anyway. When they come, we'll tell them." So they left it at that.

Don, from a hidden vantage point, had seen the car leave and—so he says—entered Jerry and Kathleen's tent believing it to be empty. But, "I'll never believe he thought that tent was empty," said Anne Marie, "I think he just wanted someone to talk to. He'd been eight days alone in the bush by then." When the couple got back to camp, Kathleen and Jerry had already made the acquaintance of Donald Kelly.

"We often discussed whether he might come around there or not." Anne Marie told me, "but we didn't really think he would—it's ninety kilometres by road—I don't know how far through the bush—but we joked about it and said, 'Oh, well, if he comes we'll just give him a sandwich and he'll be on his way.' But when I walked into that tent and saw him, it was: 'Oh my God! This is my last day on earth!' "

By that time Kathleen had cooked breakfast and Don and Jerry were having a beer. Then Kathleen made coffee. Don told them all he really needed was a pair of jeans and whatever food they could spare, but he would have to stay until dark and was sorry to inconvenience them. Soon it was so hot in the tent that Andy suggested they all go down to their trailer where they could sit under the canopy. Jerry told the children they could go play but not to get out of sight; if anyone came they were to come back and not say anything.

Don took a block of wood into the trailer to sit on and talked through the open door, the rifle propped against the wall behind him. "That gun was never pointed at anyone, nor was it ever in a position where someone could have walked in front of it; it was always safe and away—but within his reach," Andy pointed out.

Hours went by. At times Don brought the block of wood outside and sat with the others, then he'd go back in. They asked him questions about the escape, where he had been since then, asked about the evidence in his case. Talked about camping, fishing, the bush.

"You seem like such a nice fellow," Anne Marie felt free enough to say. "How in the name of God did you get yourself into so much trouble?"

He said he'd studied Psychology in prison, trying to figure that out, but hadn't come up with an answer.

Don asked if they were expecting anyone. They told him the game warden came in every day, they were expecting the Junior Rangers to come to clean the toilets, and then there was the special police force nearby, in there specifically for the manhunt and they often came by.

"If anyone comes," he told them, "talk to them as usual. Be casual, but not so friendly that they'll stay. If the police show up and shooting starts, fall flat on the ground. The police will shoot at anyone who runs—and that will be me."

Then started the drama of all the people who *did* arrive before the day was over. First the game warden. "I always go down to the road and talk with him," Andy related. "We chat about who's catching what fish, that sort of thing. Well, along he comes, but this time I stayed right where I was. He was parked close enough that we could talk, but it's a wonder he didn't twig that something was wrong because I *always* go down to talk."

"After he pulled away," Anne Marie put in, "you'd wonder who was in charge. It was: 'Why do you think he left so soon? Do you think he suspected something?' We had to settle him down, reassure him. Then he would test us.

He'd ask first one person, then another, the same thing. 'Look,' I told him, 'we have to trust *you*; you have to trust *us,* too—or it's going to be a long day.'

"We turned on the radio for the news. They had something about him, but the next hour there was nothing. 'Look at that,' I told him, 'You're not even on the news any more.' "

"Yeah, but wait till tomorrow," he grinned.

Late afternoon another car could be heard approaching. Before long, between the trees, the red bubble on the roof appeared.

"Christ!" says Andy, "they're probably coming for that drink I invited them for."

The police pulled right into the lot, backed up within inches of the trailer hitch. No one moved. No one said a word. Andy waved "Hi" to them, gave a brief nod, and sat where he was. Excruciating moments dragged by until the officers gave up and pulled away.

Again it was: "Do you think they suspected? Do you think they went for help?"

"Nah," says Andy, "we were all sitting around looking so glum, they probably figured we were having a family feud or something."

The group had barely calmed down when another car came into view, this one pulling a tent-trailer. New campers—a couple known to the two couples, three teenagers with them. They set up camp and before long were sitting around the campfire sharing their case of beer. It turned out that when this man was a teen and Don was a boy, they lived beside each other, and so there was lots of How's this person? What's that person doing now? and Do you remember the time when?

Now there were eleven "captives."

"I don't feel like I'm running," the escaper remarked. "I feel like I'm camping."

"You had to feel sorry for him," Anne Marie said. "He had such a sad look on his face."

Finally he left in Jerry and Kathleen's car, leaving instructions not to call the police until morning and taking with him the rotors out of the other two cars. He drove the car into the city, parked it on the street behind my house and went through the backyards in order to make contact with a friend. That was the night—I'll never understand why—I so uncharacteristically couldn't sleep.

Research for the book had taken me to their house, but I had got caught up in a social evening—just like Don—and, like him, overstayed. He said he would leave at dark and left at midnight; I started leaving at twenty after ten but didn't leave until one o'clock. Filled with excitement, in spite of the hour, when I got home I had to write him a note to ask how he managed to pick such terrific people, first Mr. Dupuis, and now them.

"Andy is going to see about getting the photos back from the police," I wrote, "and when he does, they'll give me copies. And Anne Marie would like to come to see you some time, if that's OK with you. I'd like that. She would be good company.

"They told me to give you their best wishes for the appeal—they're convinced you'll win, and a second trial if there is one. Said they're really hoping for you. And Andy said you're welcome at their house for a drink any time. They asked me to come back, too. How be we go together?"

The next morning, even though operating on less than five hours' sleep, I went to work on a high. Mid-morning a phone call from June brought me crashing to earth. "I'm so sorry," she said. "Sorry for both of you." She heard it on the radio: Don's appeal had been lost.

I couldn't write him. Didn't write for a whole week. Could find neither the words nor the emotional energy. My worst fear was that he had already heard through the media rather than personally, from his lawyer. He had never recovered—after twenty years—from the blow of learning by newspaper of his younger sister's death. He was in prison then, too, and she had been killed in a car crash.

Later, on Don's behalf, I consulted Arthur Maloney, one of Ontario's most highly respected lawyers. He read the transcript and determined there had been no errors in law. Given a lack of new evidence, there were no grounds for further appeal.

Dear Don,

I got another letter yesterday and enjoyed it. You keep saying you can't write, can't think, can't express yourself, yet to me all your letters are meaningful, interesting and enjoyable. I really feel quite deprived when more than four days go by without receiving one.

Well, I'm busy, busy as usual. Yesterday I saw Jerry and Kathleen and got about two hours on tape, although it was like pulling teeth from a rhino. There's no doubt about it now, we certainly see people the same way. But what you saw as his male ego, threatened, does have an explanation: as "male protector," he had his children to worry about. So, I try to be charitable. It was easy enough to see why you weren't worried about the kids once he gave them their instructions. Father's word is law. I saw that when I was there.

I love the way Kathleen spoke up to you. You go into the sleeping room of the tent, she wakes up, you ask if she knows who you are, and she tells you she can't see a thing without her glasses, hand them to her. Glasses on, she takes her stand: "You're Donald Kelly, and don't point that gun at me!" Then, when you tell her to come out to the other room, she has the nerve to tell you to turn around while she gets dressed. I agree with your assessment; when left on her own she's one spunky character.

Now I have five hours of tape to transcribe, which will keep me busy until I see the final couple after Christmas.

◆   ◆   ◆   ◆

I received your Christmas card and had to hide it. I don't think the kids are ready for all that mush. But I am!!! And so I thank you lots. It was wonderful to receive.

Your mother has gone to your sister's for Christmas. Pam drove her to the bus terminal. Anne Marie told me you wrote your mom a letter explaining why you escaped and apologizing for the problems you were giving her. They got it to her OK. But maybe you knew that.

By the way, Pam just started reading The Steven Truscott Story, so there's a topic of conversation for you. He lived with the author for a few months while the book was being written. Now why don't you do the same?

◆   ◆   ◆   ◆

So good to see you, as always. The roads were fine on the way back. No problem.

It never occurred to me until the drive back that when we were discussing prostitution I should have told you about the time a man tried to buy my mind. What do you think of that??!!

Honestly. He was wealthy and wanted to take me on a Caribbean cruise, to a concert series, basically any place I'd like to go. Told me plainly that sex was not involved if I didn't want it, said, "Sex I can get anywhere, but the intelligent companionship you can offer is not easily found." I'm not kidding you, it's true! But I guess I never could spend time with anyone unless there is something special in it. ("Something special" not being money or things money can buy.) For my birthday that year he invited me to his place for champagne and caviar and then we would go to dinner at the restaurant of my choice. I said no and did nothing for my birthday.

◆   ◆   ◆   ◆

I've been to see the last of the campers and you were right about them, too. We had a good visit. They were open, and gave ready answers to all my questions. I'll use their older boy as a narrator because I need one of the kids to tell the "inside story" about the time you spent with them in the trailer, the fooling around, the conversation (they had lots of questions, didn't they?), autographing their comic books, and them coaxing you to stay. They thought you were the greatest thing going.

Guess what your former neighbour-cum-captive said about you when you were a kid? He said you were "a good little kid, just an ordinary kid." How do you feel about being "ordinary?"

Anne Marie will come with me to visit next time. Guess North Bay would be mighty surprised to learn about that.

◆　　◆　　◆　　◆

Glad to know you received the books I ordered. I know for sure you'll like *If They Come For Me in the Morning*. (I was wondering if they would even let that one in; I don't suppose Angela Davis is considered the ideal role model. . . .) *Man's Search for Meaning* I've read twice and found it inspirational. You will relate to the concentration camp environment and, I hope, find it helpful.

I do hope you'll enjoy the one by Shirley MacLaine. I like her so much. It was written as a reaction to a trip to China she took as part of a women's delegation. She said she cried for days after returning to the U.S. because it was clear her government had lied to her. But, although she found China a well-ordered society with contented people, the lack of opportunity for individual creativity struck her, made her realize she had to take advantage of the opportunities she had, and so, at the age of 40, she resolved to train again as a dancer. It took two full years before she was ready to open her one-woman show on Broadway, which is a big success. She's so gutsy.

Fear of Flying by Erica Jong I already told you about. You will be amazed. A quick leaf through will have you reading it first, I'm sure. And then what a lot we'll have to discuss! I guess my motivation in sending you these books is so you can know a bit more of my thinking. But I'm quite sure you would enjoy them apart from that.

◆　　◆　　◆　　◆

So, the warden met with you and gave us an extra visit to make up for that fiasco. Great! If possible, I'll take advantage of it next time. I still don't have an answer to my letter to him. I hope he puts it in writing. I emphasized that this is the *second* time you haven't been given proper notice on holiday visits. It must have been a long boring day for Pam that day. A fourteen-hour trip (drive down, have lunch, and drive back again), but she didn't complain (she never complains) and I guess she at least enjoyed the driving.

I forgot to tell you I picked up a visitor on my way out last time and drove her to the railway station. And guess what? She also had the experience of going all that way on Dec. 27 just to be turned away. Her guy didn't have notification either and he's in the population. It's hard not to see a plot in all this.

I was thinking about the words to that Leonard Cohen song I told you about: "I finally broke into the prison." That's what I should have done when they turned me away. Can't you just see it? Me, climbing fences, fighting dogs, dodging bullets. . . . The image is good for a few laughs.

◆   ◆   ◆   ◆

We're back from our trip to the World's Figure Skating Championships and it was great. Besides the four evenings of competition, we went to the Parliament Buildings (my, the library is spectacular!) and to the National Art Gallery. For years I'd wanted to see their collection of the Group of Seven and Emily Carr—and wasn't disappointed. The girls enjoyed it too. Such huge canvases are certainly impressive. Once when Cheryl was in Grade Eight and was doing a project on the Group we went to the McMichael Gallery at Kleinberg, outside of Toronto, but their collection is all small paintings as I recall. At that time, the only surviving member of the group, A.Y. Jackson, was living there and he was sitting at the door greeting people as they came in. That was a bit of a thrill.

We had a nice room, not too far from the arena. I wish you had been a fly on the wall the first night. Time for bed—and the trouble started! There were two double beds and a rollout cot for the five of us (Billy didn't want to go). Cheryl and Brenda got into bed together, so it was left to Pam and Belinda who would sleep where. Would you believe it, neither of them wanted to sleep with me. They had a big fight over it! Can you picture it? A 17-year-old arguing with an 8-year-old! It was too ridiculous.

The two of them kept at it until Belinda grabbed a pillow and a blanket and announced she was going to sleep in the bathtub! She went in the bathroom, closed the door, and installed herself in the tub. But Pam couldn't let it go. She kept going in, taunting her, calling her a baby and other insults. Finally Belinda came storming out, grabbed a paper and pencil, and stomped back in with a slam of the door. We were still looking at each other with question marks on our faces when a slip of paper slid out from under the door. Pam picked it up and it said PAM IS A BEBE. A BIG BIG BEBE. With that, Cheryl, Brenda and I took up the chant: "Pam is a bebe! A big,

big bebe! Pam is a bebe, a big, big bebe!" (Obviously Belinda thought she had written "baby." I guess she figured if she left off the accents that would make it English.)

Well, by this time Cheryl was sick of the whole thing. She got up out of her bed with a big show, clomped across the room, and announced in a voice dripping with self-sacrifice, "I-I-I-I-'ll sleep with her," and plopped into bed with me with an exaggerated sigh. Now, I ask you, can you imagine why anyone would not want to sleep with me? I know had you been there you'd have made the sacrifice. And willingly, too, I dare say. ☺

Poor Belinda. Everyone laughing at her inability to spell properly and yet she has such an advantage going to French school. She can read English very well now—has taught herself—I have no idea how, it's so incredibly difficult.

Meanwhile, *my* French classes are going all right although I don't care much for his method of teaching. I hope some day to actually be able to speak French. I loved it when I was in high school and was quite good at it, but it's been a long time now. One evening I took Belinda with me and Father Degagné said, "I don't know why you're paying me when you have her at home." But she refuses to talk French with me. I guess it's too unnatural.

◆　　　◆　　　◆　　　◆

I worked at Bracebridge Monday, Tuesday and Wednesday. Billy came up from Orillia on the bus on Wednesday at noon to come here for Easter with me. We popped in to see Helen and George along the way and it was quite a surprise to find my old friend Judy there with her husband. It's a good fifteen years since we last saw each other. Jim was in my class in high school, so I know him too. We reminisced about school days, and Judy and I reminded each other about what nasty little girls we were (*very* nasty!).

Actually, meeting Judy is my earliest memory. Can you picture my sweet little three-year-old self with my angelic blonde hair, a little ice-blue ballet costume and white kid ballet slippers? We had just returned from my ballet class; my poor mother had illusions of raising an accomplished child. The woman who had previously owned that house had told me a little girl was going to move in, and it was true. It was Judy and she was eight months younger than me, my first friend. From then on we played together constantly. It was a sad day when I started kindergarten a year before her, but we continued to be best friends for the next five years.

Until Joan.

The Douglases moved next door when I was ten. That's when the trouble started. We were completely unable to be friends, all three together, for more than a few days at a time. Judy reminded me (rather thoughtlessly, I thought) of the time Joan and I got the bright idea of picketing her house. We marched back and forth, up and down the hill, past her house again and again, swinging a bell, chanting "Judy Poody, she's so snooty," until Mr. Sanderson came down, talked to our parents and that was the end of that.

Bet you didn't think I was so bratty, did you? But sometimes I was nice. Even now—in fact, I'm so nice I didn't remind her of this. One time when she and I were friends we came across Joan drinking from a fountain in the school basement. Suddenly Judy rushed forward and smashed Joan's face down into the faucet. Joan straightens up, turns to face us, blood dripping from her nose. She stands expressionless. I'm overwhelmed with sympathy, rush over and help wipe the blood from her face. Judy evaporates, and Joan and I are back to being best friends.

Next thing you know we're all back together and our new interest is publishing a one-page newspaper once a week. We do this in Joan's basement using a battered typewriter that produces barely legible print. Six copies. But I'm the know-it-all in this project and won't accept their ideas, so it's my turn to be the rejectee. When they see me in the schoolyard they taunt me: "Bette is a smart aleck, Bette is a smart aleck."

But Bette gets her revenge. One day, when no one is looking, I creep up on the Douglas's front porch and grab Joan's cardigan—a handmade one her mother had knit for her. My mother said Mrs. Douglas spends too much time sitting on the porch smoking, reading and knitting when she should be inside cleaning her house, which is a mess, so I feel almost justified. Later, at dusk, I sneak over to the corner, lift the little round metal cover to the sewer-hole and stuff in the sweater. And feel good about it, too.

Having told you all this, would you believe that I was once chosen Best Brownie in my Brownie pack? I guess not, eh, but it's true. I have the award to prove it—a Girl Guide autograph book with inscription.

◆   ◆   ◆   ◆

Today Billy and Pam have gone off to Sudbury to the library to get copies of news accounts I need for the writing.

Evie called to tell me she heard on the radio about you being on the roof. Now what were you doing up there? Just wanted a view? Do you know the James Taylor song "On the Roof"?

Did you hear about the Van Gogh painting being slashed? My heart cried.

SOMETIMES IT'S ABUNDANTLY CLEAR that life's jigsaw pieces float from the sky and find their places, not by happenstance, but by Design.

Joanne and I met in the visiting room of Millhaven Penitentiary. We chatted while waiting for our visits to arrive, then again on the way out. Joanne likes to remind me that on that occasion I talked with another visitor, a woman wearing an unusual fancy dress, which I apparently admired.

"I wear it for one of my dances," she told me.

"Ah, you're a dancer!"

"An exotic dancer," she specified.

"Ohhh! I lo-o-ve exotic dance," I enthused, all a-goggle. Joanne is still laughing at my naivety. But really, "exotic" does mean "different," doesn't it? I thought it did.

The second time we met, Joanne suggested we go to eat at a small burger place she knew, a simple eatery with a counter and a couple of tables. I may not remember the exotic dancer and her dress, but—even though I no longer eat meat—the memory of that scrumptious cheeseburger, bursting with "the works" remains vivid, a sensuous, tactile experience. Joanne frequented this place, not only because of the "down-home" cooking, but because conversation with the owner was intelligent, informative, far-reaching and—most importantly—hopeful. As Director of the local John Howard Society, he was knowledgeable about the prison system and had insight into how it creates barriers to successful reintegration into society—the opposite to the stated intention. Knowing people like him existed and were working toward better results was comforting, inspirational.

Joanne and I, it turned out, lived parallel lives. She was also in social services, was working as a Life Skills Coach with clients sent by the Rehabilitation Division of the same Ministry for which I worked. We both had stayed in unsatisfactory marriages for almost the same amount of time, and both separated at age 33. Both of us had children who were not living with us, a point of common concern. At that time her three daughters were living with their father, while I had Cheryl and Billy who were not living with me.

And both of us had fallen into a relationship with a prisoner "by accident." That is to say, initially we visited with other intentions in mind, never dreaming such a thing would—or could—happen. In Joanne's case, she and her husband and Sean had all been friends in their teens. They knew he was in Millhaven, so on the way to Ottawa while on vacation, they decided to drop in to see him. Sean asked them to keep in touch; therefore, shortly after, when he was brought back to Windsor to face a new charge, they visited him in the jail there, together and separately, and each continued after the marital separation. A year later, Joanne accepted a job in Kingston, moved there, and visited as a friend. In time it developed into a relationship that was to endure more than twenty years, in spite of hardships and obstacles that would discourage the hardiest of souls.

Joanne lived west of Kingston, in Amhurstview, only a twenty-minute drive along the lakeshore to the pen. She invited me to stay with her when next I visited. Even though I told Don she didn't drink, he insisted on buying a bottle of Drambuie to take with me as a hostess gift from him. His way of letting Sean know he appreciated the offer, I suppose. Prison politics.

Serendipity was further at play in that at this very same time a new visiting policy was introduced: visitors were now able to take their two visits for one week on Saturday and the two visits for the following week on Sunday, making four visits—eight whole hours—possible on one weekend. With a place to stay and good company, I began making the trip more frequently. I drove down Friday after work, stayed two nights, relished in eight hours of talking with Don, and—as a bonus—had Joanne's friendship. Soon I was looking forward to seeing her almost as much as Don. It was the start of many years of supporting each other through trial after tribulation, including other places and other prisons.

Having visited about a year longer than me, and much more frequently because of living nearby, Joanne knew everyone who was anyone within the system—on both sides of the bars. Like me, she didn't accept irregularities and so had had many a meeting with officials at every level, and had had extensive dealings with the Correctional Law Project at Queen's University, a legal aid clinic that provides advice and representation to inmates on issues concerning problems within the system. She would tell me the details of these incidents with a sardonic wit that had me in stitches. Cynical, some would say. We called it being realistic.

Her knowledge and experience were inspirational, to say nothing of exhausting. She recommended I read Cruel and Unusual by Gerard McNeil and Sharon Vance, an eye-opener exposé of the prison system even for those who thought their eyes were already popping. She had the Parliamentary Sub-Committee's report; we poured over the sixty-five recommendations and couldn't understand why the committee's common sense, thoughtful approach had been summarily rejected. The most important need they saw was a need for discipline throughout the system ("discipline" defined as "order imposed on behaviour for a purpose"). The discipline of authority, they insisted, must remain with the directors of institutions, and inmates must be guaranteed the discipline of justice inside our penitentiaries.

Joanne and I had personally heard all the complaints of abuse and harassment the Sub-Committee listed: waking prisoners in the night by noise and light; guards refusing to give their names, making it impossible for the inmate to put in a grievance; delaying the summoning of prisoners when visitors arrive; delaying response to personal requests; delaying and adulterating meals; calling lockup time early when only ten minutes are left in a movie or sporting event the inmates had been watching from the beginning; not allowing enough time for everyone to shower. The list is long.

"And these are the people who are supposed to be modeling the behaviour, showing how to function in society," Joanne said. For her, the most important issue was that of responsibility. "These guys are locked away for the ultimate irresponsibility, committing crimes against society, so they're put in prison where they have no responsibility at all. Someone tells them when to get up, when to go to bed, when to eat, and they don't have to work. Then, when it's time to leave, they're expected to go out and be responsible members of society."

We found the part relating to this, the Work, Education and Training section. The recommendation was that a prison industries corporation be set up, that the products of inmate labour be allowed to compete on the open market, and that inmates who work be required to pay room and board and contribute to the support of their families.

Joanne's view was that they should have to work, pay restitution to victims and assume responsibility before they're released. "All they learn in there," she said, "is to sit back and let everyone do everything for them. I see it every day in my work." Nearly half her clients were just out of jail and she had often told me how they didn't know how to do anything for themselves. We agreed, though, that nothing would change as long as all the public thinks about is the fact that they're locked away. They never think about them getting out one day, and getting out in a worse state than when they went in.

The sections that had struck me were the ones that dealt with justice within the penitentiary such as disciplinary procedures, inmate grievances, functioning of Segregation Review Boards and Inmate Committees. All needed improvement. And the Correctional Investigator should be responsible to Parliament rather than to the Solicitor General. The points regarding socialization I thought were important. They recommended that social interaction with staff, other inmates, visitors and outside groups be maximized, and prisoners should be outside their cells as much as possible. Not in the report was my concern about the effects excessive noise and sensory deprivation have on the inner being.

Years later I read that eight of the minor recommendations had been implemented.

AT SOME POINT JOANNE AND I—so alike—decided our education was not complete. We had never tried marijuana and resolved to expand our horizons, so to speak. Joanne made the arrangements with her friend Paul. He came over on a Saturday night, bringing with him—much to our surprise and apprehension—not marijuana, but hash. Said it was more convenient and more amenable to going out for the evening. What did we know, so we just went along with "expert advice."

Giddy we were before we even got started, like teens embarking on the forbidden. We inhaled and waited for the effects, if any. We had heard there were often none the first time. "They told us you couldn't get pregnant the first time either," Joanne quipped.

We waited a few minutes. "Do you feel anything," one asked the other. But we were so caught up in the general silliness of just doing it, we couldn't distinguish between what we *really* felt versus the expectations of how we *should* feel. And so, thinking maybe we felt it but then maybe we didn't, we set off for another foreign territory—a bar. This truly was "a night out"—or "out of it" maybe. If our kids could see us now!

The bar patrons stood shoulder to shoulder in the dark, shouting at each other as a rock band blasted out the walls; smoke hung heavy in the spotlights. In another circumstance our eyes would be sure to have met in a Let's-get-out-of-here look. In this instance it was a Well, we're-here-now, what-can-we-do-about-it? shrug. At Paul's urging we edged our way through the crowd up to the stage, where we stationed ourselves beside a four-foot tall booming speaker.

I can't bear noisy bars. Having to yell at your nearest neighbour is not my idea of fun, but there I was, mellow, blending in, rocking to the raucous music of David Wilcox. Obviously there were effects after all.

A few experiments were enough to satisfy curiosity, and our pot-smoking career was over.

Joanne also introduced me to the music of Bob Seger and The Silver Bullet Band. Being from Windsor, she had been aware of him from the early days of his Detroit-area success. She would crank up the stereo to top volume and blast "Night Moves" upstairs, "Against the Wind" to the street, "That Old Time Rock 'n' Roll" all the way to the pen. His words are refreshing in their simplicity, sincerity and unpretentiousness; themes reflect simple needs—the need to be recognized, need for shelter from the storm. I bought all the albums and uncharacteristically began cranking up the volume at home—to a more moderate degree, admittedly. Over the next few years we kept up to date with anything new he put out. "That kind of music just soothes the soul."

Hi,

Cheryl called last night to tell me she's been hired by the University of Texas Medical Branch in Galveston, Texas. How exciting! Her cousin Jill went there last year after graduating, so I guess it's kind of natural that Cheryl follow, considering the shortage of jobs for nurses here. It will be strange, though, to have one of my kids so far away, but maybe some day I can go visit.

Did you hear about the second Van Gogh painting being slashed? What kind of nut does a thing like that? This time it was one of the self-portraits and it was slashed corner to corner. They don't yet know if it can be repaired or not. This painting is valued at $1.3m. I wonder what he would say about that, he who said, "I care not if my paintings hang in the grand galleries of Europe. If they hang in the kitchens of working people, that's what would make me happy."

◆   ◆   ◆   ◆

It's true what you told me—it's a buyer's market right now—and June says the same. But I have to be practical. There's no sense in putting out all kinds of time, energy and money just for a place to live; there are too many more important things to do with those resources. I know if I kept the house I could build up equity in the long run, but being free is more important; I don't want all the responsibility of looking after it. When things go wrong I want to call the landlord.

◆   ◆   ◆   ◆

This evening is the most beautiful we've had this spring. I took Belinda and her little friend up to Duchesney Falls and we walked along the trails. The water is rushing wild. I had to go there to purge myself of this mood. I never understand why I can't be content like others. I look around at everyone—especially the people in the office—and I can't fathom how they can be satisfied (at least they appear to be satisfied) with their routine lives, doing the same thing every day—it drives me crazy.

I remember the first nice spring day like this two years ago. When the kids came home at noon I said to them, "Forget about school—I'm going to teach you how to be irresponsible." So I played hooky from work and they played hooky from school. We picked up some hamburgers and milkshakes, went up to the falls and had a beautiful afternoon. Later I had second thoughts about my use of the word "irresponsible." Really, wasn't that a *responsible* act? Isn't it responsible to respond to a day that should be enjoyed, rather than let it go to waste? Who decided everyone must work or go to school five days a week, nine to five? Is there no room for spontaneity?

I love to walk alone up there (but I'd let you come along if you promised not to talk). There are times when I don't want to be spoken to, or even touched, but that doesn't mean I'm not enjoying the person's company. Are you like that? Usually I walk up there about twice a week, sometimes before work if I wake up early.

You tell me all the things you know about the bush, what you learned growing up, what plants can be eaten, survival techniques, and I'm lost. When you were learning all those things I was living in the city. What does a city kid learn? Bus routes, streetcar routes, shortcuts through back lanes. The only bit of bush I knew was down by the Humber River, but that was scary because there were always girls getting raped or going missing and people said they were taken to the white slave trade. I had no idea what that meant, but it sounded pretty terrible.

◆   ◆   ◆   ◆

Once again we've written the very same thing to each other in letters that crossed. How does that happen? This time we both said we still wouldn't be satisfied no matter how many times we could visit each week. Too true.

Well, Thursday night was the long-awaited concert and our seats turned out to be good—close to the stage. The beginning was spectacular. A full house sat in hushed blackness, anticipating. Then, dramatic as a bolt of lightening, a spotlight flashed on the face alone and—in that unmistakable voice— came: "Hello, I'm Johnny Cash." How can I tell you? It was superlative, everything I had hoped for. A disappointment, though, was that June Carter didn't perform (she was sick) so I didn't hear "Jackson," which is one of my favourites.

That's the first big name star I've seen in over twenty yeas. My brother and I, as teens, used to go to the rundown Casino Theatre (a seedy place, gone now) to see such stars as the Four Lads, Johnny Ray, Hank Snow, Wilf Carter, many more.

The next night was Belinda's piano recital. She did very well and looked cute as a button of course. She can tell you about it when we see you next weekend.

◆   ◆   ◆   ◆

Here's news! Brenda has a summer job at Keewadin Lodge on Lake Temagami, where Pam worked last summer. I can't believe she's old enough to have a job and be going away on her own. I'll miss her but it's exciting. She and another girl will share in babysitting the owners' three children, aged 4, 6 and 8—two girls and a boy. She's leaving this weekend, then next weekend I'll take Belinda to her dad's for the summer.

❖　❖　❖　❖

I'm so sorry about Sunday—and no way to let you know why we didn't show. I know how disappointing that must have been, and I hope you haven't been worrying too much. You may have noticed Billy was quieter than usual on Saturday. Turned out he wasn't feeling well. When he woke up Sunday he was very sick—sore throat and fever. He said he would wait for me if I wanted to go to see you, but it was evident he was in no condition to be accommodating me, so we packed up the tents and struck out. He slept all the way back. When we got to his place I told him to tell his father to take him to the doctor. He said he probably wouldn't bother, so I went in and insisted. He said he would.

❖　❖　❖　❖

I like what you say here about thinking of me whenever you hear James Taylor singing "Your Smiling Face." That makes me feel good. Makes me smile.

Yes, the graduation was very nice, thanks. I'll show you the pictures when I get them. Everything went smoothly and Cheryl looked beautiful. I was the proud mother. This is the kind of situation that brings tears to my eyes, seeing them up there on the stage, crisply starched, their studies finished, setting off into the unknown, into adulthood—the dedication, the sense of corporate purpose. Funny how I rarely cry for myself but am touched by this kind of thing. And somebody-did-something-nice-for-somebody stories in the newspaper. And parades. Did I tell you parades? A parade will do it every time, as will almost any event or performance where people work cooperatively to create a beautiful whole.

Now my big news. I think my house is sold. With that in mind I took a good long look around and I will be sorry to leave. I really do like this house, it feels so comfortable—liked it from the moment I first walked in. But even though it's not a good time for selling, I should make $5,000 above what I paid, so I'm not too unhappy. At the same time, Pam has decided to go to Toronto to live (could the boyfriend have anything to do with it?) so I'll be looking for an apartment for three people. My numbers sure have diminished in the last seven years.

I called the Ministry of Health, asked about a transfer to their headquarters in Kingston. They said it would probably be possible but it could take two to three years. There are questions of both availability and suitability. Meanwhile, I've applied for a job in the Ministry of Education. I don't even know exactly where they need these people—it just said "various locations"—so I said I'd go anywhere from Toronto to the Quebec border, or to Ottawa. If nothing comes up I'll probably quit. Meanwhile, I got another raise this week. If I don't quit soon, first thing you know I'll be getting too comfortable and turn into a bureaucratic drudge.

Don, Beautiful One, when are you going to arrange for me to sleep over? That's what my kids do when they visit their friends.

We'll have our day yet.

The cactus remains strong and still curious.

◆   ◆   ◆   ◆

Guess what? My daughter is a hero! Brenda saved the little six-year old boy from drowning! He was wearing some kind of boots that you can walk on water with and got out too far. She jumped into the boat, rowed out and grabbed him. Imagine! Or maybe she's already told you? You seem to have quite a correspondence going.

The letter from the guys who want to make a movie about your story sounds interesting. Go ahead and see them, see what they're like, what their perspective will be, then we'll talk about it.

Pam is still waiting for her graduation pictures. If they're here before I go to see you I'll bring them, along with Cheryl's.

◆   ◆   ◆   ◆

What a lot of emotions I've gone through in the last two hours. First the happy surprise of receiving another letter from you so soon after the last one. Fourteen delicious pages! The first time I read it as slowly as I could, dragging it out more and more as I got near the end. You echoed my sentiments so closely it's quite incredible, and said them better than I could. I, too, feel I've met the first person who truly understands me and regret not having met sooner. Well, what's to be done about it? Should we lament not meeting sooner, or rejoice in having met? Your saying this warms my heart. I guess neither of us finds it easy—or maybe necessary—to commit the obvious to paper, or even say much when we talk. For my part, I know I tend to send my love letters in songs. The indirect way.

The second reading required a bottle of beer. I sat on the porch watching the rain, and for the very first time since all this started, was overcome by sadness. Wished with all my might that I could cry. Even tried to, but I guess I'm just not a crying person. Somewhere I read that a person only cries if she has hope, if she thinks it can make a difference, whereas the person in despair realizes its futility. Does this mean I have no hope?

I used to cry though. One time I had a crying marathon. It lasted three whole days. Can you believe that? I don't know how a head can possibly manufacture so much water. It was like a fountain. I was young then, only married four months. My husband left for the store in the morning and by the time he came back for lunch the pillow was drenched and the basket was full of Kleenex. Seeing him made me feel better, but when I tried to explain, the result was more waterworks. In the evening we went out for a drive and I was fine, but again, when I tried to explain—tears. Same pattern the next day. In the afternoon I managed to straighten up, wash my face, put on some make-up, and went downstairs with the intention of going for a walk. As soon as I started talking to his sister, the tears came rolling back. And so a cycle of uncontrollable crying, followed by attempts to stop, followed by more crying, was in motion. For three solid days.

We were living with Bill's mother (where he was still living when we got married). It was July, school was finished and I had nothing to do. It was a dismal existence in that house. His mother hadn't left it in years and his sister was partially paralyzed and somewhat affected mentally from a car accident. Essentially, it was a mausoleum. We were waiting to get into an apartment but the completion date for the renovations had been coming and going for some time. Promises, promises. Finally I decided the only way I was ever going to stop crying was to get out of there, so I went to my parents' cottage and waited there for a month until the apartment was finally ready. The thing was, his mother was being nasty to me and he wouldn't stand up for me. Ah, the idealism of youth! I see the situation with different eyes now: he had his priorities. I also see, looking at it from his point of view, what a trial I must have been from the very start.

I wonder if a person has a finite number of tears and mine are all used up. Or maybe I'm just a bit more mature now? I prefer to think the latter.

It's been oppressively hot so I hope the rain will cool the air. I've been thinking about walking for miles and miles in the rain with you and not saying a word. Then what would we do when we got back? Would we dry each other off or make love soaking wet? Don, I want you so badly and *right now*!

Well, now the rain has just about stopped (I didn't walk, only thought about it) and the sun is out, even though the sky is still full of dark clouds, which brings me back to a more "normal" mood—half happy, half sad.

I'm yearning to talk with you. You won't get this till Monday or Tuesday and will be disappointed that I didn't make it there on the weekend, as you were hoping. I just can't Don, for a variety of reasons. So, until we can see each other we'll just have to content ourselves with our fantasies and lots of that silent conversation.

◆   ◆   ◆   ◆

How can it be that, again, in letters that crossed, we said the same thing? "I wish I could phone you." Maybe it's not so amazing, come to think of it, because I wish that almost every day.

Well, here we sit in the new apartment—amid all the boxes. Billy came to help with the moving and will stay a few more days. I know I'm going to love this place, both the apartment itself and the setting. It's more like a private house than an apartment. The original tiny house has been raised and added to, to make four units—two up, two down. Ours is upstairs at the back, at the end of the driveway, and so we face sideways—the "front" porch and the living room overlook a country-like vista, the playing grounds behind Memorial Gardens (the arena). Very relaxing. There are three bedrooms, one for each of us. It's clean and new and I'm thrilled with it. More importantly (for my comfortable survival), the children like it too. No complaints about going from big to small.

Brenda came back from camp and—the sweet thing—with her earnings took me to dinner and a movie the first night. We saw *Heaven Can Wait* with Warren Beatty and Julie Christie. And guess what? Julie Christie played a school teacher named Bette Logan. Spelled with the "e"! What a fantasy, imagining myself looking like Julie Christie. . . .

◆   ◆   ◆   ◆

Miss you already. It was great relaxing with you on the weekend after all the work and rush of the move. The walks by the lake with Joanne helped de-stress me, too. It's so comforting to be by water. That's one reason I like North Bay—the two lakes.

As a follow-up to our conversation on Darrow, I've found the book and am sending you his address to the jury in the Leopold-Loeb case, his plea against the death penalty. It's long; I'll have to send it in sections. What eloquence! Such clarity of thought. Well, he's a hero of yours, too, so I don't have to say much. Somewhere I think I have the plea in the Scopes monkey trial—I'll have to look for it. Meanwhile, I'm back to the business of setting up the apartment. It's something I love doing—putting my own mark on it, so to speak—making it reflect my Self.

◆   ◆   ◆   ◆

Pam called last night, and guess what? She has a job already! Didn't take her long. And it's a good one, too, in the Personnel Department of Simpson's Department Store, with advancement opportunities. Isn't that great? Of course I knew she would have no problem. She has a nice forthright way about her, presents herself well, and has an excellent work record built up already, at such a young age.

Yes—what luck!—I did catch Cross Country Check-up last Sunday when they discussed Cruel and Unusual. (I was wondering if *you* were listening.) They should have called the book Cruel and Usual, though, because from what I've seen, the situations they document are not unusual at all. Joanne has sure given me an education on that subject. Her knowledge of "incidents"— what actually happened, officialdom's version, and the legal actions necessary to remedy the wrong—is never-ending. She has me quite breathless at times.

◆　　◆　　◆　　◆

Good to see you as always, and it's so thoughtful of Joanne to keep Belinda for one of the visits. I really appreciate it. Not that Belinda minds coming with me, nor does she mind the long trip. On the way back we listened to a radio drama and she was mesmerized. I hadn't thought about how children have no experience of using their imaginations that way these days, with TV being the norm.

I'm ready to start the next chapter now—the first group of captives you had. I've re-read all the court testimony and the newspaper accounts. Since it seems I'm not exactly an unbiased person, I thought I would start with the most negative, the Thompsons. (Maybe they could colour my thoughts the other way? Ha!) I drove out to their place Wednesday. Mr. T. was out front, up a ladder. He said he wasn't interested in going over it all again, but maybe "the Mrs." would talk to me. He wasn't friendly, but he wasn't rude. I went to the door, which she opened not more than a foot. She said they'd talk it over and I could call them later. I called yesterday, but you know (and I knew) what the answer was. I told her they don't need to talk about the day in question, I just want to meet them because they're in the story anyway and it might be better for them if I got to know them a bit. But, no, they don't want to talk. OK, no problem. There's no doubt the others will meet with me, so I'll reflect the story through their eyes. I just wanted to get more of a first-hand perspective, although I think what I saw in court tells it all, and the transcripts, of course.

◆　　◆　　◆　　◆

Pam and Jeff (her boyfriend) will pick Billy up in Orillia on Friday night and bring him with them for Thanksgiving weekend.

The other night I went to see Charlene where she works. She willingly agreed to an interview and I gave her your letter. She came over last night.

What a wise, confident young woman—just as you said. I love the part when she drove up and you told her to get out. She knew who you were immediately, yet had no hesitancy in telling you, "I'll get out, but you're not taking this car. It belongs to my mother." You must have wondered at that moment what you were going to have to contend with, but in the end it turned out you were pretty lucky to have her in your group. Without her at the Thompsons' you'd have had a real challenge on your hands, what with the old guy and the son yelling and swearing at you, threatening to kill you, even lying about not having a gun. She told me when you found it your eyes were blazing and all the muscles in your neck and on the sides of the face were pulled tight as can be. "He went from calm, cool and collected one minute to jumping all over the place like a nut the next." But then she added, "Of course, if *I* found a gun in someone's bed and thought they were planning on using it on *me*, I'd be mad too."

What a level-headed person. I can see why you liked her so much. (To say nothing of being attractive, right?) An independent thinker, too (her mother and her boyfriend didn't want her to talk with me), and she had a lot to say about the slant and errors in the media reports. Here are her exact words: "For me, the worst was to come. The reporters wouldn't leave me alone. For weeks the calls didn't stop. One thing about it, though, I gained an insight into reporters and newspapers. They'll do anything for a story and they don't care if it's true or not, or who they're hurting."

What made her furious was that they named her as the person who had listed the six policemen you had talked about. The newspapers had it all changed around into a "vendetta list" and she was scared about what repercussions that might have. "I wasn't scared of Don, but I didn't know who his friends might be and how they might take it because if they're like most good-hearted people they would think 'If it's in the paper it has to be gospel' sort of thing. And it wasn't a vendetta list. It wasn't as if he said, 'I'm going out looking for these guys and they deserve it.' It was: 'If I happen to run into any cops who are shooting at me, I hope these are the ones.'"

She said she didn't even give that story to the newspapers even though they quoted her. She had written it in her statement to the police, which she assumed would be confidential until used in court.

Self-assured young women like her—only 20 years old at the time—are a marvel to me. In many ways I'm still trying to get there. She'll definitely be the main narrator for that part, then I hope—if he will talk to me—to make Brent Martin a narrator as well. Need him to tell about the two of you trekking through the bush for so many hours and about going to his house.

Well, I'll finish typing up the transcript of the interview and then I'll have another long list of questions for you. Lots of work before me, but it's also so much fun meeting these people and hearing about how they handled things and why.

♦   ♦   ♦   ♦

I'm the pampered one! And how fortunate I feel, too—the little things that make mothering worthwhile. Belinda gave me breakfast in bed this morning! The menu was orange juice, a granola bar, toasted raisin bread and milk. I ate it cheerfully without telling her I need a coffee before I can even think of eating.

She and I went skating at Memorial Gardens on Friday. We intend to go every week. Plus I've started swimming at the Y again at noon hours, so hope to be in better shape soon.

William called to get info for the movie. I told him I really don't want to discuss much by telephone, plus I need to talk with you again before I do. I want to talk with him personally to see what kind of person he is and make sure he has the right perspective, doesn't want to just rehash the media version.

♦   ♦   ♦   ♦

Cheryl phoned to say good-bye; she's off to her new life in Texas. Exciting! Makes me think of me at the same age, leaving Toronto to teach in Trout Creek. Hope it brings good things for her, but I wish it weren't so far.

Belinda's piano recital is on December 3, so I'm sorry I can't come to see you that weekend as promised. I'll come the following weekend.

♦   ♦   ♦   ♦

Thanks for your answers to all my questions. Sixteen pages! I do keep you busy, don't I? And you gave me the perfect illustration of what I meant when I told you that a con artist is simply a psychology artist. I like this little example, the bit of you bringing the young lad over to your side by using him as your "helper." I'll use it in your narration. I love these nebulous areas that we can discuss forever.

♦   ♦   ♦   ♦

Pam and Jeff brought Billy up for Christmas and we had an excellent time—except for Christmas supper, that is. The six of us went to a restaurant and it was a disaster—a real disappointment because last year we went to the same restaurant and it was great. Too bad my kids don't have a turkey-roasting mother, eh? I used to, of course, but now I'm "retired."

Did Pam tell you she got a promotion already?

For Christmas Brenda gave me a James Taylor album. It has "Your Smiling Face" on it. Glad you liked your gift. I thought it was fun that each pose or expression relates to something we've talked—or laughed—about. You will remember every time you look at them. (Are they tacked up?) The photographer did a good job. I gave some to the kids, too.

Now here's a story. A couple of weeks ago I had one of those mother-experiences one doesn't relish. Oh, dear. A Saturday night. Brenda went to a dance at the Y and had asked if her friend could sleep over. Just after eleven o'clock they come in, Brenda heads straight to her bedroom and her hair is wet, so I call after her, "How come your hair's wet?" But she doesn't answer. I go into my bedroom and a few minutes later she comes in.

"I have something to tell you," she says, and sits down beside me on the bed. I see she doesn't look quite right; there's something wrong besides the dragging hair. "My friends put me in the shower at the Y."

"Why would they do that?"

"Because I was drunk." God! I didn't expect that! This is what I definitely don't want as a mother! What I never thought about when they were little and we ran around the house playing hide-and-seek, when they were snuggled in bed and I read them bedtime stories.

I start reproaching her, but before I get out two sentences, she says, "Well, at least I told you."

That stops me. At least she told me. I had to feel good about that. What a wise kid. Turns out they went to a friend's house before the dance and got into some kind of home brew. Brenda, it turns out, was more "adventuresome" than the others. Well, I didn't have to say much after that because it turns out she knows very well that it wasn't a good idea.

I heard from Joanne. Her oldest daughter, Sheri, has come to live with her so she said I should bring Brenda some time and they can hang out together.

With the holidays and all the visitors, I've taken a rest from writing, but it will be down the homestretch in the new year.

I'll mail this now but I'll probably be there before it will.

Did I ever tell you I like you? I think like is more important than love in many ways.

◆   ◆   ◆   ◆

That was a wonderful visit, and spending New Year's with Joanne was not a hardship either. A few days with the two of you would best be described as a "talkfest."

She's so comical. We talked about how we wish the visiting hours were longer. I pointed out that no matter how long they were, we would still want more; we would be greedy.

"Not greedy, just needy," she answered in a flash. Between you and her I come back full of good humour—and with sore laugh muscles.

Picked up Belinda in Orillia OK. We didn't get back till 10:30 and there was so much snow in the driveway there was nothing to do but ram the car in and deal with it in the morning. Meanwhile, Cheryl phones and tells us it's 60°F and she's playing tennis.

Miss you already.

◆   ◆   ◆   ◆

It was comforting to receive your long letter of encouragement, your expression of concern and understanding of all I have to do, the driving, etc. It means a lot to me. And I know maybe we won't always have those two panes of glass to separate us, as you say. I think about that too.

And you had good news: it won't be long until you'll be finished the Persian Garden. I wish I could hear the "conversations" you have with me over a coffee when you're working on it and the "witty responses" I make. The conversations I have in my head are plenty witty too. On both sides. Sometimes I *do* hear your "thoughts that a Puritan would gasp at," as you say here, and blush maidenly. ☺ Well, let's hope there are no more interruptions—guards messing up your cotton, you going to the hole—always something. I often think of the first time you told me you were going to do the petit point for me. You said: "So you don't forget me." Well, I don't think there's much danger of that happening.

I like the photo you sent. Good to have a new one. I put it on my bed-room mirror.

◆   ◆   ◆   ◆

Thanks for the Nietzsche quote: "In individuals insanity is rare, but in groups, parties, nations and epochs, it is the rule." We do see it all over the place, don't we?

I talked with the warden. He seems to genuinely want to transfer you into the population (at least that's my take) but, given that he did admit to you that you're in Supermax because of political lobbying, it may be out of his hands. And so I agree; we shouldn't hold out hope much longer and should try for a transfer to another region where political influence doesn't exist.

◆   ◆   ◆   ◆

Sunday I foolishly drove to Iroquois Falls to see Derek and Anne. It was foolhardy to undertake the trip at all because it was the worst storm of the season—very slippery and almost no visibility. I should have cancelled, but when I get something in my mind, I'm determined. And I hate to inconvenience people. As it turned out, it would have been better for them if I had changed the date. They were out late the night before and weren't even out of bed when I got there, so it took them a good hour to get in gear.

I took Derek's T-shirt back to him. A dirty, blood-soaked, bullet-riddled T-shirt is quite a souvenir of sixteen hours in the captivity of Donald Kelly. They found it amusing. I wonder if they will actually keep it.

Anyway, it was a good interview. I can't imagine falling asleep on a couch while basically under a gun, as she did at Thompsons', but she said sleep is her way of escaping things, of avoiding stress.

For that first twenty-four hour period, besides you, Charlene and Brent, I've decided to use as narrator Mrs. Thompson, in spite of the fact that she won't talk to me. There's enough in the court testimony, which is public record, that I can use her exact words—all the negative comments she has about you—which are needed for a bit of balance.

You'll be surprised to hear I've taken two weeks' vacation to work ahead on the writing. A solid block of time with few distractions should yield some progress. I had a couple of sessions with Ron Holmberg and he said he feels badly he doesn't see much to criticize any more. That was encouraging.

The little cartoon you drew on the paper is sweet. Why don't you do more? I love to be surprised like that. You asked about Belinda's, but I didn't see it; she doesn't show me her letters.

◆   ◆   ◆   ◆

It's been quite a day. William and Mark came yesterday. We got along well—they seem like OK guys. Whether they know how to make a movie or not remains to be seen. It's their first, but even the best have to start somewhere, don't they? So I won't hold that against them. I like their attitude and think they'll have the proper approach. I wonder if they have any money though. They asked me how much we want. I didn't know what to say, said we would talk about it. They said they'd get back to me.

Mark told me his name was refused for your visit list because of a conviction years ago for possession of a small amount of marijuana. Guess that would make him a bad influence, eh?

Meanwhile, in anticipation of their visit, I had gone to see my lawyer about making a contract with them, suggestions for terms, etc. He said he has no knowledge or expertise in movie matters but could refer me to someone in Toronto. So that left me dealing with them without any footing.

Now, wait till I tell you this. I was due to go back to work this morning, but because they seemed so keen, and because I led them to believe I was further ahead than I actually am, and because I need to go to Toronto to see that lawyer, I decided to ask for another week off work (I still had one week's vacation time left). I phoned Roy first thing this morning. He said he didn't think it was possible. I was shocked. Never expected that for an answer, he's always so accommodating. Said they needed me there; no reason why. But he said he would talk with the Big Boss and call me back. About a half hour later came the call.

"It's not possible to give you more time off right now," he tells me. "If you don't come in, we'll have to consider that you've resigned."

"Well then, I've resigned," I told him.

Just like that.

And so I went into the office, signed the letter of resignation they had prepared for me, cleaned out my desk, and here I sit. Unemployed. Tonight, to celebrate—incongruously, most will say—I'm taking the kids to see Superman, even if it *is* a school night.

I made the appointment with the lawyer in Toronto for Friday afternoon. I'll take Belinda with me and we'll go from there to Joanne's and will come to see you Saturday morning. We can talk about everything then.

So, what do you think of that?

◆   ◆   ◆   ◆

This afternoon I took the Persian Garden up to show Barb. She, too, was surprised at the incredible amount of work involved. She really liked the colours, particularly the red and the deeper blue. They're vivid—intense, but not flashy. And we discussed the symbolism, so life-affirming, spiritual. The lamp, she tells me, not only represents Life, but also Learning and Enlightenment (which makes sense). You didn't tell me about the four smiling suns over the mountain. I love them! They add a touch of levity to an otherwise serious theme. Barb says they are the sun-god Mithra and the mountain is the support for Life, what it's built on. I will treasure it always, Don, and can't think of an adequate way to thank you.

Ron gave me a little job helping him on a study he's doing for the Ministry of Health. He has developed a questionnaire and my job is to round up two groups of six disabled people (the study concerns the number of disabled people in Ontario, the kinds of disabilities they have, and the services they need), and go over the questionnaire with them to make sure all points are covered from their point of view. It would be good if I could get involved in the actual study. I'll ask him about it or if he knows anyone at Queen's who is doing social research. That would be ideal. Going from job to job appeals to me; that way things won't get boring. This is the second study I've worked on for him. The other was a comparison of people living in public housing with those in comparable private developments with regard to certain social indicators. I did all the interviewing on that one—over one hundred respondents—and helped with the tabulations.

In your letter you sound worried about me, but don't be. I *know* quitting was right. It *feels* right. It's something I knew for a long time that I would do—just needed the right time or circumstance to spring up.

> Aren't the wise ones, those who never do anything foolish,
> even more foolish in my eyes than I am in theirs?

◆   ◆   ◆   ◆

The petit point is hung! I know a person who works at a framing shop, so I had expert help in choosing the *perfect* mat and frame. The mat is cloth, a linen-like texture, the exact ivory used in the background, and three inches wide. The frame is wood, antique gold, narrow—only half an inch—and rounded. I chose not to use glass; it seemed inaccessible when we tried it, lost its feeling. Framed, it measures thirty inches tall and twenty-three inches wide, the perfect size to hang above the couch—where it is—and be the main feature of the room. I'm delighted with it. I'll take a picture and send it.

ENJOYING MY NEW LUXURIOUS LIFESTYLE, I sit down with a cup of coffee and The Globe and Mail, scan the front page, and from the bottom up leaps a heart-stopping header: "Prisoner gouges eyes out in bid for freedom." *Oh my God! It can't be him! Surely he'd never do that.* Who would do a thing like that?

In dread I approach the article. "A prisoner who gouged his eyes from their sockets as part of an escape bid was a loser on two counts—he lost his eyesight and failed to escape." *Good God! Is this insanity?* My eyes skim ahead until they fix on "Millhaven Penitentiary." *Millhaven! Would he do that? Good God, surely he wouldn't!* With dread I scan as fast as I can until my eyes pick up the words "transferred from Saskatchewan." *Breathe. It's not him.*

Relaxed now, I start again from the beginning. The escape had been planned for months. His girlfriend, from Ohio, with two male accomplices, was to intercept the ambulance and whisk him across the border to the U.S. She, however, had been the object of police surveillance for months and was arrested in downtown Kingston minutes before the gouging had taken place. The accomplices were being sought. His name doesn't appear until the final paragraph: "Dennis Dale Hunter and Margaret Prince, both 29, have been charged with conspiring to escape prison."

Margaret. . . . From the States. . . . With this I know—know with certainty—that my telephone is tapped.

I call June, ask her to come over; this has implications for her. For months she's been telling me in great detail her trials and adventures as a newly-separated woman, and they've been listening. It's humiliating. I can't phone Joanne. Her phone will be tapped, too. Joanne, I have to write.

"I can't apologize enough, Joanne," I begin, "I'm so sorry and feel guilty because I'm the one who has brought this on you.

"That call to the woman in the States I made from your place. There we were, commiserating about her living so far away, being sick and unable to visit her guy, giving our names and phone numbers in case she needed help or needed to pass a message. I don't know if she actually has cancer or not, but it turns out she was well enough to come to Kingston to play Bonnie to his Clyde in an escape attempt. According to the newspaper, she had been the object of surveillance for some time, that's how they thwarted the plan, and so we have to assume her phone was tapped when I called. That means—with me giving both our phone numbers—both our phones are now tapped, we can be sure of that. Weren't we the sympathetic dudes?

"You must have heard about it; it must be a buzz in the pen. But did you put two and two together?"

I feel guilty about having called from Joanne's place, having involved her. But she was the one who suggested it. "How are you feeling?" and "Are you coming for the thirteenth?" were the two questions I was to ask. Now I wonder if they were genuine questions or codes.

Ninety percent of phone conversation in our house is kids. Surely they skip over kid-chatter. It's infuriating to think of them being spied on, and I don't relish the thought of someone listening to every word I say either, knowing who I talk to, what I do, where I go, all my business. Even if it *is* just day-to-day stuff, it's private. Or should be. I hope they die of boredom.

On the next visit I learned the details. I should have known you can't believe what you read in the newspaper. This time, however, it wasn't the reporter's fault. He hadn't poked his own eyes out at all; someone had done it for him, but he took the blame to protect the other from being charged. They had the idea the eyes would slip back in easily, but in the end one eye had to be removed and the other was left with two per cent vision. Another prison casualty.

A FEW WEEKS LATER, I wrote Jeff (*wrote* instead of phoned, for obvious reasons) and asked him to bring some marijuana when they came for Easter.

Saturday night Cheryl called to say Happy Easter to everyone. Talking to me, she noticed my spacey delayed reactions and asked Pam what was wrong with me. Even though I had warned the children never to say anything on the phone they wouldn't want "certain people" to hear, Pam told her.

The next afternoon, as soon as he arrived back in Toronto, Jeff phoned— phoned purposely. He wanted "them" to hear what he had to say.

South of Powassan they had met a police cruiser. It slowed down, the cop took a good look, immediately made a U-turn, caught up and stopped them. The officer comes to the door, looks in the back seat and says, "You've got a marijuana plant there." The Umbrella plant (Schefflera) I had given Pam.

"Get out," he orders, and proceeds to inspect every inch of the interior and the trunk. On the floor of the front seat he finds some little grains, which he identifies as marijuana seeds. Pam explains they're from a snack mixture they had a few days ago. He goes back to his car and talks on the radio. They wait in disbelief until finally, evidently fresh from a crash course on what a marijuana plant and its seeds look like, he comes back and tells them to go on their way and drive safely.

Besides being funny, it was infuriating to know I was being spied on, police were driving by and writing down license plate numbers of cars parked in my driveway. Some time later, Joanne and I were both served notice of having been the "object of an intervention" for the past ninety days, as were Don and Sean concerning the visits. Undaunted by not hearing anything interesting in all that time, hope remained strong in their dear little hearts and they continued for another ninety days. It must have been a slow season.

Don, Dear Love, I miss you already. The visit was wonderful, as always. But will they ever give us enough time to finish a conversation? That's the problem.

It was so nice to receive the letter you mailed before the visit. Helps keep the feeling of seeing you going. Plus I still have your "visit letter" to look forward to in a few days' time.

Brenda had a great time. She and Sheri got along famously and it seems they had quite the heart-to-heart talk about mothers being involved with prisoners. She wants to go again—asked if we could go for three nights next time because it's so far for only two. She and Sheri have plans to visit each other in the summer, and she wondered if she'd be able to go to see you with Joanne in that case.

Ron paid me. I nearly fell over when I saw the amount—astronomical for the amount of work I did. Bad news, too. There won't be a job for me on the study; they're going to sub-contract it out.

Well, I can say I love my life as it is, which is a great thing to be able to say. If the money would just keep rolling in every two weeks as it does, I could live this way forever. In the morning, after a couple of hours of drinking coffee and reading the newspaper, I exercise for half an hour. Then I get out my work and organize my thoughts, and by then it's already time to prepare lunch for the kids. After they've returned to school I start working and continue all afternoon. The downside is that by supper time my head is so completely immersed in the writing that I can't come back to earth and participate in proper conversation with the girls; I feel guilty about that.

◆   ◆   ◆   ◆

If you're going to transfer as Supermax, we're limited to the three choices. I really don't find a pull to live in the Maritimes and, unfortunately, I have to eliminate Vancouver right off the top. I know it's a lovely city—I spent a week there in 1975 and enjoyed it immensely. It's incredibly beautiful, probably the most beautiful city in Canada, and no doubt very interesting to live in. But I know I couldn't survive there, couldn't endure the greyness. There's no point in even trying—it's bad enough here. I've only been to Montreal twice (a weekend visit each time) but I did like what I saw, and I've always wanted to learn French. Plus it's closer to Ontario for visits to family and friends. So that would be my choice. We'll talk more when I see you.

◆   ◆   ◆   ◆

Finally you received the Losers' Calendar the kids sent you for Christmas. "Only" three and a half months late. A "security risk," no doubt. Seems nothing happens unless I write a letter, which makes me wonder about all the guys who have no one to write complaints. Glad to see what a kick you got out of each cartoon; I knew you would. You'll love the card I just sent: "You have been the ruination of me . . . (open) . . . Thanks, I've enjoyed every minute of it." ☺

Seriously, you'll never know what you've done for me.

Have you heard Bob Seger's song "Till it Shines?" I love it. "Storm the walls around this prison; let the inmates free the guards." Love the concept.

Then he asks to be dealt another future from a brand new deck of cards. Wish *I* could think of metaphors like that—so simple yet so strong.

Are you sick to death of me quoting the words of songs to you? You did once say you prefer to express yourself in your own words. But I feel music so intensely it seeps in and becomes a part of me, then I feel compelled to share it. A "music/word evangelist" we could say.

I wish I could sing. I sing all these songs to you in my heart. If I had a voice I'd sing them to you when I'm there. (Then we'd see the blushing!) Remember I told you about cheating to get into the grade school choir? Well, in high school I redeemed myself by actually getting into it "legally" and when we gave a performance I sang my heart out with an earnestness that brought myself—if not the audience—to tears. I'm always overcome by the idea of many individuals working in concert to create a beautiful whole.

The activities I liked as a young person were either co-operative or solitary. Synchronized swimming, dancing and figure skating can all be both, and I liked them all. There was one time when I wasn't so co-operative, though, when I was about Belinda's age and I was in a tap dance number in a recital. My friend, Bev Davison, and I somehow got our places reversed. To be cool and not reveal our mistake, I figured we should just carry on in each other's position. But Bev had a different take. She insisted we get back into our rightful places, which ended up with us pushing and shoving each other and the teacher had to come out on stage and yank us off by the scruffs of our necks. My poor mother! I'd be mortified if my child did that.

Team sports were not for me. I was always scared of not shaping up, of embarrassing myself or of messing things up for others—the result of an inferiority complex gained early on when I was always near the last (and sometimes the last) to be chosen for the work-up ball games we played in the schoolyard after supper. Playing the piano I've always enjoyed, but I don't have natural talent. I got my Grade Eight and the Grade Two Theory that goes with it (quite a high level), as a result of eye-hand co-ordination. I have no "ear" but do have a feeling, which was commented on by every Conservatory of Music examiner through the years.

I worked seven hours today and now this letter, so I'd better quit and send my love.

THE LAST CAPTIVE TO BE INTERVIEWED was, conversely, the first to be taken, and the one who spent the longest time with the fugitive.

Ten minutes after commandeering a car, the escaper was stuck in a gravel pit and forced to strike off on foot. Immediately he came across Brent Martin, unlucky enough to have arrived to do a little target practice only moments before. Don says Brent had seen him, so he had to take him to prevent being reported; Brent, however, says he was just putting up the target, turned, and saw a man crossing the pit, gun pointed at him.

"I'm Don Kelly and I just escaped from the jail," he was told. At first he thought the guy was kidding, but then he looked at the clothes and knew it was no joke; like everyone, he knew the name.

"Hand over the gun," he was commanded. "Now that you've seen me, we have to find a place where I can tie you up so you won't report me."

"Take my car," Brent told him. "I won't report you till you've had time to get away."

But Don couldn't trust him, told him to start walking.

They walked through rough bush country, over and under deadfalls, through burrs and brambles, all day long—ten whole hours—stopping for a rest here and there, eating berries along the way, refreshing themselves at a creek or a spring, and never found a suitable place. They had little conversation and most of that was one-sided.

"Do you think all cops are honest?"

"I think there are both kinds," Brent replied, and that triggered a long, detailed account on Don's part of how one policeman in particular was trying to frame him. Later, when asked what he did for a living, Brent said he moved furniture, which he had done in the past, but at this time he was a police cadet, home for the holiday weekend.

In the evening a motorcycle could be heard, which gave the fugitive an idea: perhaps he can use it for his getaway. They sneak up through the bushes and, fifty meters away, spy two young fellows sitting on the ground having a smoke. Kelly is not too sure of his motorcycle-driving ability, though, especially with two guns to carry, so he has the idea that one of the guys can take him somewhere, but then if he did that, the other two would be left free to report.

The four debate the dilemma.

"We could rip up T-shirts for rope and you could tie us up and leave us here," they suggest. But Don tells them he'd hate to leave anyone there with the flies so bad. "I don't know what to do; I'll have to think on it. Where are we anyway?" and he hopes his embarrassment doesn't show when they tell him: only three miles from where they started.

The newcomers identify themselves as Troy, a local, and his friend Derek, down from Iroquois Falls for the holiday. Don tells Derek to exchange clothes with him (his prison garb makes him identifiable), then they start down the road looking for a place where he can tie up two of them while the other drives him somewhere. He's vague on the destination. This street, although on the outskirts of the city, is populated, and every house has something wrong with it: too many people in the yard; kids; too close to the neighbouring house. Finally, he realizes they're getting too close to town so they stop while he thinks. And while he's thinking, along comes the solution: a car. Troy's girlfriend Charlene, Derek's girlfriend Anne, and Troy's young brother are driving around looking for the fellows because they're late returning for the movie they had planned to see.

Don tells Troy to take the wheel, everyone gets in and they head into town, drive around city streets, meet several police cars, and he continues to think. He decides on Anita Avenue, where he says he knows someone, maybe he can leave them there. Out past the jail they go, out to Trout Lake, but when they get there he can't recognize the house. Brent says his parents are away, he can leave them there, and so, in the last vestiges of daylight they head up the escarpment.

Where a police car follows them.

"Everyone stay calm," Don tells the group. "Keep still and don't look back. If we get stopped, don't panic; stay in the car regardless of what happens. If shooting starts, duck down, but stay in the car. They'll shoot at the one to run. I'll be that one."

Silence fills the car.

"Take the next right," he tells Troy. The police make the same turn behind them.

"Keep the same speed and keep cool."

The cruiser is so close its headlights light up the interior. Two long, breathless, wordless kilometres.

"Take this next little road to the right," Don tells Troy. This would be the test.

They turn right.

The cruiser continues on its way.

At first Don thought Brent's house was the ideal place: isolated enough, yet with the parents coming back the next day they wouldn't be left too long. Then he remembered Brent's car up at the gravel pit. Once the police found it, so close to the one he had abandoned, they would come looking. So, after getting a peanut butter sandwich and a roll of butcher twine, he has them pile back into the car and into the night.

For hours they drive into side roads looking for a place he can leave them, and out again. Every house has something: lights in the yard; toys; too many cars; big men's clothes on the clothesline, until, at three-thirty in the morning, after so much stopping and starting, turning the lights off and on, the radio on and off, the motor overheats.

"Well, that just limits it," says Don. "We'll sit here until morning and pick one of these places." And so they sit in a little lane leading to several cottages on a lake, talking, until after daylight when they descend on a cottage inhabited by three more captives-to-be: Mr. and Mrs. Thompson and their adult son, Steven. Don said he would just have something to eat, have a couple of beers, and he'd be on his way. But he stayed and stayed. He didn't know where to go.

Finally, after everyone was tied up, Steven announced that his girlfriend was coming over, she would find them, and the police would be after him in no time. That resulted in him waiting another hour until she arrived, got tied up with the nine others, and—at long last—he left with the Thompsons' car. For Brent it had been more than twenty-four hours.

It was refreshing to meet Brent. He was candid in his answers and open-minded in his point of view.

"People have asked me if it had any effect on my plan to become a police officer," he told me. "I don't think it affected me one way or the other. I was never the kind who thinks 'bad guys' are all bad and 'good guys' are all good. You have to take each person they way they are."

Hi,

So, you've put in your official request for a transfer. How long do you think it will take to get approved? Should we hold our breath?

I had a good interview with Brent and didn't see him as you did at all. I think you were too stressed at the time and, really, how talkative did you expect a guy to be under the circumstances? Then later, with the gang, he was the odd man out, so, being an introvert, it was natural that he kept to himself.

He did think of various ways he could have got away from you—at the river and especially at his house—but he said he had concluded heroics weren't necessary, there really was no danger, things would resolve themselves peacefully in the end. As for his skill in bush-walking, well, you not only have more experience than him, but you certainly had a *lot* more motivation. He struck me as a sincere, even-keeled young man who doesn't get overly-excited or easily disturbed. I enjoyed meeting him. The ongoing fun of following your story.

Now, to finish writing that chapter. I do have a jumbled way of doing things, don't I? Next I'll do the part before the capture when you were alone in the bush, after Mr. Dupuis dropped you off. I have all you wrote for me on that, but still feel at a loss. I have no knowledge of bush survival and no imagination—could never write a fiction. Prepare yourself for another long list of questions. We still need to talk more about camouflaging the identity of the people you had contact with during that period. "Protect the identity of the guilty."

How am I ever going to get this book finished if I keep on writing all these long letters and burning up the road between here and Bath?

◆   ◆   ◆   ◆

Well, we had Brenda's birthday. Naturally she was surprised and pleased with your gift. Thanks to Pam, too, who helped me check out your various suggestions when she was here for Easter. (What would I do without her?) We decided your original proposal—the Polaroid—was best.

Last night Belinda and I undertook to make her a birthday cake "from scratch," as we say. Since I long ago gave up domesticity, it was the first chance Belinda has ever had to help me on such a project, so she had a lot of fun. When the others were small I baked at least three times a week, and there would be a little row of chairs lined up in front of me with my "helpers" adding ingredients, stirring, pouring, shaping, kneading, to their hearts' content. But poor Belinda has never once eaten so much as a homemade cookie from my hands. She has a delinquent mother, alas.

Anyway, the cake turned out as it should. Then came the decorating. You'd lose patience with me, I'm sure—I'm such a perfectionist. (But then, maybe not, when I think of how perfectionist you were about the Persian Garden.) We started at eight o'clock and at eleven-thirty I wanted to take off the BRENDA because it was a half-inch lower than I thought it should be. Belinda convinced me not to, and of course Brenda didn't notice the poor placement and thought it was just fine.

You'll never guess what Brenda did for her birthday. She cooked lasagne for supper, invited June over and took us all to see the movie Grease. What a kid! Last night she had three girls to sleep over. Which reminds me, when are you going to. . . . Well, I asked you that before, but no answer. Shall I assume you're not interested???

Speaking of sleepovers, what do you think of this? A few weeks ago Belinda had two little friends from school stay over, a set of twins. I did everything for those kids—played games with them, gave them a nice supper, took them to a movie, popped corn. They came early Saturday afternoon and their parents picked them up Sunday morning after breakfast—before church. Monday Belinda came home from school and told me they can't come to our house again because she "doesn't have a father." Can you believe that? Guess that's what they learn at church. . . . I'll never understand people.

IT WAS OFFICIAL; Don's transfer to the Montreal area was approved. We would go there to be together, in a manner of speaking.

Friends thought it was a terrifying leap, but to me it was as if walking from one room to another—much less of a move than the one from Trout Creek when I had no idea where I was going or who I was. The eight years in North Bay had opened life: I had succeeded at university, worked at challenging new jobs, had been active in the women's movement, participated in an onstage role with the Gateway Theatre Guild, and had had a rewarding four-year relationship with Obi, who introduced me to a vast new world of people and ideas. Then.

Then I got the idea to write a book.

One room leads to another.

Full Bloom

(May 1979—February 1985)

Dearest Love,

What a wonderful weekend that was! Everyone enjoyed it—even you, right? I feel fortunate to have found that cottage—not only affordable but spacious enough for all of us. Going to sleep listening to the lap of waves, breathing fresh lake air, is my idea of bliss. Everything was perfect—even the weather.

Have you recovered from so many visits from so many people? And you never knew from day to day—even from morning to afternoon—who would appear next. What did you think of Jeff? Between him and Billy it's a laugh a minute.

Was it good to see the kids without me there? You didn't corrupt them, did you? It was nice to be able to spend time with my friends and know you were getting visits all the same. Linda spent time on a student placement in our office seven years ago and stayed with us Monday to Thursday because she lived in Sudbury, so all the kids know her. Now she's married, living and working in Smith's Falls. They arrived early afternoon and stayed until after midnight. We were quite the gang around the bonfire—thirteen of us—so pleasant with all the various ages together. Joanne and Sheri were with us most of the time, so that was good for Brenda, while Belinda had a great time playing with Linda's two girls, one only a toddler.

I'm so happy I got the idea to do that. It was so good for me to have everyone there—a jam-packed, fun-filled weekend for all of us. Brenda used her new camera a lot, so there'll be lots of pictures to show you—including some of your totem pole. We went to the park to see it.

Now, back to writing. The capture part won't take long to do; you've already told me your part and the rest is in great detail in the court transcript. But, as I said, I hope I can do justice to the emotions. Then, after that—nothing like finishing at the beginning—the escape. So, start writing that out for me, please.

◆   ◆   ◆   ◆

Cheryl has gone back to Texas now. It was a good time, and her sisters were glad to have her here, too. She was so tanned when she arrived she looked like a different person. She brought me an album—"Exodus" by Bob Marley. It's reggae music. Have you ever heard of it? I never had. She tells me it's the big new thing in Texas. It's Jamaican, has a completely different beat—hypnotic, infectious—and the lyrics are upbeat, optimistic. Listen for him.

Yesterday I mentioned about moving in August and Belinda said, "These little feet aren't going anywhere. I'm going to Crazy Glue them to the floor!"

More worrisome, though, is Brenda's reaction. I phoned Joanne's friend in Montreal and he explained the terms of the language law—Bill 101. There are only two ways a child can attend English school: one of the parents went to an English school in Quebec; or one of the parents is being transferred or newly-employed from out of the province and has a letter attesting that the job will last less than three years. Obviously I don't fit into either category, so I let Brenda know that if we go there she'll have to spend some time in a special language-learning class before going into a regular class. She is not happy. I see it as an opportunity to broaden the horizons; a 15-year-old, however, has trouble with the long view, sees it only as being held back. Let's hope I can convince her. At the moment I would say she seems more crestfallen than defiant.

I'll hate to leave this apartment and its location, myself. But that's what I said about the house, isn't it? Adapting to new surroundings doesn't seem to be one of my problems. I heard what you just said: "Come down here and see if you can adapt to these surroundings," right? Well, if they throw me in the same cell as you, I don't think I'll have any complaints—for a little while anyway. . . .

I had a nice little letter from Billy up at Keewaydin. Says he's sick of doing pots and pans already, but otherwise sounds content. Had a letter from Pam as well. She sounds happy in her place and eager to have us down for the weekend.

◆   ◆   ◆   ◆

What good news! You've arrived! Already! I can hardly believe it's a reality. Now that's done, it's time for me to go and find my apartment. I've been telling people I'm moving to Montreal. The reactions are interesting. I don't tell the reason why, of course (except to my closest friends) so I guess I shouldn't wonder at their bewilderment. They all have the same two questions: Can you speak French? ("Not really, but I'll learn.") Then it's: How will you get a job? Which seems ridiculous because I know there's no such thing as no job for me.

> One must take one's chance and say: "I will do a certain thing and carry through with it." Well, it may turn out wrong and one may feel as though shut in behind a wall when people don't approve; but one shouldn't mind that, should one?

◆   ◆   ◆   ◆

A successful trip! We succeeded in finding you in Laval (after only a few wrong turns) and then—guess what?—after we left you, we found our apartment!

As I told you, we checked out a couple of areas the night before, but they didn't "speak" to us. Since I don't know the city at all, I phoned Joanne's friend for advice; as a result, we drove to the Côte des Neiges area, not far from downtown and not expensive. We walked around looking for *À Louer* signs. Everything looked attractive and soon we came to a nice big park with lots of shade trees. "We'll find our apartment here," I told Brenda, and she agreed.

Montreal is a city of low-rise apartment buildings—that's all you see everywhere. We walked along in front of the park and almost immediately spotted a sign in a ground-floor window, went in to check it out, and by luck the landlord was there inspecting the painters' work.

It's a nice two-bedroom apartment (one is quite small, Brenda will take it, and Belinda and I will have twin beds in the big one), has an eat-in kitchen and a big living room with a balcony overlooking the park. The street is very quiet right now because it's closed to traffic due to construction of a new subway station a short block away. When it reopens more than a year from now, there will be fairly heavy traffic (I hope not *too* heavy), but having the subway at hand will be a great convenience.

At the far end of the park is a big recreational centre. It's Jewish but anyone can join. We picked up a schedule. Programs are extensive and for all ages. Belinda can continue with her gymnastics and there's even a theatre we can go to from time to time. There's a commercial street nearby so everything we need will be within walking distance. I don't know how people can live in places where they have to get into their car for everything they do. Brenda's school is very close, while Belinda's is a good six to eight blocks away.

The rent is much more reasonable than I had expected—only $250, the same as I pay here. I gave the landlord a cheque for first and last months and the deal is done. I can hardly wait! I'm so excited to be starting off on my next adventure. I know I'm going to love it, and Brenda seems content. That's a relief.

Montreal! Here we come!

◆   ◆   ◆   ◆

Approved for Maximum already, only weeks after arriving! Shows how right you were about your chances in Ontario. We should have done this sooner, but then as long as I had the book on my hands it wasn't practical for either of us. "Everything in its own time," right? The day I walk into an open visiting room—and into your arms—will be a day in history. But before I get too excited I'd better remember it still has to be approved by Ottawa. Better not count the days.

Glad to know there's no language problem there for you, although it sounds like some of your conversations are more like games of Charades.

I'm trying to get ahead of the game—started packing things that aren't in daily use.

◆　　　◆　　　◆　　　◆

This is one confusing way to move house—dump the stuff in Montreal, turn around and come back. Did you ever see three such bedraggled-looking people on the other side of the glass? Loading a van, driving through the night, sleeping in the car and splashing water on your face in a restaurant doesn't do much to improve the appearance.

So, here I am, waiting at June's until Billy is finished his job and Paula is finished proofreading the manuscript. If we think back to the first week of your escape and my taking Brenda and Belinda to her house every day for safety, well, we have to shake our heads, don't we? All of us.

Before I even got around to seeing about getting it typed, Ron told me about something better, a new system they call word processing. One types on a regular keyboard and the words appear on a TV-like screen. The work is saved on a diskette and if there are any mistakes or you want to edit something, revisions are simple to do. So, that seems to be the way to go. He got this info at a place in Ottawa. I called and got an appointment, so we'll stop there on our way to Montreal to get a quote. I know there will be places in Montreal that do the same thing, but it seems easier to do it this way, even though I'll have to go back to pick it up. That won't be a hardship. I want to go to the National Gallery again, and Ivy is going to Ottawa soon to visit friends, so we'll be able to meet up and do something.

◆　　　◆　　　◆　　　◆

Oh, Don, I need you so badly. What can I do? Since the visit my world has fallen apart. I'm so alone, without a friend, no one to tell my troubles to, not even by phone. All I can do is pour out my heart on paper.

You saw how happy I was yesterday morning—on top of the world—couldn't have been happier. The move here, the apartment, having Billy to help me, picking up Brenda and Belinda at the train station the day before, glad to have them back, excited that Belinda does indeed like her new home and Brenda was pleased with what I'd done so far. Everything was perfect.

Then. Oh—then. Then my world fell apart.

When I got back from seeing you—devastation! Brenda announced she wasn't staying, she was going back with Billy to live with her father. Oh, God, Don, the shock of it, the hurt! How can I live without her smiling face? I cried, pleaded, tried to convince her, tried to make her realize the benefits. Told her how much I would miss her. But her mind was made up. And she had Billy for support. If he hadn't been here I'm not sure she would have come up with this at all. If the idea had been that strong, she would have just stayed in Orillia. Refused to come. That would have been the easier route.

After all I went through with her not wanting to come in the first place and then the relief when she seemed to have changed her mind. She certainly did seem positive when we came in July and found the apartment, and you told me her letters expressed contentment with the idea.

Besides being distressed—crushed—at my *own* loss, I'm worried about her going to such a non-stimulating, depressing environment. It's like living in a cave there. But what can I do? Nothing. The deed is done. I took the two of them to the train station this morning. My only consolation is that they at least have each other. Maybe two kids in the house will enliven things, make a better environment all round, and it will be good for Billy to be living with a sibling.

The only shoulder I have to cry on is yours. And that has to be done by appointment, which is not the way things work in life. And—worse—that shoulder is only figurative, since it's behind glass. Although I hope not for long.

I do have Jean and Doug here—I've known them from Kearney days, from the time I was 16. In fact, Jean stood up for me when I got married and Doug was the only guest. I haven't seen them for several years. It will be lovely to get together again but I haven't contacted them yet—want to be more on an even keel before I do.

◆   ◆   ◆   ◆

It seems kind of ridiculous to write you; I'll see you before this gets there, but it's second nature now. I'm still busy fixing up the apartment and next week I'll go to Manpower to see about starting the French course.

Belinda seems fine with her school. It's farther than she's used to but she hasn't complained. There's a hole where Brenda used to be, but what can I do about that?

Bell said it'll be six weeks or more before my phone is installed. (Have no idea why.)

Being able to see you every week—*twice* a week even!—is wonderful, a real relief. The only inconvenience (if I can find something to complain about, which I usually manage to do) is that we have to book the visits ahead here. I can see why, though; the increased number of visitors is noticeable, isn't it, with it being close to the city. The trip there is nothing for me. It's only 45 km, and I'm so close to the Decairie Expressway that it's non-stop all the way. Now all we have to do is wait for Ottawa to approve the contact visits. . . .

I'm still thinking about the psychologist saying you never should have been classified Supermax in the first place. Grrrrr!!!

THE WAIT IS NOT LONG. Three years of glass is over.

The open visit room, which can be viewed enviously through a windowed wall by the disenfranchised (the closed visit people), is a long room with two rows of low, cocktail-sized arborite tables fixed to the floor, each with four plastic chairs—movable, luckily. The Visits and Correspondence officers watch from their vantage point behind a glass wall at one end. Everything is designed to be as devoid of feeling as possible, but their psychology is of no consequence to me; it's a strategy I'm about to overcome.

Several guys have already entered the room, greeted their visitors, and I'm still waiting. What if they've changed their mind? What if there are more bullshit bureaucratic procedures to pass through? Another signature needed? My hands are sweating. Why didn't I bring Kleenex? I wipe them on the bottom of my skirt. What if the first touch is all clammy and sweaty?

Somewhere the feminist unisex vision of a new world has gone out the window. Choosing what to wear took a lot of time and thought. A brown, pencil-thin skirt that shows my new body to advantage. (All those exercises have paid off; I'm as slim as I was at nineteen.) The pale taupe blouse is slinky, gypsy style, string tie gathering a scooped neckline; over it, a matching vest in a floral pattern of muted taupes, bronzes, golds and dusky greens. I know his artistic sense is going to love the colours, to say nothing of the silky feel. Just imagining hands on it brings a quiver. My stilt-heeled shoes are the exact chocolate brown of my skirt, with narrow straps crossing over the arch. And for the first time in twenty years I've grown my hair to near shoulder length. It was very blonde at one time; now I help it a bit. I feel great. Even feel assured that I *look* great. He once said, "You look good if you *think* you do." I think he's right. I hope he's right.

The minute hand on the clock on the V&C wall has advanced only seven minutes in all this time. I'm breathing deeply, trying to contain myself, to control my thumping heart. Then it's ten minutes. Then twelve. At thirteen minutes the door clicks and there he is. I stand to face him. The moment stretches as he nears. He's within breathing distance but time stops for a click of the brain's camera. He looks good, with a spiffy new hair cut and a light grey T-shirt that accents the grey in his hair and brings out his newly-acquired tan and those brown, brown eyes. The prison-green pants I have to live with.

How often have I imagined this moment, dreamt it, longed for it? In those imaginings we come together in a blend, like a fade-out in a movie, melt seamlessly into one. That's in the movie. In real life, we come together with a jarring collision of purpose. I throw my arms around his neck in a giant bear hug, while he goes for the kiss, and we collide in the wrong places. We get that sorted out and there we are, after all this time, clinging to each other in a long embrace. Then we sit. *Next* to each other. In later prisons we would find the chairs fixed to the floor, impossible to do more than hold hands across the table, but we hit it lucky this first time. I had wondered if it would be like in the movies where touching is allowed only at the beginning and the end of the visit, but there appears to be no rule about that. In this world we can sit next to each other, his arm around me, my head on his shoulder, holding hands. We sink into that oh-so-long-awaited delicious talk, no glass between us, like real people.

We talk and laugh, laugh and kiss, kiss and caress, caress and sit quietly, absorbing the closeness. There really is a unique sense to a person, a kind of aura. I can *feel* the strength, the calm, the softness, the sensitiveness. When time is over we fall into another long stand-up embrace and then I dreamwalk out to the parking lot.

But even now I'm not satisfied. We can have only four open visits per month and a fifth if it's on a week day. Plus two closed visits. I want more.

I'm still living without a phone, but I have something better—a magic phone booth at the corner near my apartment. You put in the coins, talk for three minutes, the recording says, "Please deposit another (so many) cents for another three minutes." You deposit them, they are immediately spewed back and you recycle them three minutes later. Sometimes I've talked half an hour this way. I've called Brenda, Pam, June, Barb, Ivy, and Cheryl in Texas. This time it's Joanne. I don't understand the people who can keep everything inside. I have to hear myself say what I'm feeling. Good or bad, it has to be shared with someone close. Maybe it's not fair to gloat to Joanne about my news—she's still behind glass, after all, because Millhaven still doesn't have an open visit room. But it's Coming Soon, so I don't feel too badly.

The other news, I tell her, is that Don has started work in the welding shop, which he is happy with, and he says to say Hello to Sean, tell him things are much more relaxed than at Millhaven, they should come here too.

Dear Sweet One,

I can still feel the warmth of your arms around me, the touch of your skin, the comfort of holding your hand, of leaning my head on your shoulder. All I can say is, it was worth waiting for, worth enduring the deprivation, the long trips through storms. All of it.

The trip to Ottawa was good. Had a nice visit with Ivy, but short. Now I'm busy proofreading and making some minor changes along the way. And I got registered for the French course but still have to do the placement test.

Belinda still seems resentful at times but it's to be expected. Having to adapt to a totally new environment and being on her own must be difficult for her. She's made a couple of friends though, and has started gymnastics at the local rec centre, so I think she'll soon settle in. I miss Brenda a lot, but what can I do?

I have the apartment all fixed up now, pictures and curtains up, and it feels good. I've met two of my neighbours. The woman across the hall is my age, single and friendly. Then there's a weird guy beside me. Friendly but strange.

Why do you think the movie guys are playing games? I know they're taking their time coming up with a solid proposal, but I assume these things take time. Probably they don't have money, that's what I think. Well, we'll see what they have to say in answer to your letter.

◆   ◆   ◆   ◆

Your letter was here when I got back. Writing (and receiving) letters now seems to be in inverse proportion to the number of visits, doesn't it? It's lovely to receive a letter between visits, though, and I hope we don't stop completely.

Thanksgiving weekend at Joanne's was a lot of fun and Belinda seemed happy for the connection to old roots, too. The main activity was talk-talk-talk, of course, but we also went bowling, which was total humiliation for me. I'm too ashamed to tell you my score. Suffice to say it was less than half Belinda's. It was the first time I ever rolled ten-pins and I hate that heavy ball. I haven't bowled very often, but I'm passably good at five-pins. Do you like bowling? Are you good at it?

Well, I have little hope that Joanne will come here to visit me. She says Sean can't go two weeks without a visit. I told her you should be so lucky. I've never really told you this, but I want you to know that I do appreciate your respect for my autonomy, your understanding that I have my own life to live and can't centre it on you. Many times I've heard guys in the visiting room calling down their visitors for not showing up or for being late, and you never do that. When I don't appear or am late, you're just worried that something has happened and are relieved when you learn the reason.

We'll have our open visit on Thursday—have to be sure to use up that extra one during the week while we can, my course could start at any time. What I want now, now that we're in the same room, is a time extension. What we need is the two hours we already have for talking, then another two hours for "not talking." How about that? Do put in a request to V&C. Do you think they'll say we're greedy? Tell them "not greedy, just needy."

◆   ◆   ◆   ◆

I know I'm going to love living here. Shall I thank you for that?

Yesterday was glorious. Our wonderful visit in the morning, then lunch with that woman I drove back to town (will tell you all about it at the next visit). It was such a beautiful warm afternoon, I walked through the park in front of my place slowly, crunching the leaves underfoot, breathing in that distinctly evocative autumn smell—slightly sad, like the call of geese flying south. A strange feeling came over me: I felt I was both back in Toronto as a child and here at the same time. But with an inability to connect the dots. Bittersweet.

Why can't we talk for hours and hours? There's so much I want to say. Just to attempt this letter paralyzes my mind; the little bit I'll be able to say is so inadequate that it has me tempted to say nothing at all. Then when I'm there with you and have the chance to tell you everything, it's so lovely to just sit back, relax and be quiet, enjoy the feeling of simply being together, take in the physical connection.

Sweet Love, was it only yesterday I saw you? It seems like a week ago. I miss you more and more. The more I see you, the more I miss you.

AT THE VISIT one of the guys asked Don if I had a car, if I could give his visitor a lift back to the city. I did, of course, and it turned out she lived—in a city the size of Montreal—a matter of blocks from me. She took me to lunch at a little Mediterranean restaurant and introduced me to souvlaki sandwich, told me about several other nearby restaurants and the different foods they serve, foods I'd never eaten—or even heard of—before.

Janice had taught Sociology in the prison, one class a week for a term. After the course ended, a correspondence sprung up between her and one of the students. That continued until it seemed right that she should visit, and next thing you knew, a relationship had developed. I thought surely I was the first person on the face of the earth that this had happened to, but was starting to see that it can't be uncommon.

Janice, like me, had been an elementary school teacher in the past, in Ontario also, but she had a grant to work on a PhD. Subject: a comparison of two writers, a *Québecois* and an Algerian, and their views on the nationalist movements in their respective countries. Later, as she gradually worked her way into a full-time tenured position teaching Sociology at a college, she abandoned the doctorate.

It was encouraging to have met someone compatible so soon.

IVY CAME FOR FIVE DAYS and, a week after she left, June arrived. It was the perfect time to have visitors: I had free time and it was good to have people to explore Montreal with. We went to Saint Joseph's Oratory, an enormous copper-domed basilica built high on the side of Mont-Royal, only a few blocks from our place. Constructed in answer to a dream of Brother André who was famous as a healer, the shrine attracts pilgrims from all over North America, some of whom were climbing the 100-step stairway on their knees. And it has the macabre exhibit of Brother André's heart displayed under glass, in its original glory after having been recovered from theft. Who would want it, is what I want to know.

We drove to the lookout atop Mont-Royal, breathed in the view and walked in the park. Spent hours walking in Old Montreal where, sitting at a café on Place Jacques-Cartier, June and I watched Gino Vannelli on a photo shoot, dressed as an eighteenth century nobleman, with coach and horse. On a cobblestone road, against the backdrop of old stone buildings and quaint lanterns, it was a transporting sight.

On the Saturday night we were fortunate to find entertainment for both generations, a performance of *Annie* at Place-des-Arts. But it was the Sunday morning breakfast prepared by Belinda, featuring fried cheese, a favourite of ours at the time, that proved to be June's lasting memory of her time with us in Montreal. She's still talking about it.

WHEN I GOT THE NEWS that the French course was about to begin, I hurried up and finally went to Pointe-Claire, out in the suburbs, to see my old friend, Jean. It was good to catch up with her and Doug after so much time. Funny how with some people it doesn't matter how long it is from the last meeting, the conversation just picks up as if from the day before. During the next four years, until they left Montreal, I was to appreciate, more than I could foresee, their great friendship.

The course is full-time—9:30 to 3:00—five days a week. I start at Intermediate Level and love it. If I had my choice I would be a student forever. There are eight of us in the class, three Spanish-speaking men from Chile and five English-speaking women from different parts of Canada and a great divide between the two; each group acts as if the other doesn't exist. And the women are equally "immigrant" with the men in the eyes of the government of Quebec, immigrants in our own country, that's why we're able to take the course while receiving UIB. I'm not about to complain.

We have two teachers, both excellent. Pierrette is *Québécoise* and a real ball of fire who gets us steamed up on the referendum issue. She's on the Separatist side. Monique, from Algeria, is calm, reserved.

It's a thirty-five minute walk to school, downhill all the way, although progressively upscale, south through Snowdon, then through the mansions of Upper Westmount. I make the walk an event, take a different perspective every day, alternately concentrating on windows, doors, roofs, gardens, walkways—all different and beautiful—a kind of outdoor art gallery. At the edge of the mountain a small park affords an incredible view over Lower Westmount and below it the infinitely poorer district of St-Henri, a vista that draws me back into Gabrielle Roy's *The Tin Flute*, set in the contrast of those two districts.

From this point a stairway leads down the steep part of the mountain to Blvd de Maisonneuve, the fashionable commercial street where my school is located. Sometimes I walk home again, but most often I take the bus for at least the steepest part of the hill.

And I share it all with Don.

JANICE HAS BEEN IN MONTREAL two years, speaks French, and has a busy life heavily involved in social justice issues. Our common interests provide for stimulating conversation, and her experience in the *Québecois* culture is a help to my orientation. We spend a lot of time together and she's great with Belinda, treats her as an equal. She introduces us to several local ethnic restaurants and to the famous Brown Derby, which is halfway between our apartments. This establishment is a wonder to me with its boisterous Jewish clientele and the gargantuan meals they serve. For an additional fifty cents, meals can be shared. Even then there's enough for the three of us, considering the scrumptious New York cheesecake we share for dessert. Sometimes we go in the morning for coffee and cheese blintzes. I realize my culinary education was decidedly impoverished before moving to Montreal and meeting Janice.

Falafel sandwiches at a hygienically-questionable kosher place on Victoria Street frequented by orthodox Jews (women in wigs, men and boys sporting sidelocks, their string fringes flapping at their sides) are amazing. The nearby Quality Kosher Bakery becomes my favourite of the many local bakeries. There, one morning, the arm of my server stops me in a shock of reality. I'd read dozens of books on the holocaust, but the concept of millions suffering in the abstract falls meaningless compared to the impact of one individual with a number tattooed on her arm.

In time we explore all the well-known cheap eateries: Schwartz's Delicatessen on The Main for smoked meat on rye sandwiches, served with the biggest dill pickles in existence; Ben's on de Maisonneuve, famous for its soup and sandwiches; Prince Arthur Street where we could bring our own bottle of wine, bought at the local *dépanneur*. Later, Andros' Greek Restaurant opened on Victoria Street, near us. The three of us ate there so frequently we were greeted as visitors to someone's house. The same was true at Montreal's first Thai restaurant, also on Victoria, which we visited on the day of its opening.

But more often we ate in each other's homes. Soon after we met, Janice invited Belinda and me to supper, along with another prison wife. By that time Don had had me officially listed as next-of-kin: common-law wife. Later, when I became more fluent in French, I always referred to him as *mon mari*, even though I couldn't bear the though of anyone being "my husband" in English. One can take liberties in a second language, make words take the meanings you want to give them. To me, *mon mari* meant "my loved one, the one dear to my heart." Dorothy had had her last name changed legally to Ivan's and called him her husband although they weren't legally married. In two years' time Janice would marry David in the prison chapel. So there we were, three "prison wives," sharing a bottle of wine over supper, discussing the relevancies, and Belinda receiving a most unconventional education.

Dear Don,

I hope you enjoyed your mom's visit. I know it's kind of hard for you to juggle the three generations all together. *I don't know why you get so angry with her, though—or is it frustrated? I can see you controlling yourself. But I don't understand what causes it—must be in the history. Fortunately for her, I don't think she sees it.* It's a conflicted relationship, I can see. Still I know you feel badly about all the trouble she's had. *What I can't understand is, she never asks anything about what conditions you live under, if you're suffering, never expresses any regret about what your life has come to. She's so sunny about it all, it's bewildering. . . .* Does it insult you if I say you must take after her in your good humour and talkativeness? She beats even you on the latter, though. By a long shot.

Well, we told you all the things we did—tour of the city, show at the Planetarium, the vegetarian restaurant. But she didn't tell you about coming here on the train filled with Grey Cup revellers from Edmonton, who—by the sounds of it—were already very "jolly" by the time she boarded in North Bay. I was surprised that she would enjoy their antics. Any time you want her to come to see you, she is welcome.

Now here's news. The manuscript has been submitted to a publisher. I wonder how long we'll have to wait for news.

I took my car to the local garage. They quoted $200. Then Doug looked in the book *Lemon Aid* for me and found a garage near here and they only charged $65. So, see how much money he saved you? *I still have trouble accepting money from you, but I do realize it makes you feel good to be able to help me and to contribute to our joint well-being.* Your statement has me chuckling: "Never mind, when I'm broke I'll borrow from you."

A SUNDAY EVENING. I'M TRYING to improve my language skills by listening to a French radio station. I've been in the course four weeks but still am able to recognize only words here and there, never the entire meaning. The nine o'clock news comes on and my ears perk up when I hear the words *Penitencier Archambault*. Then I hear *tué*. I think I hear *tué*. I hope I didn't hear *tué*, or—better still—I hope I'm wrong in my understanding of the word. But I'm almost positive *tué* means killed. Time expands between words, one can die between them, die and come back and they're only on the next word. I hear a name. Sounds like "Yvon Orva." Yvon Orva. . . . I say it over and over again. Yvon Orva. . . . It's too familiar. I know this name, but something's not right. It turns in my mind like a distant memory . . . until the French pronunciation drops away and the English one emerges: Ivan Horvat. My heart sinks.

I go to the dictionary, look up *tuer*. *Tuer:* verb, to kill. *Tué:* past participle, killed. I don't want to accept this, tell myself maybe I'm mistaken, maybe they didn't say *tué*. How good is my French, after all?

I call Janice, start hesitantly. "I hate to even say this," I tell her. "If I'm wrong it's a terrible thing to say." Fortify myself with a big breath. "I was listening to the news on a French station—and you know my French isn't great—but I do know I heard *Penitencier Archambault*. Something happened at Archambault, that's for sure. And I think I heard the word *tué*. I'm almost certain they said someone was killed." She gasps. "But here's the worst," I continue, "and I don't like to say it in case I'm wrong." I take another breath. "I think they said Ivan."

Silence.

Then—barely audible—a whisper, falling—"Oh my God."

"Maybe I'm wrong," I tell her with false hopefulness.

"I'll phone Dorothy," she says. "I won't let on, just make it like a regular call. See what happens."

Five minutes later the telephone rings.

The voice is breathless, shaky. "It was Ivan," she tells me. "When she answered I just said 'Hi Dorothy' and waited. The first thing she said was, 'I was going to call you in a few minutes. Things are changing.' The chaplain called her about an hour ago. Ivan was hit on the head first, probably knocked unconscious, and then knifed. It happened in the TV room."

"Jesus."

"She sounded calm, very calm, related it all factually, like it had happened to someone else. I'm going over there. Do you have anything to drink?"

"I have an almost-full bottle of brandy. I'll ask Irene across the hall if she'll stay with Belinda and drive you over."

We spend the fifteen minutes to Dorothy's in silence. We know it could be us. Being a prisoner in a maximum security prison is a dangerous occupation. In the previous two years twenty-four prisoners had suffered unnatural deaths at Archambault. Two more were destined to be murdered before the year was out. And suicides in Canada's prisons are twelve percent higher than the national rate—to say nothing of those who die of neglected health care and lack of response to cries for help, all of which are well-documented in numerous reports.

I'm thinking about Dorothy moving here only months before to be with him. Ivan had transferred from B.C. where he had been in Maximum for seven years, but here he had finally made it to Medium—Leclerc Institution at Laval—where he had "celebrated" his last birthday, his twenty-sixth, before being summarily reclassified and sent to Archambault: "For the good order of the Institution." I picture Dorothy at the supper table, telling us with enthusiasm that at Leclerc, with the weight of pressure lifted, he was starting to do art and had been in touch with the Philosophy Department at Concordia University to get some courses started.

Things are changing. The words echo. *Things are changing,* a sentence almost mystical in its simplicity, an eloquent acceptance of fate, a stoic surrender to that which can't be changed. I marvel at her quiet maturity, a person so much younger than me.

I stay just long enough to express my condolences, oblivious to the fine spider web on which we stand at times, invisible, but strong enough to join us to our future. For at Dorothy's that night, without knowing it, I stood linked to Quakers and to Claire Culhane. Martin Duckworth was there. He had become friends with Ivan and Dorothy through making documentaries for the National Film Board; his parents were well-known Quakers. Claire Culhane was a very close and dear friend of the couple. I knew nothing of Quakers or of Claire, but time would lead me to both. Things change.

Hi,

The gang arrived safely. It's a full house at eight people—Brenda and Billy, Pam and Jeff and Cheryl brought her boyfriend. It's wonderful to have everybody reunited, and I think they're enjoying it as much as me. Right now they're watching a TV show that doesn't interest me, so thought I'd take advantage and write a few words. Will you think of doing the same? I hope so. I miss your letters.

Our Christmas was good, and thanks so much again for the turkey. Everyone thanks you. It was cooked to perfection with help from the girls. *My heart would cave in on itself, wither of bitterness, if I found myself serving as the agent of others' happiness while living in misery. How do you do it?* Your gifts always have special meaning. The Persian Garden, the cactus, Belinda's birthstone ring. And I haven't forgotten Christmas two years ago when you gave Brenda a five-dollar bill but Belinda got hers in quarters because you said little kids like to have small change to spend. You give a lot of thought to what you give and I appreciate it. *I didn't much care for Pam's bottle of Amaretto, though, with her being only seventeen. But you put thought into that, too—said you read it was developed by a woman and represented love.*

Christmas Eve I told them we'd take a tour of Westmount where we should see lots of fantastic decorations because it's such a wealthy district. We went in a convoy of two cars, up one street and down another, around and around, and hardly a house decorated. I couldn't figure it out. It was the next day before it hit me; the rich people in Montreal are Jewish.

This year, in my enthusiasm to become a *Montréalaise,* I made the unilateral decision that we'd do Christmas the *Québecois* way (skipping the midnight mass part, mind you). Our modified version was this: we ate our Christmas supper about ten o'clock on Christmas Eve; then, after the kitchen was cleaned up, we opened our gifts. That took us to just after three o'clock. By that time everyone was tired so we went to bed, although I know *Québecois* often don't do that until after breakfast.

Christmas morning we got up, had breakfast, looked at each other and said, "What do we do now?" What a letdown! Everyone felt the same. Seems traditions are not easy to dispense with. We played some games and had fun, but it just wasn't "Christmas."

◆   ◆   ◆   ◆

What a special treat New Year's Day was! To be with you from ten o'clock in the morning to three-thirty in the afternoon seems like a gift from Heaven. And I could see how happy you were, too. Surviving on junk food from the vending machine I'm not about to complain about; it was a small sacrifice. If I were a nicer person I'd write them a letter of appreciation; I've been hasty enough with all my letters of complaint. Well, at least that hasn't been necessary since we left Millhaven behind.

Five and a half hours and *still* we didn't run out of things to say. Just holding your hand all that time was the best New Year's gift I could have received. Janice and I were delirious all the way home. (Or maybe the chips, chocolate bars and soft drinks had something to do with it?)

Belinda and I enjoyed the Ice Capades. To be actually in the Forum after a lifetime of Hockey Night in Canada was amazing.

Write soon.

IT HURTS THAT HE HARDLY writes any more. I don't write as often either—it's not as necessary now—but I would like to hear from him between visits. In that way I would feel all the effort isn't on my part. He has all kinds of excuses and I "don't understand" how it is for him (probably I don't), but the heart of it is, I think, that being a gregarious person, after all those years of solitary and almost-solitary confinement he can't tear himself away from the company of others. He spends his time hanging out with the guys, which is perfectly understandable, but I don't imagine the conversation gives much inspiration for writing. And he doesn't read books any more, although he *is* current with what's going on in the world, in Montreal, and Quebec politics in particular. We have lively debates about the upcoming referendum. I tell him what our teacher, Pierrette, had to say; he tells me what the guys in there are saying (prisoners will actually have a vote), what the politicians are saying on TV, what he read in the newspapers. It's fun.

But I'm upset about not getting letters and need someone to talk to. I don't like complaining to Janice because David is so attentive, writes her often, makes Don look shoddy and uncaring in comparison even though I do know he cares; I never have doubts about that. I wish I could call June but it's too expensive—the Magic Phone has lost its magic—so I write.

"All is not perfect in Paradise," I start, and lay it out. Pages and pages of venting until, as usually happens in pouring out feelings, things become clear. One doesn't need a therapist; it's all there. Deep down I do realize that receiving fewer letters is a minor disappointment that is more than balanced by the shared understanding, the pure pleasure of being together, the fun and laughter, and the comfort of being in each others' arms.

"Although you don't say much," I tell her, "I know you worry about me in this relationship, but don't. As I've told you before, I haven't dedicated my life to him. And he knows that. When I see how Joanne lets her life revolve around Sean, how it dictates her almost every action, it brings home that that is not how I want to live. If I meet someone in the real world and it clicks, I won't let it go by because of a 'maybe sometime.' In the meanwhile, all the support and encouragement he gives, the understanding and helpful advice, are far more than I give him. To say nothing of his example of strength."

Dear Don,

You have no idea how happy receiving your letter yesterday made me. Just to see it in the mailbox was enough to make my day. Reading it made me feel a lot better about things in general, and I must have read it ten times so far. (Hurry up and send another before this one gets worn out!)

I really enjoyed it and you sound just like your old self, which was such a relief after the visit Tuesday. Right now I'm feeling as if maybe I should start to write you more fully again—maybe expressing myself on paper would help relieve the frustration. But that brings its own frustration when you don't answer. So, I don't know what I want. Just be patient with me, Don, till I work out all these things in my own mind.

I have a letter from Barb to answer so I'll continue with this after Sunday's visit. I do hope we have a good talk.

◆　　◆　　◆　　◆

I think the visit yesterday was the nicest we've ever had. And I went all prepared for a heavy scene. The time is altogether too short, though. I want more!!! Joanne tells me they have six hours of contact visits a week at Millhaven while we're lucky if we get the full two. See, I'm never satisfied. Gripe, gripe, gripe. . . . But I have so much I still need to say to make you understand. The same old things are going to crop up again and again if we don't get them resolved.

For me, disagreements are one thing; we're bound to have them. But you setting yourself up as the arbiter of what will and will not be discussed is something I won't accept. You say I make you feel like someone with his head under water, drowning, and while in that predicament I demand you talk. I understand what you mean, but have you thought of the alternative? The alternative is that I treat you like a baby, handle you "with kid gloves." Because of my respect for you, I can't do that. I have to express my feelings to you as they come up. To do otherwise would be role-playing, would be dishonest.

Sure, it doesn't hurt anybody to go easy on the other person when he's having a hard time. But it can't go one way *all* the time. And maybe you feel like I make demands while you're tied to a railroad track (your other analogy), but maybe sometimes I feel like I'm hanging onto the edge of a cliff, calling for help. Shall I just say to hell with it, someone tied to a track can't help me? Should you say to hell with it, somebody falling off a cliff can't help me? Or should we assume that somehow one or the other—or both—will get loose? Since we're both incurable optimists, I think we should keep hanging in (on?).

You described how you go to your cell with full intentions of writing and then when you get there you just flake out, which you find disappointing and hard to understand. It sounds like what I went through nine years ago. It's hard for even the person experiencing it to comprehend. You wonder if you're even the same person—all energy, strength and determination one minute, and completely sapped of will the next. I experienced it as an enormous dark cloud descending on me. The only escape was to sleep because if I didn't I would have to witness myself being snuffed out.

Things will work out the way they're going to work out. The important thing is to keep talking. I guess I want the relationship to operate as closely to normal as possible. Do I want the impossible?

On the other hand, it warms my heart to read the part where you express how much I mean to you, and a few compliments besides. At least you write those things—which is better than nothing—but I sure wouldn't mind if you actually got around to saying them some time. I'm only human, and if you're honest with yourself you'll admit you enjoy the occasional bit of positive reinforcement. Why should I be any different?

Now this will sound contrary. After talking about hanging from a cliff and needing understanding, I will now tell you that another thing in your letter that makes me feel good is where you say, "Sometimes I just feel like leaning on you and having you carry all the load I seem to feel." And then yesterday you *physically* leaned on me, and it made me feel so good to sense the ebb and flow of strength between the two of us. It really is true that one can give and need strength at the same time. Helps each of us get "re-charged." You say you hope I didn't find it heavy (your leaning on me like that). Not at all. On the contrary, it bolstered me, made me feel stronger just because you paid me the compliment of believing me capable of it.

Now Loved One, I'll close and look forward to seeing you in the morning—and hope to get another letter from you soon.

I'm including a photo of the Persian Garden, which I promised you so long ago (sorry I can't hold a camera straight). You have no idea the comfort

I get from sitting and studying it. It really does say a lot more than the words I sometimes long to hear.

◆   ◆   ◆   ◆

Guess you've been waiting to hear how my vacation is going. I'll start at the first. The trip here was great. The plane touched down at Dallas, so I got a good view of that city as well as vast expanses around Houston—plains as far as you can see, with the slightest touch of rolling hills here and there and almost no trees. Having lived in northern Ontario so long, I feel I wouldn't survive long without trees. Even Montreal has its Mont-Royal.

On the other hand, things here are nourishing in their own way: the sea, the beach, the palm trees. On the way in from the airport we passed lots of little settlements on canals beside the highway. Houses on stilts with boats hitched to "front-yard" docks. A sealand suburbia. Must be such a human way to live. Then the long causeway and bridge—more than a mile and a half—to get to Galveston Island.

While Cheryl is at work I walk and walk. The seawall is a great place to stroll. Along that stretch most of the restaurants and hotels are Spanish architecture—white plaster with red tile roofs. Beautiful, exotic. I walk on the beach itself sometimes, looking for shells, but there aren't many. On the weekend Cheryl is going to take me further out, where they're easier to find.

There's so much history to learn about here. In 1900 Galveston experienced the biggest natural disaster in the history of the United States—six to ten thousand killed in a hurricane (exact figure unknown), most of them in the accompanying tidal wave. It was after that that they built the seawall, an incredible feat of engineering in its time. Ten miles long, seventeen feet high, fifteen feet thick at the bottom, it has a concave curve designed to thrust storm waves back out to the Gulf, thus protecting most of the city. Beyond the seawall the houses are on stilts.

It's hard to understand—without the machinery we have today—how they managed to raise two-thirds of the city four to six feet by jacking up the houses and filling underneath with earth brought from the mainland. They have all kinds of information and pictures on this at the Tourist Information Centre and a slide show. The effort, I think, was herculean.

The Tourist Centre is located on the original main street, The Strand, which stands in its 1890's splendour. It had gone into deterioration but is being revived as an attraction for visitors (mostly day-trippers from Houston, only 50 miles away)—antique/curiosity shops, art galleries, several restaurants. The Strand has one of the largest and best-preserved collection of iron-front commercial architecture in the country. It's lovely—all "scrolly"—and they have wooden porches like in western movies. My ten days here won't be nearly long enough to see and learn everything I'd like to.

One thing that was surprising to learn is that the modern city was planned and established by a Canadian—one Michel Menard, who was born near Montreal. The story of his life should be a book if it isn't already—fascinating, although they say he told so many versions of his history that it's hard to know where the truth lies.

In its heyday—the late nineteenth century—the city was the economic hub of the south and home to many tycoons. There's a self-guided walking tour, which I took, to see their houses, some of which are now museums. You would love the Bishop's Palace (originally a private home—later occupied by a bishop) for the rare woods used (different in every room) and the hand-carved grand staircase. Two hundred and fifty people survived the hurricane in that house with only one window broken, while across the street the church was demolished and many perished. (Does that say something???) When we have a closed visit I'll bring pamphlets to show you all these places.

The University of Texas Medical Branch, where Cheryl works, is a town in itself. It comprises fifty-three buildings, making up six different hospitals with a staff of 6,000 and 1,800 medical and nursing students. She took me to the ward where she works (a short walk from here) and then we met for lunch at a nearby pub where Mexican food is the feature—a first for me and I liked it a lot. Also, we went for shrimp at the port. Shrimp boats come in there early in the morning, but early is not for me. At almost any time bananas from Central and South America can be seen being unloaded.

Tuesday night we went over to Jill's place (my niece). She has a cute little one-room apartment over the garage of a rich person's house on Avenue Q ½, an after-thought of a street squeezed in between Avenue Q and Avenue R. It used to be staff accommodation.

I called Janice (how fortunate to have such a good friend!) and spoke with Belinda. They're getting along fine, but I fancy she misses me. Now why can't I phone and see if *you* miss me?

Your last three letters are here with me. I love to read them again and again while sitting along the waterfront. Makes me feel close to you. Will try to answer the still-unanswered last one soon.

Oh, yes, before signing off I have to tell you this. We were walking down the street when we met a friend of Cheryl's. She introduced me and her friend said, "Your mother! She looks too young to be your mother; I thought she was your friend." "Well, she's my friend too," Cheryl told her. That sure did my ego good—in two ways.

Miss you lots and send all that silent conversation and love.

BEING AN "IMMIGRANT" TO QUEBEC brought benefits. I was allowed to stay in the language course until the unemployment benefits ran out and then was given an extension of six weeks to find a job.

I had known from the beginning that it would be impossible to get a job in social services; the mass exodus of English-speakers from the province had caused Ville Marie Social Services (English sector) to lay off 500 employees. I could have done the paperwork to get my teaching certificate accepted in Quebec, but I really didn't want to teach. Several readings of the Classifieds made it clear that there would be no job for me unless I learned to type. So, I rented a typewriter (mine had the return lever; I needed one with a return key) and bought a Learn to Type book. I'd been typing with the correct fingers all along, but I had to learn to do it without looking, and needed to increase my speed. A kitchen timer was borrowed from Jean, and I set to practicing several hours a day. Two weeks later I passed the typing test at Manpower, the counsellor phoned a company, I went for the interview and got the job. All on the same day. The thrill of it was that the job required a high degree of proficiency in French and I had succeeded in both interviews.

The job is receptionist-switchboard operator at $75 a week less than I was earning in North Bay, but since $50 of that amount was for benefits, the actual take-home pay is only $25 less. It's at a plant that assembles word processing machines—AES, the kind my manuscript was done on. The company is in the process of moving to a new building out on the TransCanada Highway, which is easy for me to get to, and I share driving with a delightful woman in the Personnel Office who, for obvious reasons, has the nickname Happy. She lives only two blocks from me and is good company.

It's not the kind of job I've had in the past—not really commensurate with my education and experience—and I'm aware most people will think I'm crazy, but I like it. There's lots of people-contact (mostly chatting with the vendors who come to see the buyers), so it's an opportunity to improve my French. And, I figure, perhaps later there will be a chance to move to the Personnel Office. Meanwhile, not having work or worries to bring home at night as I had in my previous jobs is a big advantage.

Getting underway in this job is not without its pitfalls. Hired Monday. Tuesday and Wednesday I attend a course at Bell to learn the switchboard (eight lines, sixty-four extensions, many functions). The course is in French and I understand all the instructions, but when it comes time to practice juggling calls, putting people on hold, paging, getting back to the callers, I find myself paralyzed. Thursday I tell the Personnel Manager I can't do it.

"Of course you can."

I tell her my French isn't good enough.

"Of course it is. You speak very well."

"But speaking isn't the problem; it's understanding. It's more difficult on the telephone, especially under pressure, trying to handle several calls at one time."

"You'll do fine," she says and so I find myself sitting in solitary splendour in the tastefully decorated reception area, surrounded by plants, and streams of light flowing through the vast windows. I answer the phone, receive visitors and study the functions of the word processing machine, which I find fascinating.

Before the second week is over a young fellow has attached himself to me. He comes to eat with me every day in the lunch room. I can't figure it out. He's much younger than me—late twenties, probably—so surely it's not romantic. His name is Carlos and he comes from Colombia. He's an assembly worker, and I find the fact that he "dares" to sit with me quite interesting because a great barrier of status exists between the office workers and those who work in the plant.

Carlos, it turns out, lives close to me, on the same street as Janice, just a block up. He invites Belinda and me to supper and proves to be an excellent cook and gracious host. We become friends. When I hear Bob Seger is coming to town, I ask him if he would like to go. He's never heard of him but is willing.

It's the first rock concert I've ever gone to, so I have no idea what to expect. The Forum is full to the roof, not an empty seat in the house. I can't believe I'm going to see Bob Seger in the flesh. I think of Joanne. If it weren't for her I wouldn't even know who he is.

An expectant buzz has overtaken the arena. It's building to a pitch when suddenly lights flash in a burst of blue, green and yellow and The Silver Bullet Band crashes to life. This is so captivating I've forgotten all about the star until he casually walks to the mike and the crowd explodes. Rays of purple, red, turquoise—so many colours I can't take them all in—circle the crowd slowly, around and around, giving alien faces to those in the floor seats, a spectral aura to the faceless crowd above. We're ten rows up, on the left side, about one quarter of the way along from the stage, close enough to see his face.

The music softens, the band pauses, leaves us in hushed suspense. Seger poises his hand over the strings of his guitar, ready. Everyone's ready. Then: "It seems like yesterday. . . ." and the crowd erupts. We all know that song, know every word of it (save Carlos and maybe one or two others), "but it was long ago. . . ." I send thought waves to Joanne.

The next morning I regale Don with a play-by-play, exude over the significance of the lyrics. He doesn't know Seger or his music, although he recalls some of the lines I've sent him in the past, the ones about storming prison walls and inmates freeing guards, about being too long on these islands, being far too long alone. He surely must think I go a little overboard with these things and yet he only shows interest. It's so comforting—"shelter against the wind," to quote Seger—to have someone genuinely interested in what you say, even if—*especially* if—the subject matter is unknown.

Saturday afternoon, the time of cheaper rates, I give myself the luxury of phoning Joanne. Tell her every detail. What impressed me most, I explain, is his ordinariness, how he retains it in spite of being a star. And his assurance that good things lie in the mundane.

"He sang all our favourites," and I list them, "and when it came to 'That Old Time Rock 'n Roll,' it was almost cataclysmic. That building bounced, lights pulsed to the beat, the crowd jumped to its feet, danced and sang as one. I'll probably never want to go to another rock concert because nothing could ever equal it."

Hi,

Such a lovely visit. Then, Saturday night I had Janice and Dorothy over for supper. Sunday we were invited to Jean and Doug's for the afternoon and supper. So it was a busy, good weekend.

I called Brenda. She got your letter and she's coming! Said she answered you already. Maybe you have it by now. I can hardly wait for both—her visit and the pictures. That's going to be one great day!

Just a short note to let you know she's coming.

◆   ◆   ◆   ◆

Such a special afternoon. I can't believe my fortune. The best birthday I could have had.

Did you like the new outfits I bought the girls? We shopped specially. You looked—and felt—good. I liked that T-shirt on you—tawny brings out your complexion and should look good in the pictures. With fifteen taken we can be assured that at least some will be good. Any idea when we'll get them?

It was great having Brenda here and I was sorry when she left, but the summer job was waiting. I took the two of them to the train this afternoon, so here I sit—alone. But it won't be long till I go to see them.

On the way out I picked up my birthday gift OK. It turns out to be the exact length of the couch and wide enough that the coffee table looks perfectly placed on it. When I saw it, I was worried the colours weren't right for the Persian Garden (which hangs above the couch) but the tones are muted enough that they complement each other nicely. I love the main colour—yellow? buff? cream? Is there an official name? It's soft and rich at the same time—lovely against the hardwood floor, and creates a cosiness the room didn't have.

How do I say Thank You? Now I'm feeling the happy-sad clown drawing I did for your birthday was a bit wanting. But the other part of the gift—the whole day visit—morning and afternoon—I know you liked; I still have the letter telling me that. Mmmm. . . .

◆   ◆   ◆   ◆

Alarming news from Joanne. Sean went "missing" a few days ago. Had you heard? He was in the hospital downtown and went AWOL in the middle of the night. She's beside herself with worry. Will police shoot him? Where will he go? How will he get money? I'll go to stay with her for a few days when the plant closes the last two weeks of the month and I get my forced unpaid holidays. Then I'll go on to Toronto to see Evie, to Orillia to see the kids, then spend a couple of days at my mother's cottage.

I don't know what's going on with V&C there these days. Things seem to be getting as bad as at Millhaven. We used to be all checked in and everyone notified by 1:30. Now they don't even start the process until that time. I was telling Janice how long I had to wait for you on Sunday. She went yesterday and had the same problem. It was 2:15 before David was even called—a whole hour wasted by the time he arrived. It seems like the system is designed to either make people crazy monsters or give up.

◆   ◆   ◆   ◆

Your letter with the poem in it arrived yesterday. So, you *can* be sentimental sometimes, I see. It's beautiful—brought tears to my eyes—expresses *my* feelings as well.

Belinda said the visit was "O.K." and "not too mushy." What's it come to when we have to get a kid's approval? I'm still chuckling at your expression when she slapped your face. See, that's what you get for teasing. Somehow I don't think others would fare as well if they tried that. Right?

———————————————

DON HAS BEEN SENT TO Laval Institution, where Archambault's seg-regation unit is located. Why, they didn't say. As a classification issue, they don't have to. "For the good order of the institution" suffices. We're back to closed visits.

It's a Saturday afternoon. When the visit is over—only one hour long in Segregation—I'm on my way out when the V&C officer stops me and tells me to empty the contents of my pockets onto the table. And I know I'm in trouble. Deep trouble. I comply; he tells me he has to keep the wire. I tell him I want a receipt because it's my bracelet and show him the charm that had been attached to it. He writes me a receipt for a silver bracelet.

Outside the skies are dark as if to end the world. I'm in a trance and drive past my exit, past two exits, until I wake up not recognizing anything. I'm way out in the suburbs.

After supper Belinda and I go over to Janice's so I can tell her what happened, so we can put our heads together, speculate on what will happen next, what I should do.

About three months back Don had told me someone would bring me a wire, he wanted to see what it looked like, and if we had a closed visit some time I should cut off a little one-inch piece, put it along the metal part of my wallet so it doesn't show on the metal detector, and bring it in to show him. He gave a twisting motion of his hand, which I interpreted to mean it was to open a door. With all the shenanigans they get into in there, that didn't bother me in the least. I saw it as a lark if they got into their records, the kitchen, the medicine cabinet, whatever they were after. Some time later the guy brought over not one, but three. Seeing them, I got a "bright idea." Shiny, silver-coloured, each comprised three or four strands twisted around each other with a little loop on either end. "No problem," I said to myself, "I'll just wrap it around my wrist, join the loops with a charm and—*voilà!*—a bracelet. I can just walk in with it, he can have a look, and that's that."

It was a snug fit wrapped around the wrist twice, but I managed to fasten it with a silver sand dollar charm I had bought in Galveston. And regardless of what it was for, I knew that since I wasn't entering the prison *per se* it wasn't an issue.

Minutes into the visit the charm link let go and the bracelet came apart. I didn't care. In my naivety I sat there twisting it as we talked. At one point he indicated for me to put it up to the glass where he took a long close look. Maybe that's when the V&C noticed. The rest, as they say, is history.

Janice and I agree there's no question of me importing contraband because I wasn't entering the part where prisoners are, but they'll probably harass me in some way. How, we're not sure, but they're sure to do something. We agree that since I have an appointment for the morning, there's no choice but to keep it; I have to carry on as normal.

In the morning I arrive tied in a knot, petrified, wondering if they'll let me in or not, but get booked in with no problem. Then the officer opens a door adjacent to the waiting area and tells me to sit in there, someone wants to see me.

It's a boardroom. I sit at the table, try to prepare myself. But I have no idea what to prepare for. Who's coming? What will he say? They'll ask me why I had it, what it's for. But I don't know. What am I to say? Time passes. I study the opulence of the room, the warmth of the glowing table (mahogany? something expensive), the softness of the upholstered chairs, the contrast to our space. Don will be worried, will wonder why I haven't shown up. I wait a full fifty-five minutes with nothing happening other than the ticking of the clock and the thundering of my heart. Then two huge men in suits enter. One asks if I speak French; I say I do. He rattles on for what seems like two minutes but was probably less than twenty seconds, starts walking out, asks, "*C'est bien?*"

"No," I tell him, "because I didn't understand."

"You're under arrest for conspiracy to facilitate an escape," he says.

The floor sinks. My shaking body freezes. So does my head.

He asks for my car keys so they can search the car. I know I don't have to, but I don't care, things are spinning out of control and besides, there's nothing in my car to interest them.

I sit in shivering silence across from the other guy. The room gets colder. Its vastness expands and the distance across the table widens. Finally the first one comes back, gives me the keys, says come with him, takes me to an office, indicates where to sit and leaves me there, locking the door behind him.

It's already past the time when I should be home. Belinda's going to wonder what's happened to me. She won't be nervous, but she'll be wondering. And what will I tell her about this? Finally, a woman (I don't know yet, but she turns out to be a police officer) unlocks the door, comes in and sits on the business side of the desk. She says we have to wait there. I tell her I have an 11-year-old daughter at home alone, expecting me, can I phone her? The phone is right there on the desk, but she says no. That makes me cry. What does she think is going to happen by phoning an 11-year old? I try to impress on her how important it is, but there's no way; I can't call. Ten or fifteen minutes later one of the male officers enters, she asks him if I can phone, he says I can. After the call I tell him the situation and he says we can stop at my place before we go to the jail.

The sensation of walking on a slow-motion trampoline, of being unrealistically transported on its retarded wave through decelerated time takes over as we waft down the hall, through the sliding gates, out to the administration parking lot, to the waiting patrol car. I'm told to get in the back with the woman and we take off to my place. At least they're doing this; I'm grateful, but when we get there I realize it's to search my apartment.

We get out of the car and I don't dare look up at the windows to see if any of the neighbours are witnessing this most mortifying of events. It doesn't occur to me that there's no way anyone would know, with the three of them in plain clothes and driving an unmarked car; I'm quite sure the brand is on my forehead.

In my numbness I don't know what to say to Belinda. Could there be any words that would be adequate? I tell the officers I have to call my friend to come and look after her, but they won't even let me do that. "Later," they say. I stand mute while they take the liberty of looking around, not touching, but craning their necks to see behind things; then they ask permission to look in the kitchen cupboards. I don't care. Nothing matters.

When they finish they let me phone Janice. And what would have happened if she hadn't been home? Would they have put the child in some kind of centre overnight? Made her suffer even more? Why they should take me to jail is impossible to understand. I certainly would show up to court in the morning. They can see I'm a steady person with a job, an apartment and a child to look after. They won't even wait until Janice gets there; I have to leave Belinda alone with reassurances. Is this going to scar her for life? My only hope is she's had enough good grounding up to now that it won't be that serious in the long run. My feeling is she's so wise, so "educated" from all the talk she's heard that she realizes how things go.

They take me to Parthenais Detention Centre—the city jail. I pose centre, left and right for the camera. It's surreal. He takes my hand, twists the fingers one by one onto the ink pad slowly, slowly, then onto the paper. Leonard Cohen's "Give Me Back My Fingerprints" incongruously passes behind my eyes. Then it occurs to me—and I feel ludicrously proud—that my French is proficient enough to get booked in. In fact, all communication following my initial *faux pas* had been in that language.

I ask for my phone call. Luckily I know the name of a lawyer I had heard mentioned as being decent. They look up the number for me and I get him at home. He'll show up at the arraignment in the morning and asks if I have a friend who can bring money, which I assume is for bail. They let me make another call to Janice who says she will come to meet him.

I'm in jail. Me. Overnight. In a cell. With bars. A bunk, a toilet and a sink. And a matron exclusively for me; I'm the only woman on the range. I don't even remember what they gave me to eat, but I think it was plastic. I sit for a long time contemplating nothing. A void had existed before this unreality and nothing comes after it. Finally I ask the matron if she can find something for me to read. She goes and comes back with a couple of magazines. She sits in the corridor knitting, discretely out of my face, a couple of cells down the row. She's a decent sort but I don't feel like talking. Later I decide I should pace. Not because I feel like pacing but it seems to me that when you're in a cell you're "supposed" to pace. So I pace. Five steps forward. Turn . . . five steps back . . . turn . . . five steps forward. . . . Another new experience: I've paced in a cell. Could do without this particular experience and yet—at the same time—I feel almost comfortably linked to the other side of what I've been living these years now.

Surprisingly, I manage to sleep most of the night. Escape from reality, I suppose. After breakfast and collecting my effects, we're off to court—*Le Palais de Justice*. It always did ruin the ambiance of Old Montreal with its stark glass and granite construction looming over the Old World elegance. When we stop at traffic lights people look at me, just as I have looked at people in the back seats of patrol cars.

Now I'm in the holding cells. Me in one, and ten or twelve not-so-great looking guys in four more cells, all facing a central area. Some of the guys signal various questions to me. I'm not sure if I'm interpreting properly, but I do my best to answer. Some kind of surrealistic camaraderie is happening.

Time advances like a glacier in this world. Hours pass. Nerves and having nothing to eat have me freezing, trembling in my bones. They bring in another woman. We exchange a few words here and there but neither of us is in a talking mood. Finally a guard comes with his clanging keys, opens the cell door and points me through a door. This, I'm shocked to find, expels me into a crowded courtroom, directly into the prisoner's box and they're talking about me.

"Where's my lawyer?" I ask the uniformed guy standing beside me. "I don't understand French," I tell him, because I have no clue what's being said or what's happening. "Shhh!" he answers, and the next thing I know I'm back in the cell. A few minutes later someone comes and leads me to a wicket where the lawyer is waiting. He hands me a paper, shows me the date set for my hearing—November 10, almost a month away—and the conditions of my release. It says: "No contact whatsoever between Elizabeth Logan and Donald Kelly." And that, he explains, includes letters. I can take all this, everything they've done to me, except this. Now I'm demolished. What will I do without even *letters?*

They take me down an elevator and explain a bewildering route that goes up and down and ends in a long tunnel, which surprisingly spills me out into the lobby where—to my relieved surprise—Janice is waiting. The value of a true friend. She wasted hours trying to ascertain where the hearing would be held and trying to find the lawyer. It turned out the money was for him but, because she took a dislike to him on sight, she told him she didn't bring any, even though she had brought two hundred dollars.

Not having a lead on any other lawyers, I phone my brother to see if he knows of someone. He asks colleagues and comes up with the name of a young fellow with a reputation of being sharp and looking to make for a name for himself. I go to see him the next day, and the next phase of my "education" begins. I tell him the true story, then somehow feel free to tell him I have an alternate story, which might sound better. I expect him to protest, but he's quite willing to go along with a made-up story. He listens to it then grills me on its various points to see if it would stand up under cross-questioning. That done, he tells me we'll go with the real story, but it would be better if the request didn't come from Don, better if this guy contacted me on his own and asked me to take it to show Don. So, I am now educated in the ways of "up and coming lawyers looking to make a name for themselves."

At the second appointment there's good news. At the weekly partners' meeting, he tells me, the team decided to go for a preliminary hearing and then, if it goes to trial, to put it to a jury. It's a perfect case for a jury trial, he tells me. I feel encouraged.

Then he has other news, unpredictable and preposterous. The Crown has informed him I was trying to pass the wire through the grille. More than that, it is a wire intended to cut steel!

"No way! If they say that, they're lying. Pure and simple." I'm shocked, caught in a trap. "I can't even tell you what the grille looks like, it's just there; you look through the window when you talk." I'm beside myself; I know too well from all I've heard and all I've read that in a case of "my word against theirs" whose is going to have the weight.

"Can you find out if they taped the visit?" I ask him. "If they did, I guarantee there will be no scraping noises, and no mention of it in the conversation." He says he will.

A few days later I get a phone call from Claude, the brother of one of the inmates. He has a message from Don. I go to see him at the restaurant where he works. Don wants me to know that on the day of my arrest they tried to cut a corner of a steel locker and the strands of the wire fell apart. So, Claude wants me to bring him one of the other wires and he'll test it. I ask him if, when he goes to visit again, he will have a good look at the grille and let me know what it looks like. When I go to see him the following week he has good news on both accounts. The grille, he explains, has overlapping steel slats and behind them are layers of metal mesh, so thick you can't see even a glimmer of light through them. "The only thing that passes through that grille is smoke," he tells me. And the wire won't cut steel. It just falls apart, exactly like Don heard. So, they know very well this is not a utensil for cutting steel, yet they're proceeding with the case. A case of harassment.

I call the lawyer with these two pieces of news. As to the grille, he says the fact that something is impossible to do is not a defence. Mind-boggling. With regard to the wire's inability to cut steel, he says we will get an expert witness to testify to that, if it's true.

AFTER MORE THAN TWO MONTHS of being incommunicado, Joanne writes to tell me Sean was picked up near Edmonton, is now in Edmonton Institution, and she's living there. I write immediately.

"Thank God I finally have an address for you," I begin. "I've been walking around in a blur for three weeks now, life without its definition, a body without its heart," and launch into my long story of woe, culminating with what had happened two days earlier.

I had arrived at the lawyer's office early for my for 9:45 a.m. appointment. His plan was for the two of us to take a taxi to court and do some last minute talking on the way. But he's not there, nobody knows anything about me, and I'm frantic that if I don't show up in time there will be repercussions. Finally a secretary tells me to come to the phone. My lawyer is at home, he's been very ill in hospital he says, and I'm to go to court with his partner. Then he tells me they've opted to dispense with the preliminary hearing and go directly to trial—they'll get a date today—and they're not asking for a jury. We'll take trial by judge alone.

"Jesus, Joanne, I'm standing there on the phone, fifteen minutes before court time, completely powerless—what am I to do? You put yourself in the hands of an 'expert' but the expert can't be trusted. So now the date for the Trial by Judge is set for December 18. What can I do? I miss Don so much and can't even write him. I did send him a short note, though, signed with a made-up name he'll recognize, and had a friend mail it from Ontario. But I couldn't say much more than I'm doing OK and hope he is too. And I didn't have a return address to give." Then I warn her that if she phones we shouldn't talk about anything except generalities. I'm scared if they're listening they'll find out what our defence is and figure out ways to get around it. Since their evidence is already made of whole cloth it won't take much to twist it into any shape they want.

"Damn it, Joanne, what I'm really guilty of is stupidity."

The manuscript has been rejected for the third time. As far as rejection letters go, this one couldn't be more positive. The editor, reputedly one of Canada's top literary people, says it's very well written, with an excellent control of dialogue, but the plot "seemed to get lost in the midst of attention to character dramatization." Given that my aim was to portray the different personalities and how they acted under the circumstances, I can see that that's true. The "outside story"—the details of the manhunt itself—had been neglected. She encourages me to try elsewhere ("My opinion is only one," she says), but I have no heart to submit again. Not only do I have the problems of the ongoing court case but the story is already five years old: public interest will have waned. The movie guys are still interested as far as I know but nothing concrete has been proposed.

Meanwhile, a representative of one of the electronic supply companies, Evan, with whom I've often chatted while he waits to see one of the buyers, invites me to lunch. I like Evan's manner—polite, with a polished way of keeping the balance between friendly and formal. Since life definitely needs some lightening up, I accept. Lunch is agreeable and, discovering that I, too, like jazz, he invites me to Biddle's, a popular downtown jazz bar.

At Biddle's he lets me know he's married—unhappily married—just sticks it out for all the usual reasons and so on. This news actually comes as somewhat of a relief. In spite of the fact that he's good company and compatible in many ways, I can't force myself to be physically attracted if I'm not, and so I'm spared the moral dilemma. He accepts this with good grace, and in the end we have each found something we need—a friend to go out with socially. From then on, every few weeks we take in Montreal's finest jazz at Biddle's or go to Old Montreal where we enjoy walking and eating. After sampling several restaurants, a small Hungarian one featuring gypsy music played by a three-piece band becomes our favourite. For the rest of my time in Montreal this friendship and social life continues.

The next court appearance brings the first good news—at least potentially. The judge, at the request of my lawyer, revoked the order prohibiting communication by mail. I write as soon as I get home. My heart won't stop racing until I see if he gets it or not. I won't expect an answer for two weeks minimum; they will certainly hold it up while making a decision. Every day when I open the mailbox I dread seeing an envelope with the CPS logo; if I see that I'll know what it says.

My Dearest Loved One,

Two hundred calls come in to my switchboard every day—and yesterday one was from you! What it meant to hear your voice I can't tell you—nourishment, an infusion. Then, on top of that, today, the glorious feeling of relief when I opened the mailbox and saw your writing on the envelope. I didn't know whether to tear it open and devour it or open it slowly and savour it. I opted for the latter. The familiar lined paper, the well-known handwriting, the anticipation of its words—almost more than I could bear—brought a rush of nearness.

You, too, are in low spirits. What can we do? It's a "wait and see" game right now: me, with this ongoing court thing (now it's set for January 22), you with the never-ending segregation issue.

I'm glad to see though, that Pam and Belinda's visit helped. I managed to pry out a word-by-word description of the conversation from them. Young people are so non-verbal. You must have been tongue-tied yourself when you asked Belinda what she got you for Christmas and Pam piped up: "Get him a razor and a pair of scissors!" Wow! How did that feel? They told me your appearance was a little (ahem!) "unkempt." *I'm joking, but I'm worried. You must be very down to let yourself get like that.*

Glad to see you're reading again. No, I haven't read *Shogun*, and—sorry—don't feel tempted. Joanne was reading it last year; I looked through it but was attracted to neither the subject matter nor the length. But then I'm presently reading *The Covenant* by Michener, which Cheryl gave me for Christmas, and it must be as long. You're still trying to get me to read Asimov. Maybe some day—at least a sampling. But for now, I have to read only things I *know* I can lose myself in.

Our trip to June's for New Year's was especially pleasant—a breath of fresh air in two senses. The weather was extremely cold with lots of snow, which I enjoyed—contrary to here where we have warmer temperatures but bone-chilling winds that have me shivering non-stop. I'll never get used to it. While there, we were treated to an ice fog so dense we couldn't see the houses across the street—a spectacle I'd never before seen.

Brenda came with us but she stayed at her friend's place, so I just saw her some of the time. June and I took the three girls bowling, which was fun for everyone, and being five-pin, my score actually went into three digits. ☺ Since we were only there three nights, I didn't see any of my other friends and only talked to Barb on the phone, but it felt good to be back in North Bay.

One good thing about Quebec is that it seems almost everyone gets the full week between Christmas and New Year's off. Did you know that? And this time my holidays were paid, thank goodness.

I miss you so much, Don. Three whole months now. Every time I hear, read or do something interesting, the first thought that pops into my head is "I must remember to tell Don that." And then the reality hits: I can't. At least now I'll be able to tell you by letter. It's a small mercy, but for the moment, a gift.

You say don't let things get me down; well, that's pretty hard to avoid. But, I know you're suffering just as much as me, probably more. Letters will help us both.

> It does one good to feel that one still has a brother who lives on this earth. One sometimes gets the feeling: Where am I? What am I doing? But then such well-known handwriting makes one feel firm ground under one's feet again.

Write often. I want to feel grounded.

◆   ◆   ◆   ◆

Another phone call—a whole two minutes this time (at least that's what it seemed) but precious seconds wasted getting Brigitte to take over the switchboard for me. Oh, well, I dare not complain when it's the best we can do. Didn't even have time to tell you the hearing is now slated for March 31. It was the Crown that asked for the remand this time. My guess is they really have no case and are hoping to come up with one. Do you think our problems are related? Mine causing yours, or yours causing mine?

Joanne wrote that she found a good job with the provincial government in no time—social worker in the Child Welfare Department. Sheri (her daughter) has joined her and is also working. Sean says you should try for a transfer there and she tells me I'd have no problem getting a job in social services. Is this something we should consider?

My friend Elena is staying with us for a few days, which is a good diversion for me. She couldn't find a job as a lab technician here after we finished the French course, so went to Medicine Hat. We're having a good catch-up and tonight we're going to do the Old Montreal bit.

It's hard for me to imagine living Elena's story. Her family is Hungarian. In 1956 her father took part in the overthrow of the communists. Success was brief, if you remember, and when the revolution was quashed, he needed to flee the country. Elena's mother, on the other hand, wanted to stay and so it was decided (can you imagine the turmoil that must have gone into such a decision?) that Elena—at four years old—would come to Canada with her father while her two-year-old sister would remain with her mother. And that's how they've lived all these years until two years ago when she and her father went back for a reunion. On the personal level, the visit went well, but she was bemused to find them contented living under communism.

Everyone has a story.

◆   ◆   ◆   ◆

I'm so glad you read that page of articles in The Globe and Mail; it makes me feel we shared the experience. The whole weekend was fantastic. To actually see all those paintings "in the flesh," so to speak, to stand in front of them—stand at the oracle—what can I say? Like having a transfusion. Twelve years I've wondered how I could get myself to Amsterdam to see them, and in the end they came to me!

You probably know more than me—those articles seem to have covered a lot of ground from what you told me. *Vincent Van Gogh and the Birth of Cloisonism.* I quite frankly had no idea what cloisonism was, but guess you did before me. I thought using Van Gogh as the focal point was stretching it a bit, but who am I to dispute the Art Gallery of Ontario? Gauguin's style is very much that—a stained glass look, areas of flat colour separated by heavy lines. Explanations of technique, to me, though, are of only mild intellectual interest; the *feeling* their spirit evokes is what counts.

Oh, Don! Can you picture the little drawbridge with a horse and cart going over it and women washing clothes at the riverbank beside it? The brick on the walls of the bridge are fresh, luminous, like they were fired yesterday. You want to reach out and touch them. The water, swirling in circles where they're doing their laundry, you can *feel, experience.* Stand before this picture and you have a direct link to the Sublime.

The outdoor café at night with the cobblestone street and the stars above, the yellow house he lived in, his bedroom, the sunflowers—so many of the ones we've seen on calendars and posters—were all there. Can you imagine how overwhelming it was? If I hadn't been with Carlos, Pam and Belinda, I would have stayed all day. There were over one hundred paintings on exhibit, forty-five Van Goghs, but not enough Toulouse-Lautrecs to suit me (nor you, because you told me you like him).

We stayed at a guesthouse on Spadina that I've stayed at a few times before. Billy came over Saturday afternoon and we all went out for supper. He's doing fine, getting good marks in his electronics course. It was a good time; I could forget my troubles for a whole weekend.

Carlos and I continue to be friends, as you can see. He's had Belinda and me to supper three times but I don't dare ask him in return because he's such a good cook. Back in October he gave a big party for a relative visiting from Colombia and invited me. That was only the second time since I came here that I've been out in the evening without Belinda.

The guests were all Colombian except me, so it was like going to a foreign country: the conversation, Spanish; the food, Columbian (very tasty); the music, Latin American, which I found extremely irritating after two or three hours—same beat on and on—no variety. And in spite of having three different teachers, I couldn't learn to dance to it—much to my shame because I've always been a good dancer.

◆   ◆   ◆   ◆

Your two letters this week warmed my heart. It's so good for me, too, when someone has been to see you. So now you know from Pam about the latest remand—to April 23. My lawyer this time. "A conflict in his schedule." Is there to be no end to this? Five months now. What can I do? Everyone tells me I should change lawyers but it has gone down this road so long and has taken so much money with it, how can I? And who would I get? Another "recommended up-and-coming" one???

You say you've written Claire Culhane, that she had the same problem as me and should be able to help. But I don't know who she is. Tell me more, and send me her address.

William called. It seems you finally got across to him loud and clear. He now understands that he is to deal with me, that you have given all rights to everything concerning your name to me. I told him I wouldn't consider selling anything but the movie rights, he can forget about all those other things he put in the contract—literary publications, radio and TV broadcasts, theatrical presentations, T-shirts, coffee mugs, blah, blah, blah. . . . (Said it, I think, a bit more diplomatically than that.) Also told him the upfront money isn't enough. We left the door open, but I don't think he's going to come up with a better offer. We'll see.

◆   ◆   ◆   ◆

Today I went to the Botanical Gardens, my favourite place to go to be alone, think and get renewed. The spring flower display is on—several rooms exploding with colour, fragrance and freshness. But in the end it's the cactus room that pulls. Warm, soothing, not many people, it has a settled sense to it, is conducive to quiet contemplation. There, I sit and talk to you, tell you everything I've been doing, how much I miss you, tell you not to worry; like the cactus, I will endure. And you will, too. I know that. Ask you how many shades of green you think there can be. Can the number be infinite? Is that possible? Look for human characteristics in the shapes. Ask what you see. Who is strong? Who is angry? Who is lonely? Which one am I? Which one are you? I never question whether you hear me or not, I'm just sure you do. Well, I *know* you do because you answer. ☺ There are several Curiosity Plants—huge ones. They talk to me, remind me of my birthday gift and why you gave it to me.

◆   ◆   ◆   ◆

The case is remanded to May 21—the Crown this time. And every time it's
another day off work. I've had to be absent so many times that I decided to
tell Manon the problem. She was sympathetic, but I can tell by the Personnel
Manager's fish eyes that Manon went straight to her with the news. So we can
say good-bye to any chance of advancement in this company. Did get an $11
a week pay raise a while back, though. That helps.

◆   ◆   ◆   ◆

That phone call—short as it was—did wonders to boost my spirits. It's so
good to hear your voice and have a precious moment of reassurance, which I
know works in both directions.

I heard from Claire. She'll be coming to Montreal in September and we'll
meet then. Janice tells me she's very well-known and well-respected.

◆   ◆   ◆   ◆

Can you believe it? May 21 has come and gone, and the case has been
remanded to July 13. The Crown again. What are they doing? I'm convinced
they're trying to come up with pieces that don't exist.

Pam's visit went into the holiday, so it was a five-day weekend. I decided
to invite a few people over on Friday night—a disparate but interesting group:
my old friends Jean and Doug (Pam has known them all her life; in fact they
kept Cheryl when Pam was born), Janice, Dorothy, Carlos and his friend,
Alain. Pam made chili while I was at work—that was a big help. It was a nice,
relaxed evening with easy conversation, even though most didn't know each
other and translations were necessary for the two who don't speak English.
Jean and Doug are willing to go to see you if you like. It's wonderful to have
such good friends.

◆   ◆   ◆   ◆

Here I am in Edmonton, and enjoying everything. It's great to spend time
with Joanne, pour out my heart. Try to explain all this to someone who hasn't
seen what she's seen—well, I just wouldn't bother.

Went to see Sean. I didn't know evening visits even existed; how practical
for working people. He sends his good wishes and says you should try for a
transfer here.

Here's a story that will bring a chuckle. The night Sean "went missing"
from the Hotel Dieu Hospital in Kingston. Two-thirty in the morning. He
tip-toes past the sleeping guards, peeks out the door—no nurses in view—

hurries to the stairway, dashes down the stairs, checks out the lobby (all clear), and casually walks out the front door onto the street. In his pyjamas and slippers. No worry, his friend will be there waiting with a car.

Dernières grandes paroles.

He looks up and down the street. Nobody.

Trying to look as inconspicuous as one can possibly look while walking down the street in pj's in the middle of the night, he searches for a phone. (He has his contact list and some coins ostensibly for the vending machines in the hospital). He comes to a booth outside a restaurant, calls, but there's no answer. The optimistic view is maybe the friend *did* come for the pick-up and at this very moment is driving around the area and—sooner rather than later—will spot him.

He walks smartly along the sidewalk trying to exude confidence, normalcy, but he knows he can't stay on the street in this garb much longer, so when he comes to a park he enters it and leans against a tree for camouflage and to think.

Just then a young fellow comes jogging across the park and sees him.

"Hey, man," the guy says, "what are you doing here in your pyjamas?'

Sean looks him over. He's young, casual, probably a university student. Looks cool. He makes an instant decision.

"I'll be straight with you," Sean tells him, and proceeds to relate the whole story, that he's a prisoner, was in the hospital, got away, his friend didn't show up with the getaway car, and now he doesn't know what to do.

"My van's over here," the guy says. "We can sit in there while you think."

So Sean goes with him to the van and once they're settled the fellow says to him, "Hey, man, I bet you'd like a toke." So, they sit there smoking up and discussing what's to be done. Sean has other phone numbers with him, but the closest person is in Toronto, and that's a good three hours away.

"What we can do," the guy (who does prove to be a university student, a Law student at that) suggests, "is, we can go to my place, you can sit outside because I have roommates, I'll go into the house and phone for you."

So this is what they do. The student goes back and forth from the house to the van, making contacts and passing messages, and eventually gets someone willing to pick him up. A meeting time and place—a corner of the park—is arranged. Then—do you believe it?—I know you do because you were offered unbelievable help when you were out, the guy gives Sean a whole set of clothes—jogging pants, jacket, running shoes, baseball cap, the whole kit, all old but serviceable, and they sit there talking and smoking until it's almost meeting time. Then the student drives him back to the park where Sean sits in full view (getting very light out by now), waiting for the rescuer. In parting, as a Thank You, Sean gave the guy his watch. That will be some memento. Wonder if he'll tell this story to his law partners one day? ☺

Once in Toronto he connected with his so-called friend. (Some "friend," I say. He hadn't even come for the pickup at all.) Sean stayed at this guy's place for a few days then made his way to Alberta where he stayed with other friends not far from Edmonton—just long enough for a "vacation," shall we say?

The past three days, Joanne and I, with two whining, squabbling teenagers in the back seat, took a trip to Jasper, down the Icefields Parkway to Lake Louise, and back to Edmonton. Her two younger daughters had been living with their dad in California; they came for a visit a few months ago and refused to go back, so they're living with her now.

The first night we stayed near Jasper in a log cabin in a lovely forested grove. Unfortunately it was raining too hard to even think of walking on the beautiful trails. By the time we arrived at the hot springs the next morning, the rain had reduced itself to a drizzle, but all of us were disappointed in the springs. It's just a swimming pool—not the natural setting we had expected—and they're not even hot. "Warm" would be a more adequate description. I tried to be positive and concentrate on their reputed beneficial effects. Do you suppose the magic can find its way through the pores to the spirit? That's the part that needs healing.

The tops of the Rockies, for most of the trip, were shrouded in dark clouds, but it was intriguing, in an artistic sense, to watch them roll down the mountainside in various formations. It took some imagination to visualize Lake Louise in its calendar image; when we were there it was dark, rainy, and totally deserted. That night we stayed at a place along the Bow River and a moose came right into the yard. (A frequent occurrence, the owner told us.) In the morning the sun finally came out—a glorious morning—and it was the first time I've ever experienced the anomaly of standing in both warmth (the sun) and coolness (the air) at the same time. The girls went horseback riding while Joanne and I walked up onto the edge of the glacier—a wonderful feeling of restorative calm.

It's been revitalizing to spend these days with someone who understands how things happen, has heard it all. Mostly I enjoy her cynical laugh. It's easy to be cynical, hard to keep the laughter. She brings it back.

A couple of times when Joanne was at work I took the bus into town to look things over with a mind to living here. It looks fine—is big enough to have everything I would want. Joanne always lives on the outskirts, but I would live in the centre of things.

◆   ◆   ◆   ◆

Did you get the postcard I sent from Ausable Chasm? What a lovely weekend we had camping there. Belinda enjoyed it as much as me. We went for a boat tour on the river—beautiful and refreshing. Being the July Fourth weekend (I hadn't thought of that), there was a spectacular fireworks display Saturday night on a nearby hill. Then it rained all night and we woke up floating. Nothing like a pup tent in the rain. Undaunted, next weekend we'll go to Vermont.

◆　　◆　　◆　　◆

We have a new household member! A kitten. Belinda has been bugging me for ages, but I don't like cats. In fact, when I was young, kids would terrorize me by chasing me with one. (My mother told me a cat came through the window and into my crib when I was having my nap one afternoon and scared me.) Kittens are OK, but they do have a way of growing into cats.

June convinced me. She said now that Belinda is on her own with no siblings, she should have a pet if she wants one. So, I decided to get her one for her birthday and Saturday morning we went to the animal shelter. A shy, all-white one at the back of the cage, not mewing like the others, caught her eye. Only when she took it out of the cage for the "touch test" did we notice that one eye is green and the other blue. That convinced her. After much discussion, we decided to name her Puddin'. Needless to say Belinda is thrilled. Truth is, I like her a lot, too.

I was reminding Belinda of when she used to carry around a piece of fur, stroking it, talking to it, and would put it to sleep in a shoe box at night. It was her kitty-cat. Hearing that at twelve years old brings a blush to the cheeks, as you can imagine.

◆　　◆　　◆　　◆

I've met Claire now. We met in a coffee shop downtown, and what a delightful person she is; we clicked from the get-go. Such energy and determination. I don't know how she has the stamina to keep on as she does (she's not young—about 60, I would say) and not be consumed by anger, with all the obstacles she meets. Her knowledge of the system is vast and she did have some useful suggestions for me.

She's on her *third* book! The second one, called *Barred From Prison*, is a detailed account of the riot at B.C. Pen in '76. She told me where I can buy it, so I'll go there soon, but she gave me the summary. With other members of the Citizens' Advisory Committee, she stayed in the pen three days and nights acting as go-betweens between the Inmates' Committee and officials. (The I. C. had demanded they be called in as observers in order to prevent something bad happening such as the year before when C. O. Mary Steinhauser was killed by staff in their so-called rescue attempt.) Anyway, the situation was resolved to everyone's satisfaction (more or less). You probably know all about it.

Then came the kick in the face. Five days later, they were still taking shifts, monitoring conditions until things got back to normal (which, of course, they didn't because the Commissioner of Penitentiaries, under pressure from the guards' union, soon negated the agreement, but that's another story). At the end of her shift, because regular mail collection hadn't yet resumed, several prisoners gave her letters to drop off at Visits and Correspondence on her way out. This was done in the presence of guards. She showed them she was putting them in an outside pocket. On the way to V&C, with the letters poking out in full view, she was stopped and accused of taking out contraband, escorted out of the prison, and told never to return. Another committee member came forward, told all and sundry she had delivered letters in the exact same manner the previous day, but it made no difference. Claire was declared *persona non grata* at B.C. Pen, and soon after at almost every federal and provincial institution in B.C. The story gets long and complicated, I'll tell you more after I've read the book. The one she's working on now is to be called *Still Barred From Prison* because she's still barred in B.C., which is ironic because as head of the Prisoners' Rights Group she founded, she visits freely everywhere else in Canada. That's why she's here now—visiting prisoners.

The first book was about her experiences as a nurse during the war in Vietnam and the campaign she later waged to try to stop Canada's involvement in it (massive arms sales, supportive endeavours such the hospital she was supposed to administer, which, when she complained to Foreign Affairs that it had no patients, was told it didn't matter, all that mattered was the appearance of it being there). Her report was suppressed at top levels so she went door to door to MPs' offices, lobbying to get it before the House. When that didn't work she camped in front of the Parliament buildings with members of the Voice of Women, chained herself to a chair in the House, and finally, as a last measure, wrote her book, *Why is Canada in Vietnam?* What a woman!

Now she works full time on prison issues with help and donations from people who care. I told her next time she comes to Montreal if she needs a place to stay, she's welcome.

◆   ◆   ◆   ◆

I see Carole quite often. She has a boy, Nicolas, who is three years younger than Belinda and they get along nicely. I've had them over for lunch a few times, and we've been up to their place. Did Pierre tell you she's a singer? The voice of an angel. Plays the guitar also, and writes some of her own songs. She sings in clubs sometimes when she needs extra money and has been on a TV program from Toronto, 100 Huntley St. (which I've never seen or heard of—it's religious). Friday night Belinda and I went far out in the east end to hear her sing in what we thought was a non-alcoholic night club but was, in fact, a centre for handicapped people—several, severely so. I have to admit I was a little uncomfortable but Belinda seemed unfazed. Nicolas was there also and it turned out to be a pleasant evening with snacks and socializing and an opportunity to see another side of life.

Carole, along with two other women who have guys on the inside, started an organization for families/friends of prisoners a while back—*Carrefour Macadie*. It's mainly a support group, but they also help out with various problems, have a bit of a resource library, and do some education. There's a meeting every Wednesday night, to which I've gone a few times, and enjoy—makes me feel less isolated and closer to you. It's mainly wives and girlfriends, but there are also family members and a few newly released guys. I like the people and feel good there, even though I'm the only Anglophone. I don't even know if anyone speaks English or not. My French is good enough now that no one feels a need to change for me.

Diane is the leader. She's a dynamic person and another who met her guy on the inside. In her case, she was visiting for a religious organization. That's the only put-off for me; she often talks about God, invokes his (?) help. (Maybe I should try that? What do you think?) She leads the group in a sharing session (any news or feelings people would like to share), then Carole or someone else sings a few songs. Then we have tea or coffee with cookies and informal chatting. It's a very long trip to get there, but it's worth it. I come home renewed.

◆　　◆　　◆　　◆

I've made contact with the *Office des droits des détenu(e)s* (Prisoners' Rights Office) about my problem and the many you've detailed in your letters. A lawyer will come to see you. Meanwhile my case has been put off until November—what else is new? More than a year of missing you. The less said about that, the better.

◆　　◆　　◆　　◆

This afternoon I strolled down to Snowdon Post Office to buy some stamps. The warm weather, the scrunch of leaves underfoot, their smell, reminded me of a ritual we had every fall when I was a kid—one day only, the day of

Teachers' Convention. My brother and I and our closest neighbour-friends raked the leaves into huge piles on our front lawn, jumped and rolled in them, threw them at each other, ganged up and buried someone. Yells for mercy pierced the air—real or fake, depending on whether "the victim" had succumbed willingly or not. It was extraordinary fun.

I got to thinking of all the old "city things" of my childhood. I'll bet you've never seen a "sheeney man." When he passed it was an event in our young lives. Long before he actually came into sight, his plaintive "Rags! . . . Bones! . . . Bottles!" filled the air, accompanied by the clip-clop, clip-clop of his horse's hooves. When we heard that, we came running in anticipation of the passing spectacle: the wooden cart, the horse, and the strange man.

When I think about it now, I realize this man's dignity was at odds with his appearance. He had tangled hair topped with a crumpled black hat, and his grey-streaked beard was long and shaggy. A ratty multi-coloured blanket was pulled up over his knees, no matter the weather, and his drab suit had seen better days—many better days. But he sat tall and regal, completely unaware of the sight he presented. We thought him very peculiar indeed, yet he was so exotic and remote we didn't even think of laughing.

The sheeney man bought and sold almost everything, but looked very poor. My mother said lots of people like him and the popcorn man were actually rich and lived in expensive houses in Baby Point (pronounced "Bobby" as in "*lah*-dee-*dah*"—a district of expensive houses not far from where we lived). Trying to imagine these guys wheeling their carts down those high-toned streets made me incredulous on that point even though I seem to have been taken in on many another.

At noon hour the popcorn man parked his cart almost across from our house, where he had the custom of students from two schools. The funny thing is, June and I could very well have stood shoulder to shoulder buying popcorn because she attended the commercial school across the street from us, although we didn't meet until North Bay.

I've been walking a lot. These warm evenings, when I go to meet Belinda at the Y, I leave early, walk around the district, looking in people's windows. I'm bound to see in at least one living room, a group of Jewish men in prayer shawls, bobbing forward and back, forward and back, in prayer. It's another world.

All this city walking makes me feel glad I'm here, which is ironic because I had such a desire to get away from the city when I was a teenager. In my mind "city" was equated with "materialism." It took some years before I realized they don't have to be twinned; it was just that at that time my world vision didn't extend beyond my mother's value system.

These autumn meanderings, although they bring good memories, are accompanied by a certain sadness, a feeling of loneliness—or "loneness" perhaps (is that a word?). A solitude that registers both as a lack and as a feeling of satisfaction.

◆   ◆   ◆   ◆

It was torture to be up in Ste-Anne-des-Plaines, having coffee at the nearby restaurant with my sister-in-law, only metres from you, when Gary went to see you. At the same time, it made me feel connected—a pleasant, warm feeling. Good thing he's a lawyer and could get in without prior approval. I have all your news now, and let's hope you stay at Archambault. I hear from Janice that they're preparing the trailer for conjugal visits—for all the good that's doing us.

Did Gary tell you I've started work at another company? Still receptionist/switchboard operator. Happy quit AES about three months ago and went to Micom, which also assembles word processing machines. In fact, both systems were invented by the same person, Steve Dorsey.

When Happy quit, I had an interview for her job. The reason given for my not getting it was that the other person had studied Personnel procedures at college. Well, maybe, but I can't help but think the real reason was the trouble I'm in. So, I was glad when Happy called and asked if I would like to go to Micom. Given that they were offering fifteen dollars a week more than I was getting, plus it's much closer to home (not far at all), it was an easy decision to make. The reception area of this place is small and dismal, though. That part I don't like. Also, Micom is a considerably smaller operation, so I'm not nearly as busy, which is a negative, although for now learning the new word processing system takes all my spare time. The people seem fine, and it's nice to see Happy every day again—cheerful, as always—plus there are several others here who used to be at AES; there appears to be a raiding operation going on.

◆   ◆   ◆   ◆

Got your letter yesterday and am sorry to see you're back at Laval, although you say it's for the best. If that's the case, well, then, OK. I just thought it might be better for *me* if you were at Archie.

Nobody's ever heard of a case that goes on and on like this. Now the November date is put off till December 17. And, as you know, one sits for hours and hours waiting for her one-minute appearance. Will this ever be over? Ten dates in fourteen months and not finished yet. I no longer even dare hope the next will be the last.

Dear Love, I miss you so much. Sometimes I feel my guts will spill out on the sidewalk, my heart will burst out of my chest and bleed all over the furniture. . . . Or maybe I'll just slowly disintegrate. The only thing that saves me is the endless conversations I have with you. In that way I feel as linked as ever—mentally, spiritually—a closeness distance can't deny. I tell you all the things I'm doing, what I'm thinking, feeling, relive past conversations, laugh at things we laughed at. Even in these extreme circumstances, I'm happy for what I've had with you. *Je ne regrette rien.* Although I do admit the present reality is definitely a situation of deprivation.

There's the philosophy that adversity builds character. I said that to Ron once and he answered, "Yes, but what kind of character do you want to be?"

◆   ◆   ◆   ◆

Finally—finally!—one part of the burden has been lifted. Did you think it would actually happen? They finally finished with my case today. The whole story is one of disillusionment: all the delays, the shoddy "evidence," and especially the lawyer. Claire says there should be a special place in Hell for lawyers, and I can see why. (Lawyers and journalists, she says.) First he says we'll have a jury—it's the perfect case; then it's no jury. Then we'll ask the court to go to the visiting room to see the grille so they can see nobody would even attempt to push something through it. Not done. Why? I don't know. Then he was going to get a copy of the list of my personal effects when I was taken to *Parthenais* because the charm was still in my pocket. Not done. Right up to today he let me think we were calling an expert witness to testify about the wire—namely, that it doesn't cut steel. Fifteen minutes before the case is to proceed he tells me no expert. No expert; no reason. I've never felt so completely powerless. Screwed and tattooed from every angle.

In the evidence, the first thing that amazed me was that although the V&C testified the visit was taped, they didn't offer it in testimony. "And why not?" you ask. Because the V&C doesn't speak English!!! That's the reason he gave! Can you believe that??? The judge speaks English. Most of the trial was in English. Anyway, the sound of something grating the grille is independent of language. They didn't put the tape into evidence because there was nothing incriminating on it. Nothing in the conversation and nothing in the way of sounds. Pure and simple. *Point final.* I've seen now—first hand—how things work.

Next was the wire. They presented it to me for identification and—guess what?—just like you said, it was torn from their attempts to cut with it. I pointed that out, asked the judge to look at it, but he didn't bother. Nor did my up-and-coming-lawyer-who-is-trying-to-make-a-name-for-himself say anything to help on that point. Well, I know I don't need to tell you how these things go, but it was an eye-opener for me.

They asked me the name of the guy who gave it to me. I told them I know only his nickname. The lawyer said that made me look bad. Why is that? Does everybody know the full name of everyone they meet only once? I don't even know Carole's last name—hasn't occurred to me to ask—and I know she doesn't know mine. Janice came with me for support. She says the lawyer and judge probably come from a segment of society where people are always formally introduced—first and last name—and think everyone's like that. So, I "looked bad."

In the end it was "a finding of guilty, with no conviction registered." This so I will be able to get a job in social work if we go to Alberta. I'll give the lawyer credit that he at least got me that.

◆   ◆   ◆   ◆

We can say there's a good side to all your trouble; at least you get to see the Classification Officer and he lets you make a phone call. I know my crying didn't make you feel any better. "Don't let things get you down," you say. Well, that's kind of hard to do. Here I am in Montreal expressly to be with you and I'm a million miles away. I know you, too, are down—never been this down in your life, your letter tells me. Just remember I love you and we'll keep having all our silent conversation and fantasies. That's all we can do for now.

◆   ◆   ◆   ◆

You ask if moving to Edmonton is what I want, if you should try for a transfer. For myself, yes. I'm quite sure I could adapt almost anywhere, and in Alberta I could get a much better, more satisfying job that would pay better, too. But can I force another move on Belinda? And should I take her—and myself—so far from the others? That would be a tough decision. Let's wait until we see how things work out for us here in the next few months before we decide. Shall we hope for better times in the new year?

Ah! It just came to me! "Hoping for better times must not be a *feeling*, but, rather, must be an *action* in the present." Do you remember that? OK, then, no "hoping"—only action. In the New Year, I'll start my campaign to get the visits back. For now, I send my love and lots of that special conversation.

I, too, "want one more look at you," as you say.

"Watch closely now. Are you watching me now?"

◆   ◆   ◆   ◆

Getting through a second holiday season without seeing you was a joyless prospect, as I expect it was for you. For solace I turned to the person who helped in the past, and re-read Van Gogh's letters. And once again he proved to be inspirational.

It's a mystery to me why people see him as depressive and even crazy. Of course, that's how he's been portrayed in the media and we know about media, don't we? If they took the time to read what he actually said, they could do better than just perpetuate the stereotype. He tried hard to shape himself into what others expected him to be, particularly his father, but finally, after much anguish, took the courage to follow his own leadings. That's when he became "peculiar" to those still in the mould. It was less than a two-year period at the end of his life (and then only intermittently) that he had problems that can be classified as mental illness. An underlying melancholy did pervade his life—that's incontestable—but isn't that to be expected when you're philosophically at odds with almost everyone around you? Overall, the reality is that he was forever optimistic and never lost faith that he would succeed. I think he killed himself, not in madness, but in a sane calculation: fear of future attacks, and that his illness would cause a financial drain on Theo, now that Theo had a wife and child to support.

Well, your letter shows your cheerfulness and optimism have deserted you (and it's no wonder—I don't judge you on that) but please try to rouse yourself. Try—for my sake, for the sake of seeing each other again—to be less negative and stop making more and more trouble for you. Get busy and file grievances on all those charges you're telling me about. I'm about to start working on getting the visits back and you'll have to get yourself into a more credible position, be standing on firmer ground, when you try from your end. *Can't you see how all these charges are making it worse? How they can go against us?*

Miss you so much—more than I can tell you—but to continue "with a brave and cheerful spirit" that is what is important and what, I hope, will bring results.

I send my deepest and most sincere affection.

I ATTEND ONE OF MY many free concerts. This one, a piano quartet, is at the Salvation Army Citadel on a Saturday afternoon. At intermission I'm standing out on the steps getting a breath of fresh air and debating the ethics of leaving. The first two selections were lovely but the final piece is by a contemporary composer, the very mention of which sets my nerves a-jangling.

(Have they run out of melodies these days?) But being a free concert, it seems unappreciative to bail out like that.

I'm approached by a fellow who starts a conversation: Did I enjoy the Mozart? He did. The Brahms, he thought, was a little weak, but he doesn't like the next composer at all. I'm worried about it myself, I tell him. Well, then, would I care to join him for a coffee at the restaurant across the street? This looks like it could be interesting, I think, so accept. Why not?

We order a coffee and a danish. He's about my age and reasonably attractive even if his name is Fred. The conversation proceeds easily, about music, what kind we like, what concerts we attend, and he tells me about lots of free or cheap ones, where to get the information on them. He's a high school teacher and has lived in Montreal all his life. I tell him I've been here less than three years. Well, then, he says, he can show me around, be my guide. In fact, how about tomorrow? How about going to Ste-Agathe, take in the scenery, the lake, and he knows a nice little restaurant where we can eat.

Whooooa! Ste-Agathe! Duddy Kravitz country! In one short sentence I've been transported into both the *real* Montreal and the world of novels. If ever there has been a character more vividly portrayed in Canadian literature than Duddy Kravitz, I haven't met him. I certainly have walked St-Urbain Street where Richler's characters still sit on every balcony, still frequent the same corner store. And now the chance to go to Ste-Agathe, where Duddy worked at a summer lodge and, brash and ambitious, bought up a whole lake.

It all looks good. He's educated, loves music, is apparently single, and is eager to show me the sights. It looks good, that is, if you overlook the irritating tch, tch thing he does with his tongue and teeth. But then I think of June and her advice against going on first impressions. At first she didn't like Ken at all and now, there she is, living happily with him in Florida. So-oooh, I decide to give it a chance.

The arrangements are made: he'll pick me up about ten in the morning, we'll have coffee at my place (he'll bring bagels) then we'll drive to Ste-Agathe where we'll look around the area a bit and have a late lunch. I picture a cozy restaurant on the lake.

In the morning he arrives with the bagels and cream cheese. I've been here all this time and didn't even know you're supposed to toast them and put cream cheese on them. He has a quart of milk with him that he wants to leave in the fridge, says the little store in his building might be closed when he gets back.

Just after he arrived Belinda left for a day-long gymnastics event at the Jewish Y, but in ten minutes she was back; it was cancelled due to plumbing problems. So she will come with us. And I'm not sorry at all because the tch, tch is already getting on my nerves, even though I'm trying to get past it.

After all, without Fred, when was I going to learn how good toasted bagels with cream cheese are? And when would I see Duddy Kravitz country?

The drive up into the hills of the Laurentians is beautiful, but Fred, it turns out, has a distinct tendency to grab more than his fair share of the conversation. Never mind, I tell myself, he's probably nervous. At Ste-Agathe we have a glimpse of the lake before going to the "nice little restaurant," which, it turns out, can only be described as a diner: a counter, arborite tables, vinyl chairs, a tiled floor and a boring menu. He orders fried eggs with bacon and toast. I can't believe it! Not having any real choice to speak of, Belinda and I go one step up the sophistication ladder and order hamburgers and fries.

Belinda is sitting beside Fred, across from me. He is hunched over his plate, slurping up the dripping egg yoke. Loud slurping noises punctuated by equally loud smacks. Somehow this man has the facility of slurping, smacking, tch-ing and talking all at the same time. Belinda gives him a sidelong glance and looks over at me, her opinion clearly registered. The two of us raise our eyebrows in concert, roll our eyes, and give that helpless little "what-can-you-do?" shrug. He continues to slurp, smack and tch, oblivious to the pantomime taking place before his eyes, which he would see if he had the presence to look up once in a while.

We came back directly from the restaurant without sightseeing, not that I wanted any by this point, and it was only when we parked in front of my place that it hit me why he had brought that milk with him. He wanted an excuse to get back in. We came into the apartment, he went in the bathroom and when he came out I was standing there, waiting, with the milk in my hands. That was the end of Fred—and any inclination to "go beyond first impressions."

Never in the history of dating has anyone been more appreciative of a daughter's company. We laughed for months over "our" date with Fred.

Dear Don,

It was good to get your letter *but—I won't write this—you spend one paragraph telling me you can't write then write five pages detailing every charge you're on. It seems you* can *write. Why can't you write something more meaningful to* me, *something more like conversation?* Hope things go your way at the disciplinary hearing.

Do you realize it's now two full years since we saw each other? In one sense it's a hole in the pit of my Self and I miss you intensely—the fun we had, the sharing, your support of me in so many ways. And yet at the same time I feel a closeness, a shared understanding, almost palpable in its reality, linking me to you, soothing. And no one can take that away. *Even so, you have me on a seesaw. One minute I'm angry at the lack of letters, think you should be trying to encourage and support me; the next minute I see how it must be for you and the reverse comes to the fore.*

You say this is the lowest you've ever been in your life, and that cuts me, *sinks me with despair.* I don't know what I can do except keep assuring you of my love, of the great faith I have in you as a person. *Yet I want* from *you. Want more. Need something—anything.* Your words, "In the '70s I kept up a correspondence with more than sixty people; now I can't bring myself to write to one," make me try to understand *but I'm caught in my own mesh, my own needs.* Try to think of how much I need to hear from you, and how appreciated it is.

◆   ◆   ◆   ◆

Since you told me the institution refused National Geographic I did all the usual complaints—letters, phone calls—you know the drill—and got it settled (I hope). Let me know when/if you receive it. Really, it's hard not to see a diabolical plot in all these petty things.

◆   ◆   ◆   ◆

You're bouncing back and forth between Archambault and Laval so fast I can't keep your address straight. Thank God you weren't at Archie during all that barbarism. As for the threat of putting you back in the SHU, if the C.O. says there's no basis for it and he's never seen anything like it before, try not to worry; it's probably mind games.

Belinda went off to Galveston by herself for mid-winter break, but the morning of her departure the poor thing woke up sick with a sore throat. I packed her off anyway, confident she'd have a good nurse in Cheryl when she got there. Thankfully she felt better in a couple of days and is having a great time. Pam and Brenda and a "friend" of hers (a guy—very cute, very nice and polite) are here and we're having a good time, too. Went to the Botanical Gardens today and took lots of pictures. Hope they're good; I plan on sending you some.

◆   ◆   ◆   ◆

Remember when we first came here and I told you how completely different the Quebec culture is, how they have their own star system—singers, actors, poets, artists—who are unknown in the rest of Canada? I found out it works both ways. When a friend from work couldn't use her tickets to see Ella

Fitzgerald, she gave them to me and I invited Carole, thinking as a singer she would be thrilled. Imagine my shock when she said she didn't know who Ella is! Unfathomable! But then there was the Ray Charles concert I went to, remember? The attendance was so poor he had to beg the audience to "tell their friends." Anyway, Carole came along and amid the dozens of standards, recognized—in her words—"a couple." For my part, you can imagine how ecstatic I was, even if our seats were in the very last row of the top balcony.

◆   ◆   ◆   ◆

Things go along as normal. Even the ache in my heart has become normal. My job is fine, but I had to get rid of my car. It's a shame, too, because it was still in excellent shape mechanically, but I trust the advice from that garage I've gone to ever since we came here. They said the bottom was so rusted out it would just crumble in a crash. At least I did manage to get $250 for it. Advertised in the newspaper.

I really don't need a car here. I'm a two-minute walk from the subway, and it's a short bus ride to work. If I want to go out of the city, I'll rent one. As for going to see you, it will be a long bus ride, but it will be worth it. *Just stop getting all those damn charges!*

JOANNE AND SEAN GET MARRIED in the prison chapel. She sends me a picture of them lighting a candle. He's handsome in a dark blue suit; she's lovely in a turquoise dress, which is perfect for her blonde hair and blue eyes. I write back, not quite sure what one says under the circumstances. Congratulations? Best wishes for a happy married life? I don't know the protocol. Lucky Don and I have no aspirations in that department. Neither he nor I think a relationship should be defined by a piece of paper. In fact, he disdains legal papers of all kinds and couldn't understand why I wanted a contract for the book, said we had our understanding and that was that, his word is his bond kind of thing. He signed it, though, to please me.

I write her an extraordinarily long letter, pour out all my frustrations and doubts. I miss my times with Joanne—always so easy to talk to. Janice is great, but David never gets into trouble. I feel more comfortable telling Joanne these things, how disappointing the letters are, how he seems to have a persecution complex. "They're" doing all these things to him; he does nothing. Logic tells me he can't be innocent *all* the time, but then, I go around the circle again and wonder. . . . I do know, after all—by experience—how things can get turned against a person.

I tell her how Don met with the Director, was told we would get the visits back in a month if he didn't have any serious problems before then. It's been three months and he keeps getting charges. Many are obvious nonsense (staying too long in the shower, for example), but having a piece of a screwdriver hidden in his cell???

"I think he's so despondent," I tell her, "that his thinking gets off track. He once said—and I think there's probably merit in this—that if a person isn't paroled in five to seven years, they should send him to the psychiatric hospital because he'll be ready for it by then. Sometimes I think it'll drive *me* nuts."

Then I tell her about the lawyer from the *Office des droits des détenu(e)s* who went to see him about all these charges and they tried to prevent her entry. She had to make a big fuss, call for the keeper and finally the warden, before she got in.

"It does make you wonder; everyone knows a lawyer has free access. Then my friends Jean and Doug submitted the papers to get on his visit list, but the papers got 'lost,' and they had to start all over again. It's not a game for the faint of heart, is it?"

Joanne will understand. She's the one who told me twelve per cent of men and twenty-six percent of women have serious mental health problems when they enter. I hate to think what the statistics are when they come out.

Billy came over from Toronto on his motorcycle for a weekend, which had me frantic. I drove him up to Laval to see Don and sat waiting in the parking lot, a jumble of conflicting thoughts and emotions. So close, so far. A month later it turned out my worry about the motorcycle had some validity but had been misplaced. While making a left turn at an intersection in the city, a car running a red light hit him and his leg was broken in three places.

Twice Diane from *Macadie* went to see Don and took Belinda with her. Belinda told him we were going to see Shirley MacLaine for my birthday. He told her to take money from the bank account he had started for her two years back—he would reimburse her later—and, knowing how I love lobster, treat us to a lobster supper before the performance. We ate at an expensive restaurant on trendy Crescent Street, and the show was outstanding.

I sent out dozens of letters to religious organizations, NGOs, MPs, support groups, anyone who had been suggested to me as a source of possible help to get the visits back. About half didn't answer, some answered with sympathy but didn't know what they could do, and a few sent letters to the warden. But it was the expertise of the Correctional Law Project at Queen's University that had the ultimate influence. Carole with me for moral support, I drove to

Kingston for a long meeting with one of their lawyers. He listened attentively, took all my information, and without hesitation gave his legal opinion.

When I got home I went straight to the *dépanneur* for a bottle of wine and called Janice to come for supper.

"He's very sure," I told her excitedly. "Says they can't do it. He'll write a letter to the warden from a legal point of view, and if that doesn't work, he'll take it to court."

From everything Joanne had told me about the Law Project, I felt confident it was only a matter of time. Within a week I received a copy of his letter. I waited a few more days to be sure the warden had received his copy, then called him. He wanted to see me. I went to the interview and was granted closed visits.

My dear Love, Don,

How can I begin to describe the emotions of finally—*finally*—seeing you today? Two years, two months and nine days—but who was counting? ☺ And then—after all that time—"seeing" was all we could do. What a racket! It was exhausting, trying to compete. Made me feel helpless, just sitting there looking. (I *dare* complain! You'd think I would be thankful for small mercies.) The noise reminded me of when you once wrote: "The English talk quietly in small groups, while the French gather in large groups and yell like they're trying to communicate with someone in the Gaspé." Well, that was about it. And of course no one would ever think of putting in soft surfaces to deaden the clatter.

For the moment, though, I'll be content with being able to do no more than look. *But what a letdown when you walked into the room, ungroomed, no smile, looking as if it were too much bother to walk to the room. Heart-shocking questions attacked me: Is this what I did all that fighting for? Don't you love me any more? We sit there looking and looking with, seemingly, nothing to say. Or too much to say. And you showing nothing, until finally, at the end, that last little something in the eyes. I take that home with me.*

It's unfortunate my job restricts us to weekends when the room's bound to be full like that, but over the holidays I'll be able to come on weekdays. That's something to look forward to. Being limited to one hour, with you in Seg, is another misfortune, but dare I speak of misfortune when I've just become so fortunate?

There's no end to my complaining, is there? Well, "I don't want much; I just want more." Remember? From *A Star is Born*. Let's hope you get into the population soon so we can have more time and then—before too long, I hope—contact visits.

I love you, Don, and seeing you again made worthwhile all the efforts to get the visits back.

"See you"—and maybe even *hear* you???—next Saturday morning.

IN THE VISIT ROOM, I had the chance to inspect the famous grille. It was enough to make me furious all over again. It's necessary to put your head right down on the ledge/table in order to look up through the overlapping steel louvres. From there layers of metal mesh can be seen, so dense that not a spot of air shows through. As the guy said, nothing passes through that grille but smoke.

The visit letter arrives. "The one thing they should never do with a convict," he tells me, "is ruin his visits or letters." Only then do all those charges become clear. He was rebelling, in the limited means at his disposal. Should I fault *him*? Or the system? Or both?

And so the long deprivation was over. I would have done anything not to have been forced to go through all that time without him; yet, at the same time, it was an experience I feel thankful for. I knew already, from all I'd heard and read, that these things happen, but I learned *first hand* how a person can be convicted by false evidence and how she can be deceived and betrayed by a lawyer. How many people are behind those walls because of similar, and worse, circumstances? And with more dire consequences? In the end I can say it was an education I value.

I began attending meetings of the *Office des droits des détenu(e)s*, sitting mostly mute at the table, feeling somewhat of an interloper because of my lack of contribution, but I got a lot out of it. It was refreshing to be with intelligent, clear-thinking people with a solid vision of how a thoughtful, caring society should function. The lawyers and staff person all lived at near-poverty level in order to do their work—a true inspiration.

At that time the consuming activity was with respect to the aftermath of the killing of three guards in a riot at Archambault. Over supper and a bottle of wine I tell Janice about the abuses that have gone on: beatings; excessive tear gassing, even directly into the mouth and on food; guards peeing on food and on prisoners; guards keeping prisoners awake by banging incessantly on cell doors; refusing to give clothes, or giving clothes soaked in cold water. I'm breathless recounting it all. It goes on and on. Naked prisoners forced to kneel before guards and shine their shoes; prisoners forced into scalding hot showers; a mock hanging to the point of near-suffocation; access by lawyers refused for over a week while journalists were invited in on the third day so they would report the official version.

"Even if we can understand the guards feeling justified in avenging the deaths of their buddies," I tell her, "there's no justification for *administration* turning a blind eye. And they've smoke-screened every investigative body that has come along."

Investigative reports are issued by the International Human Rights Law Group in Washington and the United Church of Canada, both of which condemn everyone from the Solicitor General down. The International Federation of Human Rights, based in Paris, is called in by the *Office*. I went to the meeting when its representative, Thierry Maleville, reported his conclusion: torture as defined by the United Nations had indeed taken place.

The Moderator of the Presbyterian Church wrote a Letter to the Editor in The Globe and Mail saying this is a matter of social concern that affects every Canadian because it is society who put those men there. This being the case, a public inquiry is necessary to find out what went wrong and what needs to be changed.

"In your dreams!" I write Joanne. "There was something called the MacGuigan Report which clearly enunciated what's wrong and what needs to be changed. And what happened to it?"

I expected Don to shake off the past two years, put a lilt in his step, come bouncing into the visit room, smile on his face, as if nothing had happened. I expected, too, to receive a flood of cheery, amusing letters full of laughs as in the past; in short, that he be as happy as I was to get the visits back. His lack of enthusiasm I took to be a lack of caring, and felt lost. After all, the move to Montreal was to be with him, but in three and a half years we had had not much more than a year of active, rewarding relationship. Over the first few months of 1983 the visits were mostly disappointing, his negative attitude impossible to deal with. He was a different person, none of the old good humour, the *joie de vivre* I'd always found so amazing. If I had been clear-thinking and not so full of my own problems, I would have recognized how depressed he was; his letters had shown it, yet lost in my own concerns I was blind to his.

At the end of February he saw the warden about getting contact visits; the warden said Get back to me the first of April. "To hell with it" was Don's reaction, "I'm not asking again. Do you think I'm going to say Pretty Please?" That didn't sit well after all I'd done.

At the same time I hated my job. Sitting trapped in that drab, brown-walled, brown-carpeted space with nothing interesting to do, was depressing and demoralizing. Talking with visitors and job applicants passed part of the day, but Micom wasn't as busy as AES had been, and it was a dead end job. Besides that, I had constant backache, which had me at the doctor's repeatedly. X-rays produced a discouraging diagnosis: convex left scoliosis; dorsal kyphosis; moderate multi-level degenerative disk disease; arthritis. But I knew the real problem was sitting on that chair all day long under air-conditioning, aggravated by the unstimulating environment. Finally I quit and my own assessment proved correct when I continued to do word processing in other offices pain-free.

It was a miserable time but I had my friends—Janice, in particular. We continued to see each often, sharing our thoughts, feelings and frustrations (my disappointment in Don's attitude; her dashed hopes for David's progress in the U.S., which meant abandoning plans to have a child). She would tell me about her classes, the students and their reactions to the subject matter (Sociology of Women and Sociology of Sex), her activities in the teachers' union, and the numerous protest marches she participated in. Belinda and I went on one, a Take Back the Night demonstration in which we marched through the Plateau district shouting, *La Rue! La Nuit! Femmes sans peur!* Trivial Pursuit had come along. We played it with gusto, revelling over all the memories evoked by the questions. The fact that I was more often the loser than the winner didn't lessen the enjoyment.

Carlos continued to invite Belinda and me for supper, unusual, delicious meals, made especially pleasant by the ambiance he created with his tasteful table presentation and soft Hispanic background music. In return we took him to Beauty's on Mont-Royal Avenue, a small noisy restaurant with 40's décor, where long lines freeze outside in the dead of winter for the chance to eat all-day breakfast. The Beauty Special—toasted bagel with smoked salmon, cream cheese, tomato and onion—defies duplication. Then we walked St-Laurent Blvd, ("The Main"), the dividing line between English and French Montreal, a festival of quirky people and eclectic shops.

With the resumption of visits, the Wednesday night meetings at *Macadie* became less necessary; accordingly, I attended less frequently and eventually stopped. Carole and I remained friends. We went to see Oscar Peterson perform his Canadiana Suite with the Montreal Symphony Orchestra in a spectacular free concert at the Forum. This time, as a *Montréalaise,* she knew far more about him than I did. Gradually, though, after some time, our friendship faded.

Having my old friend Jean nearby was comforting, friend from all the stages, all the joys and sorrows, past and present. We often spoke on the phone but actually saw each other only infrequently. Belinda and I were both thrilled when twice they took us to see the Expos play baseball at the Olympic Station. Mascot Youppi and his antics added to the fun. It was a sad day in 1983 when she and Doug left for Toronto, one of Doug's many transfers in his career with the CNR.

Hi,

Here's a riddle for you: Why did it take the woman two hours to get from the visit room of Laval Institution to the bus stop 200 meters away?

. . . . . Tick-tock, tick-tock . . . . . (Thinking time here.) . . . . .

Give up?

Between the visit room and the reception area is a little hallway and a washroom. On my way out I went to the toilet. Then, down a short hallway to the exit door. I pull the handle and—nothing, Shake it as hard as I can. Absolutely nothing. It's locked!

I knock, wait, but there's no response. Knock louder. Nothing. Yell as loud as I can, kick the door with all the force I can muster, again and again— but nothing. I'm locked in. *Those stupid bastards. I probably shouldn't give them the satisfaction of reading this; they'll probably be pleased with themselves.* I go back to the other end of the corridor, to the exit from the visit room, thinking I might be able to raise someone from there, but that door is locked too. So there I am, locked between the two doors and nothing to do but sit on the floor and wait for an hour and a half until they open up again. I wasn't pleased, believe me, but what could I do? *I should report them but of course I don't dare lodge any complaints at this stage, do I?*

So there I am—me, the big security risk—and they're not even keeping track of me. It was damn lucky for me that it was a morning visit and not afternoon. Imagine then! I'd have been there the whole bloody night. Wouldn't that have been something?

Joanne had a similar experience at Edmonton Institution back in the winter. (Similar as far as security, is concerned.) She and her friend went for an evening visit when a huge storm blew in unexpectedly. Other visitors lived close by, but Joanne had what on a good day is an hour's drive. She knew she'd never make it and refused to leave. V&C didn't know what to do with them. "We can stay in the trailer," she told them, because she knew one was empty. "Ah, we can't let you do that," was the automatic response, but in the end they acquiesced.

In the morning she and her friend helped themselves to breakfast and waited. No one came. Finally, after nine o'clock, she phoned the keeper, asked him when someone was going to come and get them. He was totally shocked. No one had even told him they were there!

We're both scratching our heads over the way they make visitors feel they're such a danger, yet it's a game—important when they want to make a case against you and non-existent when there's a situation that has potential.

◆   ◆   ◆   ◆

Oh Don! It was like going home, returning to one's roots, being grounded after so long afloat. Just to sit next to you, to be able to touch, kiss, after all that time. You felt so good. No words to describe. And I, for one, am optimistic about the reclassification even if you aren't. *Why do you continue to be so negative, still the same hopeless outlook? You've got the C.O. trying to get you to Medium, and you refuse to get excited, or even believe. Only two more years until you're eligible for parole—but I'm not supposed to mention that. "They're" never going to give you anything.* It's apparent that at least one of "them"—the monolithic entity you always refer to—the C.O., sees something in you or he wouldn't be working to help you advance. *But saying that, even, I know, will anger you.*

I'm counting the hours until Saturday afternoon and we can sit next to each other again.

◆   ◆   ◆   ◆

I got your little visit note and was happy. In the same mail I had a letter from Joanne telling me Sean's back in Millhaven. She's living in Toronto and will commute from there. No stagnation for us, I told her when I wrote back—a long letter, you can be sure—had to tell her how the Law Project got the visits back for us. *Also poured out my conflicted thoughts and questions about free will vs. determinism because I'm exasperated with your attitude. Free will: "O.K., we know they put themselves in there." Determinism: "But there's something else, something went missing somewhere, something went askew other than the individual himself." Back to free will: "Still, there's no getting around the fact that ultimately we choose our own lives." That's what I try to tell you. But you won't listen.*

Claire's friend arrived for her week-long stay. She goes to Archambault every day—got special permission through Claire's influence. She's good company. Besides the Prisoners' Rights Group, she's involved in the anti-poverty and feminist movements, so there's a lot to discuss. What I find fascinating is that she likes her job cleaning a school at night because it leaves her mind free to plan the actions she's going to take. I'm so lucky I get to meet such interesting people.

"FRIENDS, PARTLY THROUGH their own experiences in prisons of the seventeenth century, became concerned about the treatment of the accused or convicted. . . . Subsequently they worked for reform of these prisons. Today Friends are becoming aware that prisons are a destructive and expensive failure as a response to crime. We are, therefore, turning from efforts to reform prisons to efforts to replace them with non-punitive, life-affirming and reconciling responses.

"The prison system is both a cause and a result of violence and social injustice. Throughout history, the majority of prisoners have been the powerless and the oppressed. We are increasingly clear that the imprisonment of human beings, like their enslavement, is inherently immoral and is as destructive to the cagers as to the caged.

"Prison abolition is both process and long-term goal. In the interim, [we must] reach out to and support all those affected: guards, prisoners, victims and families.

"We recognize a need for restraint of those few who are exhibiting dangerous behaviour. The kind of restraint used and the help offered during that time must reflect our concern for that of God in every person."

Excerpts from Minute #93
Canadian Yearly Meeting, 1981
Religious Society of Friends (Quakers)

Dear Love,

I missed our visit on the weekend but I'll have lots to tell you when I see you.

Quakers, it turns out, do not wear grey, nor do they wear dour expressions. So much for our theories, although you knew more than I did. But they didn't start prisons as you thought but, rather, changed them into their modern form. (Even that's not much of a recommendation, is it?) Before that, prisons were places of containment until fines were paid or punishments meted out. Quakers felt confinement would be a more humane sanction than the cruel corporal punishments of the day and campaigned for the change. Then they got the bright idea that if held in isolation convicts would have time to think about their crimes and become penitent. Hence the word penitentiary. I'm told that the first prison built under the Quaker model had a small walled exercise yard for each cell to facilitate total isolation. Even talking to oneself, whistling and singing, were forbidden and, ironically, brought on their own harsh punishments.

Prison abolition, I should tell you, in the terms of this conference, doesn't mean opening the gates and releasing everyone tomorrow. ("Too bad," I heard you say. ☺) It means dismantling a system where eighty percent of offenders have not committed a violent crime and are not dangerous to the public. They would be made to work in order to make restitution to their victims and support their families. The idea is that fifteen percent should receive counselling and/or education to prepare them to do this, and five percent might have to remain incarcerated. What do you think of that? Does the five percent dangerous tally with your impression?

Billy came over and met me near the university for supper on Saturday. He's doing fine. I had to borrow money from him to come home by bus. Going there I was frantic the whole distance. A fierce wind was blowing and the van we rented was too light—or too high off the ground—something—and swayed wildly onto the other lane, scaring me half to death. I guess I looked like a wimp to the group, but there was no way I was coming back in that van.

Well, I'll tell you the rest when I see you.

EIGHT OF US FROM THE *Office des droits* attended the first International Conference on Prison Abolition (ICOPA), held at the University of Toronto. Over four hundred participants—NGOs, academics, civil rights lawyers, activists from religious organizations, several former prisoners, even a representative of Corrections Canada—gathered to discuss the subject. The agenda followed three tracks: an analysis of the present system; how abolition would work; how to get there. I was impressed and inspired by the clear-headed thinking of every speaker. Not "do-gooder" ideas based on sympathy or soft-heartedness, but practical visions of a justice system that would benefit society as a whole by bringing together victims, offenders, their families and members of the community, in order to find solutions that would answer everyone's needs. Transformative Justice.

One of the main speakers, the Executive Director of Mennonite Central Committee, Jake Epp, said, "The inmate who wants to get through prison alive and healthy does not dare to become rehabilitated." Prisons teach survival skills: lying, cheating, bullying, denying emotions, being cunning—qualities that are the antithesis of those needed for success on the street. Darwinism at its most refined: adapt or die. One assumes that, as the former head of two prisons, he knew his subject.

When I registered, the woman at the desk exclaimed, "Oh! You're so lucky! You're billeted with Ruth Morris!" That meant nothing to me and my blank face must have shown it so she explained that Ruth was one of the main organizers of the conference.

Busy as she was, Ruth made a point of travelling back and forth with me and, the trip being more than an hour each way, there was lots of time for talking. She and her husband had put up bail for so many people over the years, she told me, that the Ontario government had asked her to set up a program in order that poverty not be the only reason people were detained before trial. And so she was Director of the Toronto Bail Program. Her forthright manner, earnestness, clear thinking and cheerfulness were impressive. She, like her husband, had taught at university level and she had a vast store of facts and statistics to back her thinking. But the spiritual basis of her work was the driving force, she said, the belief that there is "that of God in every person."

Over the three days of the conference I had the opportunity to chat with several Quakers. Another with whom I was taken was Madeleine, who was from Massachusetts and had a tragic story. Her son had killed his father, which left her both a victim of crime and family of an offender. He had been diagnosed schizophrenic before this happened. Now, instead of being in a hospital, he was being held in prison where his mental health was steadily deteriorating. She had been fighting for eight years to get him into a facility where he could get treatment. Such quiet strength. We kept in touch for several years.

I liked these people, liked their way of thinking—my kind of people, I thought—and determined to find out what it was about Quaker beliefs that attracted them. To that end, I researched and found there was a meeting in Montreal. However, without a car, going and coming to Laval by public transportation took up three hours of my day on top of visit time, and Sunday mornings I was able to get a ride with another visitor, the mother of one of the guys. The choice, therefore, was easy.

Hi,

You finally made it to Medium and don't I find something to gripe about? For me, it's a demotion: one closed visit a week and *one* group visit a month. That's not much. Who do I complain to? OK, it doesn't have an open visit room because it was built as a Maximum, but surely they could make one! It wouldn't take that much money. But there I am again, after all this time, still expecting things to make sense.

◆   ◆   ◆   ◆

So good to sit next to you yesterday after so long, and having food to eat made it seem almost human. And it was fun to give the weights a go—something Belinda could show me up on, eh? The whole thing felt almost normal. Good to see you looking so good, too. Getting outside more and running are having their effects, I see. Motivates me—think I'll start weights at the Y in the fall.

I spoke to Cheryl again. In the end she was designated essential staff—very essential!—Acting Head Nurse. She was not pleased, knowing her boyfriend and friends were having a Hurricane Party at her place while she had to work. So far they think about twenty were killed. Very extensive damage—a Category 3—but the seawall did its job and held back a twelve-foot surge. (Can you visualize it after all my descriptions?) She said they're selling souvenir T-shirts with ALICIA, WHAT A BITCH! printed on them.

Miss you already. How about a letter?

◆   ◆   ◆   ◆

I have to say, judging by the handiwork I saw in the visit room, you do a good job of barbering. Maybe you take a long time but, lucky for you, your customers *have* a lot of time. ☺ You'll get faster, don't worry; you're just learning. And good to see you excited about participating in the Scared Straight program. That's so worthwhile. As for the language problem, I don't know what to say. It's funny, after four years and how many prisons, this is the first time it's come up. Maybe it's restricted to particular people who will eventually get transferred out. I hope it regulates itself one way or the other. Too bad you don't seem to be able to learn French. *The problem I would like regulated is letters—not enough of them—and when you do write, all you do is fill pages with protestations of not being able to write. I resent it, resent that I'm the only one putting forth an effort here. I've tried to tell you so many times. What do you do except walk down to the visit room, while I spend hours going there and back?*

IN THE CLOSED VISITS, for a bit of variety, and to make believe we are real people, I take Trivial Pursuit cards with me. Instead of spinning for categories, I hold a card up to the window, he reads me the questions until I get one wrong, and then I ask him his questions until he misses. I keep score on a paper. We're so evenly matched that it makes for a lot of fun, and then there are all the spin-off conversations and laughs about related facts or memories.

"What is a person who lives in Liverpool called?" Neither of us knew the answer to that one. But the V&C did! On my way out he unabashedly told me he knew it: Liverpuddlian. In my next letter to Joanne, I tell her the story, tell her I'm still laughing. "At first I was angry, but in the end decided to be charitable. It's his job to listen, after all, and no doubt we did a good deed by cheering up his boring day. Maybe next time I should ask if he wants to make it a three-way game? What do you think???"

I QUIT MY JOB, and wondered why I didn't do it a long time before. But things have to come to you first. When there's a change that needs to be made, I always feel I'm standing there ready, waiting, but don't know exactly what form it should take until the answer presents itself, as it always does. The thing is to recognize it and grab it. In this case when a woman came to the office to replace a secretary who had been injured in a car accident, I got talking to her, found out how being employed by an agency works, and realized: This is *it!* This is what *I* should do! And so I registered at a temporary placement agency, passed the word processing test at Intermediate level, and started immediately. And the pay was twenty percent more than I had been making.

Dear Loved One,
    Hope everything is fine with you. Miss you, as always.
    Our trip to Quebec City was excellent. Did you know the old section is the second oldest settlement and the only walled city in North America? It's a magical place to visit, and our guesthouse was comfortable, convenient, and tastefully decorated in early 19C style.
    Strolling through rue du Trésor, the artists' area, Cheryl was taken with a painting, impressionist in style, a street scene reminiscent of the very area in which it stood. The more she looked, the more she wanted it, but it was expensive. Purchasing it required some thought, so we retreated to a bar. Went back to see it again and, yes, it felt right. Expensive, but right. The deal was made but, because it had just been completed that morning, the paint was still wet, so he said to come back to collect it in the evening. When we arrived it was waiting, well-packaged for air travel. Jean-Louis, in high spirits at such fortune, invited us, along with two of his friends, for a celebratory drink. An exceedingly jolly evening ensued: seven of us at the table—three who had no English, one who had no French, me doing my best in between, and Belinda the only one able to understand everything—if everything was indeed intelligible. At one point Jean-Louis left the table, disappeared, and

came back fifteen minutes later with a small oil painting for each of the three of us. So touching, and a lovely memento. A weekend to remember.

◆   ◆   ◆   ◆

Belinda had an adventure not many of us have had (save a few like you, who've seen it from the inside). Yesterday she was in the bakery across from her school when a woman rushed in with a troupe of little kids, very excited, explaining that they needed a safe place because there was a robbery happening in the bank next door. Hearing that, Belinda went and took a look. There, in plain view, wearing pantyhose over his face and holding a gun, was the robber. He turned, faced the window—faced her—which sent her smartly back to the baker's. Minutes later they heard shots, looked out and saw a police car parked askew, its doors open, and another car roaring off—the robbers, she assumes. She didn't even seem nervous about it.

◆   ◆   ◆   ◆

We had an enjoyable few days at my brother's. Then, Boxing Day we went to my mother's for the annual extended family get-together, a boisterous affair with everyone trying to outyell my mother, who is not content unless her voice is the loudest. Pam and Brenda were there—all is well with them. I phoned Joanne every twenty minutes from the time we arrived (wanted to plan my getaway right from the start) but it seems she forgot we had plans (or didn't care) because she didn't come home until mid-evening. So it was a long day.

Gary and I were sitting talking when he started looking through an old photo album. We came to a picture of us standing on a dock with our parents (I'm 8, Gary is 6) at a cottage we used to rent before we bought the one on Lake Couchiching. There we are, the four of us, arms around each other, everyone smiling. Gary looks at it a long time then says slowly, in a low voice, "We must have been happy at one time." Do I need to say more?

I wonder why you and I rarely talk about our childhoods. Do we want to forget? Or are they just not worthy of mention? You told me of one incident, though, that remains vivid. When you were telling me, the look on your face morphed into your four-year-old face with its sad dark brown eyes. You're standing at the bottom of the front steps and your mother is in the doorway, telling you No, you can't come live with her. I try to avoid seeing the next image, but can't: you, trudging back to your grandmother's across the street, not knowing why. And you still don't. Why don't you ask her? About your father, too. Or you could ask your sister, maybe she even remembers him.

You don't know who your father was, but neither do I, even though he lived in the same house. That photo—and that remark—got me to thinking. It can't be that I always hated him, because I remember having great fun playing Whistling Game. He would start whistling a tune, and Gary and I would try to name it as fast as we could. The first to guess would then take his or her turn. I had to hum, though, because I could never whistle worth a darn. I remember, too, going to ball games with him at High Park and going on our bicycles to see his parents.

The really bad times didn't start until my teens. Night after night his place at the supper table sat empty, and my mother would start. Basically she was yelling at the walls, but we were the ones who had to listen. It would be eight or eight-thirty before he arrived, the worse for drink. Never falling-down-drunk, but drunk enough to enrage my mother. (He did manage to hold on to a very responsible job as Chief Accountant for the Toronto Hydro.) The screaming reached a fever pitch for the half-hour or so before he went off to bed—her doing the yelling, him answering only the minimum. I identified with her, took on her view, saw him as the cause of all our problems and hated him for it.

When I was 16 he went missing and it was in the newspaper, which was humiliating in the extreme. My friends didn't say anything, so I didn't know if they knew and were being polite, or didn't know. After about five days I heard my mother and aunt in whispers behind closed doors saying he'd been found at a ball game in New York City. But I knew that made no sense. Police don't go to that extent to find an ordinary person missing only a few days. And how could one individual be spotted in a crowd that size anyway? Nothing was ever explained; it's still a mystery .

Another mystery is what happened at his wake. People thronged to it in streams. When the floral tributes lined all four walls from ceiling to floor, a second room had to be opened up to accommodate them. You'd have thought it was the funeral of a public personage. Who were these people? Who was the person they knew, the person they honoured and respected, the person not seen in our house? To this day I don't know what that was about.

Only after his death (I was 21), when the yelling didn't stop, did I come to question things. She had yelled at us to some extent all along, but now we were her only target—although Gary took the brunt because I was already married and living in Trout Creek. Seeing that, I had to ask myself: Did the drinking cause the yelling, or did the yelling cause the drinking? Or did they just reinforce each other in a co-dependency, as we now say? In the end it's clear they were two very unhappy people, wrong for each other, who were forced to stay together because of the social strictures of the time. A pity.

Well, those are my fond memories evoked by Boxing Day at my mother's. Duty done for another year. My cousin drove us out to Joanne's, which proved to be on the edge of nowhere. I don't know how people can live in the outlying areas like that, where you have to get in your car every time you want to go somewhere. Suburbs are such bland places—no personality. "Little boxes made of ticky-tacky and they all look the same." Only in this case, big boxes. Nevertheless, it's a nice apartment in a nice building (we availed ourselves of the exercise room), and it gives her fast access to the 401 to go to Bath. Sean is fine, by the way—nothing new to report. He wants to know if you got the kite he sent.

Well, it's good to be a "lady of means" and be able to take ten days off work without pay. (As if I had a choice.) Seriously, it feels good to know that in the new year I'll have any number of interesting jobs coming my way and on own my terms. I never dreamed there would be so many benefits to being a temp.

Lucky for me, your letter arrived before we left. I brought it with me so I won't forget you!! Ha! I'll repeat your closing thought: "Waiting patiently with how much impatience." Me, too. Waiting, waiting . . . with how much love. . . .

And, you know what? I've had it with this Trivial Pursuit business. I want to play Serious Pursuit!

GARY, VAL AND THE CHILDREN come at the mid-winter school break for an overnight on their way back from their annual ski vacation in Vermont or the Laurentians. It's become a tradition. They arrive Saturday afternoon and off we go for supper at Andros' Greek Restaurant where Gary and Andros greet each other as old friends. Everyone looks forward to the food and we linger over a bottle of wine. Even the kids are content.

Sunday morning we go to pick up our breakfast at the Fairmount Bagel Factory, located in Duddy Kravitz territory where the streets are filled with Hassidic Jews in black fur hats, long black jackets with white fringes trailing out the sides, black pants and shiny black satin topcoats.

The "factory" is not much bigger than a shed, ramshackle and probably dangerous with its open fire in a very old, crowded, wooden building. A factory, though, in the sense of how much they produce and how fast. Enormous mounds of dough are mixed in metal tubs, the mass so huge it takes two strong men to lift it onto the floury wooden counter. There, they cut it, first into manageable portions, then—chop-chop-chop—so fast you'd think it was being done by machine—it's cut to bagel-size, twisted into shape with the flick of a wrist, and thrown into boiling water. When they have risen slightly, the rings are fished out, placed on long wooden slats, and sprinkled with either sesame or poppy seeds. Then the circus act begins. The slat is precariously lifted over the fire, the bagels are flipped from it and, in a true wonder, land on the grille in a long straight row. When that side is cooked, the worker somehow slides the slat under the whole row (how much practice is required to learn this skill?) and flips them to the other side. When that side is done, the board is once more slipped under the whole row and they're dumped from it into a flume, which slides them down onto the counter where the clerk throws them, piping hot, into paper bags. We drive home with the aroma of freshly-baked bagels wafting through the car, and an extra two dozen for Gary and Val to take home with them.

There's an ongoing debate on who produces the better bagel, the Fairmount or the *St-Viateur*, only blocks away. The bigger question is whether Montreal's or New York's are better. I told Belinda we can never move from Montreal because how can we live without bagels? We have them only because of the large Jewish population, second largest outside of Israel next to New York. Evie and I went on a search in Toronto once and found some on Spadina Avenue, but they proved to be "imported from Montreal."

DON WAS RECOMMENDED by the Classification Officer for an eight-hour pass to my place; it passed a board and our hopes were up. Then it went for the warden's approval. He refused to handle it, passed it to Ottawa. There it was refused. The people who deal with him on a daily basis have a good opinion of him and good relationships with him. That higher-ups have the authority when they don't even know the person, is discouraging. But he handled it better than I did. Maybe his hopes weren't as high. For me, it was a bitter disappointment but in the end, just seeing that much trust placed in him represented a big step forward.

More disappointing to him was Belinda's recent attitude. She didn't want to visit any more; I had to beg her to go to the last social. He thought of her as his daughter, perhaps somewhat unrealistically, but she was only seven when she met him and she was always very affectionate toward him. At fourteen, though, it didn't fit with her priorities. Nor with what she thought a mother should be doing, no doubt. A recent incident had revealed the relationship to her in a different light. Not even realizing it was something that needed to be kept more or less secret, when her friend asked where the picture of Don and me on the kitchen wall was taken, she answered truthfully. And got an unfavourable reaction. Only then did I realize I had made a big mistake in not warning the children about others' opinions. Instead of telling them of the prejudice against prisoners and what some people might think, I had hoped they would form their own ideas from their own observation and experience. Which showed a certain unwarranted optimism on my part, as well as a double standard, because *I* certainly didn't tell everyone in *my* life about the situation. It also showed an inability to learn by experience. When I was going with Obi I expected the children to accept it as natural, which they did until they ran against friends' opinion of me having a black boyfriend. One would think I might have been more savvy after that.

I was sad about Belinda's alienation. Don wrote her a seven-page letter but didn't tell me what he said.

ON THE MAY HOLIDAY WEEKEND I rented a car, took Belinda to Orillia, then drove back to stay with Evie in Toronto. I called Joanne, she told me Sean's latest prison problems, so I suggested Ruth Morris might have some useful advice. Ruth said she could meet Joanne at Friends' House after Sunday meeting. So Joanne, Sheri and I went off to meeting.

Toronto Friends' Meeting is located in a lovely old house in the Annex district, big, with oak-paneled walls, very elegant. We arrived a few minutes before eleven o'clock, took our seats in the back row, and waited.

The meeting room, a modern addition at the back, is set up with four rows of chairs in an open U-shape, facing a beautiful flower garden viewed through a wall of windows. A table sits in the open space, for the leader, I assume. Eleven o'clock comes and goes and nothing happens. Sixty or more people sitting there in total silence and nothing happening. It's enough to make you squirm. Sheri, in typical teenage fashion, gets to giggling. She's tittering away on the other side of Joanne, and that gets the two of us going. It's contagious; we can't help ourselves. We're tee-heeing, sniffling, fairly rocking in efforts to contain the forces, yet muffled snorts manage to escape hands clutched over mouths. No one pays mind. Everyone continues to sit in apparent relaxed contemplation.

Still no minister, yet no one is looking at the door in expectation, no one is asking her neighbour what should be done. After an excruciatingly long time it occurs to me—perhaps a memory from some distant book or movie—that this is what is *supposed* to happen, strange though it is. Then it becomes easier, although sitting with others in silence is not something that comes naturally; socially it's considered a failing if you can't find something to say to fill the void. Another fifteen or twenty minutes and I'm surprisingly comfortable.

A man rises and speaks of Benigno Aquino, how he had returned to the Philippines to oppose the government the previous Fall, had been shot down the moment he set foot on the tarmac, how that had touched off non-violent protests, and how those protests had recently increased in response to the apparently-fraudulent re-election of Marcos. "The efforts we make in this life," he concludes, "often appear ineffective at the time. The work we do for one cause or another often doesn't yield results that are evident. It may well be, though, that those results will come in time, later, maybe much later, maybe even after we're gone."

No response. Everyone remains completely still. Ten minutes later another person rises and gives her message. More silence. Most peculiar.

Minutes later there's a bustle, people are shaking hands and a woman comes and stands at that table. She welcomes everyone, the newcomers in particular, and asks them to introduce themselves. Announcements are made, and everyone is invited to tea in the dining room. While Joanne meets with Ruth in the sunroom, I check out the bulletin boards, all overflowing with announcements: upcoming events, protest marches, petitions to be signed, clippings of socially-relevant news articles. Evidence of an active, dedicated community I needed to know more about.

In the afternoon, when we talked it over, Joanne and I agreed that each of the spoken messages was impressive, worthy of further thought. We were quite mystified, however, about the process.

Dear Don,

The opportunity of a lifetime and I let it go by! "Dear Chicken," you start your letter. Well, I'm that; I can't deny it. It was proven. And you thought it was "an offer I couldn't refuse," didn't you? What did that do to your ego? But, damn, how could I walk in there in front of all those people? Even worse, walk out again? *You went to all that trouble to arrange an unlocked room we could go into and then I wouldn't co-operate. Turns out my sense of propriety is a stronger force than the sex drive—to my great disappointment.*

I love the description you quote from one of the guys, who was apparently watching my reactions when you were trying to convince me: "The look of someone at a midway, going into a tunnel of thrills, unsure of whether she will laugh or be scared." That about sums it up. Was *everyone* watching? Damn, you really set me up, didn't you? I wonder what I'll think of all this in twenty years? One comment for sure will be, "It was never boring."

◆   ◆   ◆   ◆

We've decided to move. Only two blocks away, but a better building— newer, with bigger, brighter windows—and it's a quiet street. The rent is $40 more, but I hope the landlord will be better, namely that he will attend to cockroaches if any, which this whole district seems to have.

So exciting to know you're about to "graduate" from the nebulous classification of pre-Medium (which I have never understood) to full Medium. We're closer to the end of the tunnel and it makes me happy. Not a long trip this time, only next door, but it's a considerably shorter walk for me from the bus stop. Let's hope it has a proper visit room.

◆   ◆   ◆   ◆

Cheryl and Pam's visit was very nice, relaxed. The weather was so balmy we did lots of outdoor things: walked up *Parc Mont-Royal* to the lookout; went to *Île Notre Dame* and *Île Ste-Hélène* to relive our Expo '67 experience; and checked out Old Montreal from a historical point of view, as opposed to the "just soaking up the atmosphere" meandering we usually do.

The thing I like about the job where I am now, at the Head Office of the Bank of Montreal, is that it's located in Old Montreal. Every morning when I come out of the Metro, the wonder of it hits me, and I have a "pinch me, can this be real?" feeling. Lunch hour is spent walking around in pure pleasure. Yesterday we had a bird's-eye view from our office window as the Pope emerged from his Popemobile and entered Notre Dame Cathedral across the road. Sometimes I just can't believe how lucky I am to be living here.

Falling Leaves

(October 1984—February 1989)

AT THE NEXT VISIT I learn there's more to the transfer story. And it's not good. He tells me in mouthed words and cryptic written messages he holds up to the glass that he expects "trouble" at the other prison. The word is a euphemism because it refers to the worst kind of trouble he could have. There are enemies who will be waiting for him. He doesn't tell me the details and I don't ask; some things you don't want to know. He absolutely refuses to tell the authorities, and I am severely warned not to tell anyone in the system. Better dead—with his honour intact—than ask for protection. The Prison Code. We're living in different universes and they're nowhere close to being parallel. And so I'm living in dread, paralyzed in two ways – paralyzed emotionally and paralyzed as far as taking action is concerned. The only way I can handle it is to hold myself icy cold.

A week later I get a call from the CO. Don was transferred the day before and this morning there was an "incident" in the yard. Don wants me to know I should visit only in the morning.

I go to see him and after he tells me what happened and his options for the future there's nothing to say. Or there's so much that needs to be said that attempting it is futile. We just "hold" each other across the table in long periods of silence.

He had been transferred on Monday. Tuesday he knew he had no alternative but to go into the yard, no matter what. He hadn't finished the first lap when two guys started toward him. He knew by the position of their hands that they had shivs in their pockets. He ran, kicked the door full force and the guards let him in.

He won't hear of being put in Protection and so the only option is a transfer. After talking things over extensively with the CO, who seems to be a good guy, and taking everything into consideration—his classification level, me, the whereabouts of the "wrong" people—it's clear that a transfer back to Kingston is the only real option. And so we sit wordless while the vocabulary of silence encircles us, draws us together, closer and closer.

There's more: he's likely to run into some of the same group in Ontario. He asks me to tell Sean—via Joanne—that he ran into the wrong crowd and will transfer back to Ontario to avoid them. Prison politics. Sean has influence. What can I do? I'm stunned. In shock. Powerless. And the luxury of choice does not exist.

It becomes official: he will go to Kingston, to Collins Bay, but it's decided it would look better if he waits for a regular transfer run; if they make a special run for him, questions will be asked. So he stays two more months, which means he remains in a potentially dangerous situation all that time. I hate to bring him to the visit room, but he wants me to come, wants to see me, says it should be OK. He has me send "political" (I call them) Christmas cards to allies in various prisons. No message, just a regular card and sign his name. Interesting to see how things work. It's another world.

MEANWHILE, AS AN ANTIDOTE I find my work enjoyable. It's odd, because people (even myself to some extent) think I should be doing something more in keeping with my education and experience, but I like the people at the agency and by this time I've passed further tests and been promoted to Senior, which brings more pay. And I love the variety. It's not always plain typing; sometimes there are mathematical or sorting functions to do, rearrange sections of reports to make a presentation more visually appealing. Endless variety in the work itself as well as different people and different locations.

At Abbott Laboratories I typed a report on the nutritional product Ensure, which was in its clinical trial stage. Working on that was like reading a book with a plot. And I met a new friend there, Hilde, who liked the same authors and activities, and has travelled everywhere. She's from Germany but met her *Québecois* husband in India. Later he went to see her in Germany and then she came to spend time with him in British Columbia. She was at the end of her visa, wanted to stay longer. The only way to do that was to get married. And so they did, and still are. After finishing at Abbott, we stayed in touch, met for coffee, and a few times, with Belinda, took in the cheapest "dinner and theatre" evenings in existence: a free play at the National Theatre School located in the down-and-out lower end of St. Lawrence Blvd, preceded by a stand-up hot-dog and French fries from a similarly run-down take-out place next door.

A friendship was developing with another woman at Abbott, Christine. She lived in the suburbs, so when we went to see Anna Mouskouri at *Places-des-Arts,* she drove to my place and we went from there, by Metro. On the way back, after eleven o'clock, we had just rounded the corner onto my street and she asked if I felt safe in that district. "Very safe," I told her, "I never even think of it." With that she lets out a scream. I turn to see her struggling over her purse with a young fellow and another about to grab mine. Belinda and I had just taken a self-defence course, which had filled me with confidence. I crouch into an aggressive position, shelter my bag in the pit of my stomach and let out a Karate yell, or facsimile. At any rate it was enough to scare my guy off and once Christine's aggressor saw that, he let go of her bag and they took off. No doubt the fact that they were fourteen, fifteen years old was a factor. The stone of her favourite ring was lost in the struggle, though, and after that she didn't want to be friends with me any more.

Dear Don,

Your visit letter arrived and I'm glad to see you enjoyed the social and the visits as much as I did. It's a long time since we were able to have four in a row. But you're too much of a party animal for me! How can I make all the dates you're giving me? I'll be there April 10 for the parole hearing, that's for sure, April 20 for the Sports Social and May 25 for Family Day. As for June 10? Well, I'll have to see if I can clear my calendar for that one. Ha! (And ha! again.)

In a more serious vein, last Sunday I finally went to Quaker meeting. Whereas there were many people at the one in Toronto, there were only eight at this one. But it was easier to sit in silence with eight, I found, or maybe I just knew what to expect. Again, I liked it and liked what they call ministry (spoken messages), but it's a puzzle to me why they call themselves Friends because they aren't friendly at all. There was tea at the kitchen table after the meeting and no one even spoke to me. I could have spoken up, of course, but the conversation was beyond me: world issues such as the Israeli/Palestinian conflict, the boycott of South Africa; changes at McGill University; news of people they know. It was rather rude, I thought, but I did like the meeting itself and also the book I borrowed from their library, so I'll go again tomorrow.

Quaker history and beliefs, you'll be interested to know, are revolutionary in nature. It started in mid-17C with George Fox going about the English countryside preaching that there was no need for the clergy. You can imagine how that went over. His message was that since there is "that of God in every person," there is no need for an intermediary. If you follow that line of thought, the concept necessitates the equality of all people—men and women, black and white, rich and poor—so women had equal standing within the movement from the very start. This belief explains Quakers' history of working on issues of social justice such as abolition of slavery, votes for women and now, abolition of prisons. And the belief in the equality of all means it's a non-hierarchal organization with no ordained or paid ministry; every person has the potential to minister. For these heretic views Fox was arrested a total of thirty-six times in forty years and spent six years in prison.

Early Quakers refused to use status titles such as Sir or Your Honour and refused to doff their hats to people supposedly superior, behaviours that showed a "lack of respect" serious enough to get them jailed. Eventually they were banned from even meeting, which they defied, so went to jail for that too. These prison experiences opened their eyes to conditions, leading to their work in prison reform in the past and abolition now.

The God on my Sunday School cards—an old grandfather with a long white beard—turns me off completely, as does the vengeful God of the Bible. You'll be surprised to learn I've actually read the whole Bible from cover to cover—Old Testament and New. Read it when I was 19 in order to decide things for myself. Didn't really come to any kind of conclusion because, to tell the truth, I didn't understand much, but plowed through it anyway.

I have no interest in any deity or spirit that is personified. However, in my reading of Quaker literature up to now, the concept of God is more often expressed as "The Light" and that has a lot of appeal, seems soft, connected, not remote. Another thing I like is the belief that "the Truth" has not yet been revealed; we are on an ongoing search for it. And so they're open to new ideas and new interpretations.

Only one person spoke last Sunday, a visitor from Ithaca Meeting in New York State. She teaches problem kids at the secondary level and told of an exercise she gave her class. The students were asked to make a sentence by using the letters of the centre row of keys on a typewriter—ASDFGHJKL—as the first letter of each word. The sentences, she said, ran the gamut from despair to violence to anger to comical to optimism, and the one she especially liked was: Always swift doves fly, gliding happily, joyfully keeping love. There's something so light in it, it lightens my heart just to repeat it. The "keeping love" is almost mystical; I try to go further with it, but it just stands there, pure, impenetrable. The point of her message was that we can be given the same set of circumstances, in this case the letters, but it's up to each individual what she or he makes of it. A simple statement that evokes a lot of thought.

As for the sentence, I probably would have come up with something like "Any stupid dope fries good ham juggling kitchen lamps." But then, I'm not so profound.

A PATTERN HAS STARTED. I go to see him and that wonderful comfortable connection is in place. We've missed each other and enjoy being together. I get a nice letter shortly after, saying how good it was to see me, and then nothing. Weeks go by, and nothing. Then I'm discouraged, resentful, start thinking why should I bother. Why should I be the one to do all the work? Make all the efforts. It's a seesaw that goes up and down and doesn't stop.

The next social comes along and one of the members of Montreal Meeting tells me of a Quaker in Kingston who may be able to host me. I call her, she won't be home that weekend, but I'm welcome, she'll leave the key under the mat and I can help myself.

Sunday afternoon I find myself low on money for the trip back and decide to phone Sheri, ask her if she can cash a cheque. The Hello, however, most surprisingly, is Joanne's. She had just walked in the door, hadn't even taken her coat off yet.

We meet at a coffee shop and I pour everything out to her—my discouragement and doubt, encouragement and certainty—all mixed up in a soup bowl. Should I continue in this game, or not? (Yes! I say after I've seen him; No, I say, later, when time goes on, goes dead.) Joanne has good news. In a month's time she will move back to Kingston, having found Toronto too expensive.

THE NEXT SUNDAY AT QUAKER meeting the silence is intense when a woman rises.

"Sometimes it's so difficult when a decision has to be reached, especially when both choices seem to be creative." That perks me up; *I* have a decision to make.

"To know which is the right choice, we should look for signs in the little things that happen, maybe the words of a child, or a co-incidence." Co-incidence? It's a co-incidence you're saying this, I think.

"Some people say there are no co-incidences; the things we take as co-incidence may, in fact, be signs." Tears are streaming down my cheeks. I have the sentiment she's speaking to me alone. How could it be that, at a certain moment—at that particular moment and no other—I decided to give Sheri a call? What were the chances that at that very moment—and no other—Joanne should walk in the door? The fact that she'll be moving back to Kingston and I'll be able to stay with her again, I take, not as a co-incidence, but a sign: I'm meant to continue.

THE CASE MANAGEMENT TEAM (Classification Officer, psychologist, John Howard guy and a fellow from the Parole Board) has worked extensively with Don in preparation for his day parole hearing, and he feels fortunate in having such a good team. But certain necessary milestones have not yet been crossed (first escorted passes, then unescorted ones) and so the team has prepared him for a two year bump; that is, he won't get another hearing for two years.

I go to the hearing with him. The board reiterates what is necessary but says he can re-apply any time the release plan is in place. And so he is heartened.

Dear Don,

I got the photo you sent of us at the lake. Thanks. It's a great reminder. Oh, I was supposed to put quotation marks around that "lake" bit, wasn't I? But when you look at it, you'd swear it was the real thing, not wallpaper.

Some day, maybe. But I wish you had trimmed your beard. Guess I'll just have to tell people that when you're on vacation you don't like to bother.

It was a wonderful day from start to finish. So good to relax with you and just have a good time. The food was good and (with a little imagination) it seemed like a social event one might go to anywhere. I do feel quite encouraged after all the bad times we've been through. It was good of Jenny to drive me. She went out of her way to pick me up and drop me near here and she wouldn't even take money for gas. So many good people out there.

This past Sunday I went to meeting. I like it more and more. I find there's always some deceptively simple (profound) message to take away and ponder for days. As for the way it operates, what I've been able to figure out from my reading and observation is this: they sit "waiting expectantly" for a message that comes out of the silence from the Divine. When someone feels he or she has an inspired message, something that would be helpful in the sense of contributing to people's spiritual growth, he or she rises and delivers it in language that is to be simple and concise. No one should speak immediately after; the words should have time to sink into the silence, be absorbed. The thought can be—and often is—expanded on in the course of the hour, but it should not be directly refuted.

Some meetings the hour goes by and no one speaks. Then, sometimes, not always, an incredible thing happens: the silence becomes palpable. A sense of unity takes over and yet—at the same time—one feels completeness within the Self.

I'm so impressed with Quaker thought, the process and the people. Wish I had met them earlier. But then how and where would I have? I guess one just has to wait and the right thing comes along at the right time. Even so, even though I knew nothing of Quakerism until now, it's uncanny how much of the thought has been mine all along.

In other news, Saturday I went by bus to Mt. Mansfield in Vermont with a hiking club. There was one little detail I didn't realize in advance. "Hiking" actually means mountain climbing, whereas I thought it meant a walk in the forest. However, I made it to the summit (after being pulled out of snow up to my hips by the guide) where—visibility less than twenty meters in a wild snowstorm—I felt the power and exhilaration of having scaled Mt. Everest.

It was a nice, casual, friendly group—all Francophone—the natural type you would expect. Next time is Mt. Cascade in N.Y. State.

Have you been seeing a lot on TV about the fortieth anniversary of the end of the war? What has it come to when we can actually remember—and clearly, too!—forty years ago?

You, living in unpopulated areas, wouldn't have the same kind of war memories as me. We had air raid practices with blackouts. It was pleasant, though, not scary. The family huddled around the radio in the dark, listening to detective stories and mysteries like Perry Mason, The Thin Man, The Falcon. We had to put a towel over the radio because radios had a light on the dial then (do you remember?—they were also a piece of furniture then) and military police would go around checking for any glimmer escaping pulled drapes.

We had air raid drills at school, too. When the siren rang we marched our designated route down to the basement where we stood in straight lines, singing songs (Waltzing Matilda is the one that stands out) until the All Clear sounded. It all seemed very ordinary at the time, nothing to worry about. The Air Force drilled in the schoolyard across the street from our house. My brother, three years old at the time, marched proudly alongside, a kind of mascot. I can see him yet in his little air force look-alike suit—or is it the photos I'm seeing?

The day the war ended I was in Grade Two. The picture is still clear. The wooden box telephone on the front wall rings, the teacher answers, listens through the little round listening device, walks slowly back to the front of the class—no visible emotion—and tells us in a monotone that the war is over, we can go home. Her equanimity, in retrospect, has me wondering. Maybe she had someone who wouldn't be coming back? Anyway, we all ran home in excitement and my friends and I went to the corner store, bought red, white and blue streamers and decorated our bikes.

Several months later our family went to the Coliseum at the Exhibition grounds where we met up with my father's family (his parents, his younger brother with his wife, and the wife of his older brother, all practically strangers to me). Lining the stadium, above the top row of seats, were huge cards, each bearing a letter of the alphabet—A, B, C. . . . The crowd numbered in the thousands, tens of thousands maybe, making it difficult to find a place under "L" where the nine of us could sit together.

Over the next half hour a din of anticipation engulfs the arena, rises in a crescendo, then—over it all—a blast of horns, the rumble of drums. The crowd hushes. A long moment of anticipation, and then a marching band enters from the far end and the crowd erupts in a thundering roar. Behind the band come the troops, maybe twenty abreast, marching home from war. At ground level rigid lines of soldiers in uniform, in perfect step (how could they contain their excitement?); in the stands, pandemonium—cheering, yelling, crying, laughing. My eight-year-old self found it part-exciting, part-mystifying and somewhat terrifying.

The soldiers march around the perimeter of the field and come, eventually, into formation in the centre where they stand passively, my Uncle Jack among them. Then, suddenly—there must have been a signal of some kind—troops break rank and rush helter-skelter, each toward his own letter of the alphabet, while those in the stands run down the stairs, jump over seats, yelling and waving name signs, until in a great scramble of hugs, kisses and tears, families and lovers are reunited.

Not long after that my father's family was invited to supper—the only time I remember them being in our house. I didn't even wonder at that then; a kid just accepts what *is*. In retrospect, though, it's easy to see we were what these days is called a dysfunctional family.

Now I type so quickly I tend to get carried away. But it always feels so good to talk to you—even on paper. Being back to long distance communication is discouraging, but I know it wasn't by choice. We have to live with the hand we've been dealt. "Deal me up another future from some brand new deck of cards." That's what I want. Bob Seger: "Till It Shines."

I only have one letter from you since the social. I hope there's another coming.

WE GET THE DATE for our conjugal visit. No watching eyes, no listening ears. Three whole days of blissful privacy. My head is swimming with scenarios: X-rated, tender, wild, loving. I want it all.

Then the worries come flooding in, the insecurities over my saggy 47-year-old, soon to be 48-year-old body. Can I contrive to keep it hidden? We go into the trailer at eleven in the morning; it's almost the longest day of the year, it doesn't get dark till nine-thirty. I certainly can't wait that long. My only hope is that they have dark drapes on the windows. Have they thought of that? I doubt it.

I feel like a bride. A long-betrothed, old-fashioned, virginal bride. And I want to look the part—or at least a modified version of it. I envision myself entering this state of being as something untouched, in both the literal and figurative senses. I want to come out changed. Touched.

Shopping is my least favourite activity in the world, but for this I will shop. It's a mission, has significance. On the third foray into mall-land I find an ivory-coloured dress of cotton twill, wrap-around style, held together by only a piece of Velcro at the waist. There's also a button, but we'll leave it undone. After nine years of waiting, lovers should be able to come together by magic: no zippers catching, no buttons being obstinate, no pant legs to trip over. Destiny should be able to take its course without obstruction.

I find stockings and shoes to match the dress. Ivory—semi-virginal—only slightly tainted.

The magical day arrives. Feeling tremendously bride-like I walk, not through a rose bower, but through a metal detector. And my suitcase is submitted for inspection. I'm expecting the placemats, candles and candlestick holders to be declared contraband but they pass. Then I'm escorted up the aisle—er—through various corridors—until we come to the place where Don is waiting, looking particularly ungroom-like in the same old clothes I see every time.

What a strange, strange thing to love someone so long—nine whole years—before being able to express it fully. The Velcro doesn't have to wait very many minutes to do its thing. The curtains don't do theirs—the room is far too light—but who cares? Worry is such a useless thing.

Heavenly, too, it was, to do what are otherwise mundane activities, the daily chores of everyday life. He was in his glory cooking, doing the dishes. I took a picture of him in his apron. "I'm going to send this to the North Bay Nugget," I told him. "Tell them: 'Now what do you think of your Extremely Dangerous Person?' "

Time and freedom. Commodities we'd never had before. Freedom to do what we wanted, when we wanted. With no one watching, or listening. We Play Trivial Pursuit in our own time, play cribbage. We're so evenly matched we have to play game after game to determine a winner. Watch TV. Even deciding what to watch is fun. Make love and make love again. I wake up in the night with the arm of the one who loves me around me and can't believe my fortune, know I will bask in this moment forever. Three whole days of wonder—seventy-two hours—June 10 to 13, 1985. Three days in history.

For Don, however, it was to turn out not so happily. When he got out of the trailer, he had a message to call his sister. In the visit room that afternoon he told me the news: their mother had died. I was surprised he was so upset, yet glad he was showing it. After all this time I was just starting to see what a hurt, shy and nervous person he was. Maybe it took that long for him to trust enough to show it.

Back home I go to see my doctor. She knows about the visit—Janice and I both go to her—she knows our stories. As soon as I walk in, her face lights up in a big smile. "Well, you look better!" she beams. "A good lay keeps the doctor away."

I write Don. "Honestly! That's what she said! Her professional advice! The only thing is I don't know how to fill the prescription when it's needed, which will be mighty often now. Maybe you should work on another unlocked little room, an offer I may not want to refuse this time." ☺

THIS BIG NEWS merits a phone call to June. She was there from the start; she *has to* hear about this. I tell her every detail (sparing the intimacies), how great it was to talk to our hearts' content, to eat together, even cleaning the trailer before leaving was fun. More than worth the wait. Then, to be honest and complete, I get to the bigger picture, to the ups and downs.

"It's an 'up' now and I hope it stays that way," I tell her, then I get to the sore point.

"Remember when I used to get three or four letters a week?" She definitely remembers. In the beginning the receipt of each one had me phoning her, breathing every detail. With her my only confidante, it was exciting, titillating.

"Well, that's changed," I continue, and tell her how I try so hard to explain to him how important letters are to me now that I see him so seldom. He says he understands, he's sorry, and he hates to see me discouraged, but he just can't write.

"I don't see why," I complain. This is getting to be an expensive phone call. "Well, I *do* see why." She listens. Always the listener; never the judge. I go on to tell her how he's so taken up with what could be called a social life, going to all the various groups, his job, his friends, he's in his element now, knows lots of people and is known by everyone, has status. And language no longer limits his ability to socialize. He's in his world, and something is changing.

"He's so enmeshed in prison things, all the dynamics—who said what, who did what—much of which seems infantile to me. He has his world. He lives in that world; I don't. I think he's becoming institutionalized."

She doesn't say a word, waits for me to continue. Although she's never come out and said so, I know she's never really understood this relationship. I wish she would realize my judgment can be trusted, that he's really a good person, a sweet person at heart.

"He's never been anything but kind and supportive to me, and never demanding. So, don't worry about me."

I know she'll keep on worrying.

Hi,

Your letter arrived. Glad to see you got all the postcards I sent. The trip was great—couldn't have been better. Long, though, with more waiting than travelling. Three hours in Toronto and then nearly four and a half hours waiting for Cheryl and Scott to pick us up in Pittsburgh. His new plane is nice—a six-seater (the one we flew in at Christmas was a four-seater). We followed the route of the Ohio River southward and I was surprised to see so much river traffic—barges hauling goods.

Scott keeps his plane at an airport at Huntington, W.V., in what they call the Tri-State area—where Ohio, Kentucky and West Virginia meet. Ashland is not far away. It's too bad we didn't arrive a day earlier; we could have gone to a Judds concert. The whole town was excited about it because they come from Ashland.

For my birthday we went to a restaurant in an old railroad station and I ate—guess what?—lobster! The next day Cheryl took Belinda and me to Carter Cave Park—about 40 miles from there—where we had a 45-minute tour of X Cave (so named for its shape), my first cave. At the juncture of the X was the huge stalactite formation you saw on the postcard, in the shape of a chandelier, with dripping water (the mark of a "live cave" apparently). It was chilly down there at 55 feet below ground and, being dimly illuminated, a bit spooky,

Early Saturday morning, in our role as rich people, we jaunted off in our private plane for an overnight at Myrtle Beach. (How some people live!) We stayed at the Myrtle Beach Hilton (where else?) in a beach-view room on the eleventh floor. (The four of us shared one room to save money.) I spent hours jumping in the waves and got a serious sunburn. I'm a water baby, you know. Did I ever tell you that? When we were in high school Evie and I were on the synchronized swimming team.

On Sunday, about an hour before we were to leave, I was devouring the last bit of ocean (not literally) when the Life Guard called everyone out of the water. Down the beach a group of people had congregated so I went to investigate. A boy about 16 or 17 was lying on the beach unconscious, oxygen tubes in his nose, his leg bandaged, but blood running through on the sand underneath. He had been bitten by a shark. (I had been playing out further than anyone with no thought of danger!) Our lifeguard said the flesh was ripped right off on both sides of the calf. I keep picturing this kid—good looking, blond curly hair, muscular—and wondering how he will be, if he will recover, if it will change his life.

All in all it was a great time—there and in Ashland—and we hated to leave. Janice met us at the airport and took us to her place for supper, where, over our usual bottle of wine, we gave her the play-by-play.

The disappointment of it all was that, on coming back, there was no birthday card from you.

◆   ◆   ◆   ◆

So sorry I missed your phone call, but hope you had a good chat with Belinda. She didn't say much, just told me the date—September 30—for the trailer visit. That's not long! Only nineteen days. Mmmm. . . . I'm imagining things already. . . .

I have a surprise for you. I'm starting a new job. It's a surprise to me, too; the serendipity of how things work constantly amazes me. I wasn't looking for a job at all, was satisfied with what I was doing. *It* came to *me*. Ron Holmberg recommended me to a friend of his who is acting as a recruiter. He called, it sounded interesting, I went in for the interview, and took it. I'll be working for a psychologist who does psychological, aptitude and interest testing as part of candidate screening for a large company. Administering the tests, analyzing the results and writing reports on the findings will be my job. It looks good. It's a small office—only him and a secretary, and it's only one bus to get there (walkable on a good day). The pay is the same as I'm making now but I'll get statutory holidays and vacation time so it will actually be more in the end, and I'm certain to like it. I start immediately, but told him I have "something planned" in the next few weeks and will need to be absent a few days. (If he only knew!!!)

While there I started learning the word processing system they have. Both AES and Micom are going downhill these days because now everyone's starting to use word processing programs on computers. They think it's a big advance and have no idea how slow, laborious and cumbersome it is compared to doing the same thing on a dedicated word processor. I'm going to be extremely frustrated trying to work on it.

THE NEXT NEWS has me writing Joanne in a fury.

"Damn! Damn! And double damn!" I slam onto the page. Then catch myself, explain I wanted to call but I knew it would be a one-hour rant, figured pounding the keyboard would be better—better for *both* of us.

"At work today someone from the prison called and told me the conjugal visit has been cancelled. Seems Don got into the homebrew and was charged. Isn't that a fine how-do-you-do? With *four days* to go! Couldn't he stay out of trouble until it was over? How much does he want it, anyway? Has he no foresight? Of course, he always thinks he won't get caught. Says that's why the threat of prison doesn't work as a deterrent—they just think they won't get caught. I don't know what's with him these days. It seems the closer he gets to advancement, the more he does to prevent it."

Three pages receive the brunt of my anger and frustration. I pour it all out, every grievance, every doubt, vent until—once again—I come around to: "Exasperating as it is, at the same time, I have to admit if I'd been in there that long I sure wouldn't mind a drink or two. It's so hard to know where the line is between being forever the 'understanding female' and demanding what's right for *me*. It's not easy. And it's not clear."

The second conjugal visit comes three months later, six months after the first. I approach it happily, excited, with high expectations. Don comes in like a bear in both attitude and appearance. He's antagonistic, on edge, unpleasant. I have no idea what's wrong and he won't say. I don't think it has anything to do with me because he would say if it were. Maybe it's some issue to do with the Inmates' Committee of which he is now chairman, but again I think he would tell me that. I have the feeling he doesn't know himself. Being in prison that long doesn't do a person any good, that much is certain, but it sure would make things easier if I had some insight into the problem. Even his appearance isn't good. Usually somewhat vain in this regard, he's scruffy, his beard is untrimmed and he needs a haircut. Another visitor once remarked his looks are "somewhere between Kenny Rogers and Grizzly Adams." This time he's somewhere between Grizzly Adams and a grizzly bear.

By evening things have calmed down and the second day everything is back to normal. All the food he ordered is there (we had talked it over), and he's in his element cooking—loves it—and I luxuriate in having meals prepared for me. There's lots of good conversation, laughing, all the fun of being together, and of course a few "intermissions." He's elated about Brenda's imminent arrival, although disappointed Belinda didn't want to come. He loves them, he says, as the daughters he knows he will never have. Brenda arrives on the morning of the third day and we have a great time playing games, chatting, watching TV, all three together. She stays the night and all ends on a happy, optimistic note.

THINGS CONTINUE IN THE SAME pattern. I enjoy being with him, feel good, am encouraged, get a nice letter a few days later and then things go blank. I feel he doesn't do his part, decide I'm no longer going to do everything, am on the verge of quitting when something always happens to change it.

Our first escorted pass comes in March 1986. I enter the reception area of the prison at ten o'clock and he's there waiting, drop dead handsome in a light grey three-piece suit and a navy topcoat. His hair and beard (very grey now) are trimmed to perfection and exceptionally attractive against a well-tanned face. He's gorgeous. Every bit as gorgeous—more gorgeous—than when I made that comment so long ago, when I never once envisioned a moment such as this.

Don had asked a guard he likes, Robert, to accompany us. He proves to be good company, thoughtful and sensitive to the occasion. He's dressed in a similar manner, which is done purposely so there is nothing odd in our appearance as we go about town. We drive around town slowly on a conducted tour, finishing at the waterfront park where the totem pole he worked on is located. We sit at water's edge drinking in the fresh air, the quiet, the greenery, holding hands in the world. Even if I don't live in that sensory-deprived environment, this is as splendorous to me as it must be to him. A transfusion. Robert sits waiting in the car.

For lunch Robert suggests several restaurants, giving us a description of the benefits of each. We decide on the one known for its tasteful service, which he thinks probably has adequate choice for a vegetarian, which I've been for the past two years. It proves to be a quiet yet well-patronized establishment and the lunch is leisurely and delicious, the conversation pleasant and interesting. And I get to pay. For all three, which irks me, but apparently this is what's done. Can't buck tradition.

We go to the biggest mall, walk around window-shopping, taking in all the developments of the past few years. Don buys a shirt, dark green. You'd think he'd have had enough of green by now. Is there significance in this choice? We want to tour the Sir John A. MacDonald house but when we get there, find it closed for the season. The best we can do is take a few pictures in front, to prove we were there.

Sublime it is, to do ordinary things that ordinary people do. And Don is so natural, calm, and his usual all-round good company.

I'm optimistic now and looking forward to the coming progress—a few more escorted passes, probably three, they say—then some unescorted ones before he can be recommended for day parole. It seems there really is a future, and it's less than two months before the next pass rolls around. Don asked the same guard to be his escort, but Robert explained that he had accepted the first time as an exception; he particularly likes Don, but doesn't want others to get the same idea. And so Don asks Alex, who proves to be every bit as pleasant and perspicacious as Robert.

We spend the morning at the John Howard office and are surprised by a cake for Don's birthday. Several of the staff come to join in—pleasant, agreeable company—and we sit around chatting and drinking coffee. Then we go for a long lunch in a busy restaurant with a warm, friendly atmosphere. We sit for an hour and a half discussing, enjoying a delectable meal and, especially, the company: Alex, Barb (the woman from John Howard) and her young daughter, whose presence makes it so natural, human. I don't even mind paying for five people.

It was a day of dreamwalking, of being in the real world, of knowing I'm right. The day floated off into slow motion. We strolled along the waterfront, so nourishing, and being there with him—the wonder of it—of being in public, doing everyday things—had me transported to a place that surely must be called Perfection. I wanted to walk further—walk forever—disappear into the future. Alex was within sight in his car, but Don was so nervous about not doing everything right (for once in his life!), he thought we should go back to the car. So we did. And soon a perfect day floated into memory.

IN THE USUAL TURN OF EVENTS, things go bad. He's in the hole on charges again. I don't even know or understand all of them: possession of contraband, making home brew, not obeying an order. He has an excuse for every one. It does seem some are petty or even manufactured, but all of them? Not likely. What does that say for his desire to progress?

He thinks they're trying to send him back to a higher-level prison. It's all incomprehensible to me. Why is he even still in prison? What purpose does it serve? He's not going to get any "better"—get "cooked"—get "done." Can something be more done than done? More finished than finished? Such a good person with such a potential for happiness and enjoyment of life to have wasted so many years in prison, and in his life on the street, to my way of thinking. Yet I know he can live a nice quiet, ordinary life and be no bother to anyone when he gets out.

"I remain convinced," I tell June in a letter, feeling I've probably worn out both Janice and Joanne on this subject, "no matter what anyone thinks, that he is a good person and worthy of my faith. Whether or not we can get along as a couple in the long run is another issue. I'm not the easiest person to get along with, am fiercely independent, and am not sure I want to live with anyone in any case. All that part remains to be seen. But for the simple person-to-person part of it, I am not wrong."

There *is* one thing, though, that I don't go into, a question that has been creeping in lately, nagging for recognition: if he had been in the population when I met him—had been busy like he is now, taken up with so many activities, had been among so many friends, been involved in the Inmates' Committee, would I have fallen for him in the first place? That's a heavy question. The reality is that when I met him—and for three years after that—he was in the Special Handling Unit, in almost-total isolation, surviving in conditions that set the stage for stimulating conversations about books and ideas, things we heard on As It Happens or read in the newspaper. It's ironic that when his physical world was miniscule, his mental world was vast. I miss that kind of contact. That warm band of understanding that was created then exists still, in the emotional sense, but its basis—what it was founded on—now appears only in vestiges. What keeps me going is the realization that the inner person, the core of a person, doesn't change.

Hello Don,

I received your letter. And how do you think I'm supposed to feel about this news? Accept it without comment? I just don't understand how you can do this. Does it mean nothing to you? The *second* time now that you've lost our trailer visit. Is following the rules too much to ask when that's the reward? *Don't I mean more to you than that? How much does having the trailer visit mean to you anyway? Nothing, apparently. And here we are, more than a year past your parole eligibility date and you still haven't even had unescorted passes.* You say I'm living in Fantasy Land, that you'll have to serve at least seventeen years before you get out. Well, you're making sure it's that long. You predict it and then you make it come true. Six months now since the last one, and who knows how long before the next, the way you're going. I'm really so angry I'll refrain from saying more.

◆   ◆   ◆   ◆

Guess what! I'm a grandmother! I can't believe it. (Does that mean I have to retire to the rocking chair?) Pam had a baby boy. Jason. Born on Sunday. "Sunday's Child"—like me. "And the child that is born on the Sabbath day is bonny and lithe and good in every way." That's me all right. Don't you agree? ☺

The day he was born I got the news early in the morning, before going with my hiking club to Lake Placid. I was so bursting with excitement that I went up to two women in the group—complete strangers—and told them. They looked at me like I had just arrived from space.

◆   ◆   ◆   ◆

Back from Orillia now. Stayed for a week, helping Pam. Rolls and rolls of film were taken, which made me regret again that I have so few pictures of my kids—almost none—as babies and growing up. Not nice for them, either. Do you have any of yourself as a kid? I suspect not with all the moving around you've done. I don't know why I didn't take more. The only thing I can think of is that picture taking wasn't part of my growing up experience; there are no photos of me as a baby and very few later on. On the other hand, you'd think *that* would have made me conscious of the importance of having pictures. Maybe I was just too busy to think. My husband obviously didn't think either. I'm sure he has no pictures of himself of a child—I never saw any, anyway. We did take movies, though, and only after I got my things from the house did I realize he had hidden the camera and films along with a few other items. So, I guess at least the kids will be able to see them when they want. That's a consolation.

Can you believe Belinda is 16 already and has a summer job? I taught her how to operate the Micom; she registered with the agency I worked for, passed the test, and is now working for them. At twice the minimum wage. My last baby off to work. She has one more year of CEGEP and then will be off to university. Not here, she tells me—has to try her wings. What can I say since I've tended to use mine from time to time?

Cheryl called. You'll remember after breaking up with Scott she moved to Lexington. But she hasn't been happy there so she's moving back to Galveston next month. She wanted to know if I would go there and help drive her car back. I'm thrilled she asked and look forward to it.

◆   ◆   ◆   ◆

Did you get the postcard I sent from New York City? I had no idea I was going there! But I'm not the only stupid one. I asked several people (including you!), "What am I going to do in Newark, New Jersey for five hours?" and no one was more informed than I was.

Imagine my astonishment—and the thrill of it!—when on the circle for the landing I found myself looking down on the Statue of Liberty! And then a breathless view of the city. In the airport it took some minutes for me to come to my senses, but finally I realized that for five dollars I could buy a bus ticket to Grand Central Station. We went through the Holland Tunnel into Manhattan; I saw the Brooklyn Bridge, the Manhattan Bridge, the World Trade Centre, the Empire State Building, part of Park Avenue and a corner of Central Park. Can you imagine? Such a bit of serendipity! I went into Grand Central, walked along 42nd St. and Lexington Ave.—streets names I've known all my life. They're real! Sights I'd never seen before popped out at every turn: vendors selling hot pretzels and smoked sausage from their carts; a shoeshine stand; many street people, some drinking openly; streets that never see sunshine.

Today I'm just resting while Cheryl is at work. When she comes home we'll continue with the packing. Tomorrow she'll give me her car for sightseeing. Just a note for now, to tell you I got here OK and am thinking of you. Will write more later.

◆   ◆   ◆   ◆

Here I am, in Galveston, sitting on the deck at my niece's, looking out on Galveston Bay. She now lives west of the city, in a beach house on stilts. The weather is hot and humid—81°F when we got here at nearly eleven o'clock last night.

The movers were more than twenty-four hours late arriving, which was a big stress and meant we had two long days of driving—from eight o'clock in the morning till late at night both days—and couldn't go into New Orleans as planned. A disappointment, but with Cheryl starting work Monday morning it couldn't be helped.

The trip was enjoyable, and spending the time with Cheryl was good. Cruising along with us the entire distance was Fleetwood Mac. From the fervour of the sing-along beside me, my guess is that they send coded messages to her, like the ones that come to me from Bob Seger, James Taylor, Leonard Cohen and others.

It was a picturesque route through a variety of landscapes. Superhighway all the way, with hardly a town in sight. Did see Nashville in the distance, though. The soft open hills of Kentucky and Tennessee rolled into magnificent big ones in northern Alabama, with amazing forests. We stopped for the night at a motel just south of Birmingham. Seeing the turnoff signs to Montgomery and Selma was surreal. Somehow—I know it doesn't make sense, is naive—yet somehow it seemed to me as if all those places with their civil rights struggles occurred in TV-land.

Abruptly, near the end of Mississippi, within a short distance of thirty miles, we found ourselves in swampland, going around bayous; evergreens had become willows shrouded in Spanish moss. Beautiful, but somewhat eerie. West of New Orleans was otherworldly: a hundred miles with no houses, no towns, no people—just the road built high up over swamp in an incredible feat of engineering, and long, long bridges (the longest was eighteen miles).

Lured by a series of billboards advertising the Old Fish Market Restaurant, we turned into a town and found it. We both ordered Blackened Catfish, which sounds bad but was scrumptious. Catfish seems to be the popular fish of Louisiana.

Crossing the Mississippi was a thrill, then, near the Texas border, ranch land began. By the time we got here I had seen so many dead armadillos on the road (and vultures eating them) that it's easy to understand the joke:

Question: "Why did the armadillo cross the road?"

Answer: "To see if it was possible."

Today Cheryl will take me to see the apartment she has rented. Who knows when the furniture will arrive? She goes to work tomorrow, and I fly back.

Waiting for the movers gave extra time for sightseeing around Lexington. Cheryl drove me around the countryside—the heart of horse country and remarkably different from that around Ashland. Pastures everywhere, all of them enclosed by the classic white-painted wood slat fences. I had to try hard to see the blue in the grass, but "think" I did. Houses, barns and well-manicured grounds were all the picture of prosperity. We can say there is a lot of money in horse country.

We went to the Kentucky Horse Park, which is quite extensive, comprising several museums. The Parade of Breeds was interesting, a half-hour show where they bring out several breeds and explain how their characteristics suit them to the purposes they serve. One of them was a Lipizzaner, which was a thrill to see because they always seemed to me, from my reading of novels as a young girl, to be mythical. Sometimes my heart wants to burst for the need to have you with me, at my side, to share these things. But I "share" them by telling you in letter and by thought waves—the only ways I can. It's a consolation.

I'm wondering how you are, if you have any news yet on your status. Hope you're holding up OK. I try not to worry, try to be optimistic and hope for good news when I return. Claire Culhane is staying at my place. The instant she spied my Van Goghs on the wall she exclaimed, "Ah! We're soulmates in more ways than one!" What an excited conversation that led to. Turns out she has a male friend—fathom this!—who often sends quotations to *her!*

Look forward to spending time with her when I get back. How she keeps calm and a sense of humour is more than I know. You would, though; you have that quality yourself—so foreign to me.

AFTER OUR FIRST MEETING Claire put me on her mailing list. Frequently the easily recognizable trademark envelope would arrive, the previous addressee's name and address struck out and mine written to the side. In its first life the envelope had been carefully opened by knife; in its second incarnation a strip of scotch tape closed the slash. Inside would be several photocopies of articles of interest—news from the system, actions she had taken—each photocopied on the back of used paper and cut to size, all stapled to an explanatory note written or typed on a strip of paper. Not an inch of paper was wasted. With a mailing list in the hundreds, this was a lot of work. Claire was not only thrifty—doing all this work on next to no income—but, being ahead of the rest of us, she was mindful of the need to conserve common resources. Every action she took was testimony to a fully integrated life.

Her third book, *Still Barred From Prison: Social Injustice in Canada* had been published the year before. All this time—since 1976—she had been freely visiting in prisons everywhere except British Columbia and, in fact, had excellent working relations with the Commissioner of Penitentiaries. It was time, she and her supporters felt, to take action. A suit was launched against both the provincial and federal systems. Each backed down days before the slated court hearing and she was readmitted to all B.C. prisons.

The next year Claire came to stay with us again, this time for a month, and it would be impossible to have a guest who took up less space—physically or psychologically. She slept on the couch in the living room, her little overnight bag (her entire luggage) hidden from view at the far end. She had one change of clothing, washed out her T-shirt and underwear every night, yet she had an uncanny knack of never being in the bathroom or the kitchen or on the phone when they were needed. Socially, she was unobtrusive—friendly and chatty but not "in your face." And always good-humoured.

Short and stocky, she had grey wavy hair as wayward and unruly as herself, although I'm not sure she tried very hard to "rule" it. Handmade beaded necklaces given to her in appreciation by native prisoners often decorated her simple, second hand clothes. If she had an important meeting or a speaking engagement she would throw a brightly coloured scarf around her neck in the illusion that her T-shirt had been transformed. A specially-dabbed smear of lipstick completed the picture, and off she went.

Her energy was boundless, and when she came in at eight or nine in the evening, she would tell me about her day: a meeting with a lawyer at the *Office* or with a warden; a visit with a prisoner or two; a talk to a Criminology class; or perhaps she had had lunch with an old friend, having grown up in Montreal. Almost every day she had dealings with officials regarding problems in the prisons. "The best fight in town," she called it. If she needed to talk to the Commissioner of Penitentiaries, a Member of Parliament, or even the Solicitor General she would phone their office briefly and they would return her call because they were on toll free lines.

"And do you know what the bastard said?" she would ask rhetorically, her dark eyes crinkled up in a pixyish grin, the voice soft, light-hearted. She always called them bastards, yet it was with affection—or at least with understanding if she couldn't muster the former. I admired her ability to deal pleasantly with people whose views we considered unreasonable, thoughtless, even inhumane at times. Her solid sense of what is right kept her on an even keel.

Claire's involvement in prison issues had begun in 1974 when she took a volunteer job teaching a Women's Studies class to incarcerated women. The following year, a month after the hostage taking at B.C. Pen that resulted in the killing of C.O. Mary Steinhauser by staff, prisoners were staging a sit-in to protest the extreme conditions they were still enduring. Claire joined demonstrators in their support, was branded "pro-prisoner" and her class was cancelled. That lit her fire; the fight was on. She, with others, founded the Prisoners' Rights Group.

We talked about our children's attitudes toward unconventional mothers, the time we spent working on causes when the children would have preferred we be home, the resentment they can have. I had worked in the women's movement and the anti-poverty movement in the seventies; Claire had been a ceaseless activist in many causes. "Well, I figure," she said, "if they're not on drugs and they're not in jail, I've been a success."

A success she must have been because for her seventieth birthday, her two daughters, along with many supporters, had commissioned the writing of her biography. She asked me if the author, Mick Lowe, her ex-son-in-law, could stay overnight. He was going to interview her and she was going to show him around the city, point out the places important to her early life.

Mick, for his part, was also a charming house guest, and it was a thrill to look through his finished manuscript for *Conspiracy of Brothers: A True Story of Murder, Bikers and the Law,* which was in a box, ready for submission to the publisher. A compelling read that was voted Best True Crime book of 1988 by the Crime Writers of Canada, it was the story of six bikers and the strong evidence that they were wrongfully convicted. The title reflects the conspiracy that took place on both sides, by the bikers and the police.

Mick's biography of Claire is called *One Woman Army.* And that she was.

Joanne, over this time, had also become friends with Claire. When, a few years later, she moved to Vancouver as an inducement for officials to transfer Sean there (things appearing to be a dead end in Ontario), she stayed temporarily with Claire in her tiny apartment-cum-office and helped with the work of the Prisoners' Rights Group. Every conceivable space was given over to a well-ordered filing system—cabinets and boxes—and extension cords running everywhere to accommodate phone, computer, fax and copy machines, on top of the usual household necessities. A mirror was set up at her desk in the living room so she could work and watch the news on TV at the same time. Speaking at Claire's funeral in 1996, Joanne described how on her first day, while searching for a tea towel, she discovered that even the kitchen drawers were stuffed with files.

A year earlier another of Claire's famous cut/taped/stapled missives arrived. "Can you believe this?" she wrote, and I can still hear the soft lilt of her voice, see the sparkle in her eye. "The bastards gave me the Order of Canada!"

And sure enough, attached were photocopies of newspaper articles on the investiture. At first, she decided not to accept it, she explained, thought participating in an "establishment" event wouldn't be appropriate, and she worried about what the prisoners might think. But family and friends convinced her that she deserved the honour and the prisoners would be proud of her. She died, however, feeling that all her work had been for naught, that she had been unable to change anything.

Dear Don,

Two weeks now since I saw you and still no letter. Have you recovered yet from your humiliating loss at crib? Never mind, maybe next time I'll let *you* win a couple of games. Ha!

Things are fine here. I spoke to Jacob about the raise. I didn't get the raise but I got something better—time. From now on I'll be working four days a week for the same pay, which is effectively a twenty percent raise. I look forward to a more relaxed life with lots of time to get things done at home, and going to see you won't seem so "squeezed in."

Pam and Jason—who's four months old already—came for the weekend. Saturday the four of us drove to Quebec City and walked ourselves into exhaustion through Upper Town, down into Lower Town (where the streets are so narrow laundry is strung overhead from one side to the other) and then—stroller and all—we climbed the stairs on the edge of the cliff up to the cold and windy Plains of Abraham. Terrifying for Pam with her fear of heights.

THE FIRST CONFERENCE on penal abolition had been a success. Two years later its successor was held in Amsterdam and since then it has convened in various countries almost every two years. In 1987, Montreal was the host city and Ruth Morris came to stay with me. A person who "witnessed to her beliefs," as Quakers say, her life was a reflection of her spiritual understanding. She wasn't naïve, though. Her trust in people had been betrayed at times, and she wrote with compassion about overcoming betrayal through the power of faith.

"Abolition is such a Utopian goal," I told her, "with so little hope of becoming reality. How do you keep working on it?"

"We are not called to be successful," she told me, "we're called to be faithful." An oft-repeated Quaker expression, but it was the first time I heard it.

Three years later, dying and too sick to go to Ottawa, the Lieutenant Governor of B.C. came to their home (she and her husband had moved there for retirement) to present her with the Order of Canada.

QUAKER HOSPITALITY is a nourishing thing. Kirsten and Ghislain called and asked if they could come to stay a few nights. I had met them only once at Friends House in Toronto when I stayed overnight and Kirsten was Resident Friend. We became friends and in later years I often stayed with them in Toronto on my annual trips home from Thailand and Mexico.

An attender of Edmonton Meeting phoned one evening, explained that a Toronto Friend had given him my name. He was doing research for his thesis and needed a place to stay in Montreal for a week. Could he possibly stay with us? Of course he could.

Steve's research was on the rescue (or capture—depending on your point of view) and deprogramming of young people who had become involved in cults. An easy and accommodating house guest, Steve regaled us with stories about the people he had interviewed, things he had learned, dangers he had encountered, all of which made scintillating contributions to our evenings.

One afternoon Belinda came rushing back into the apartment on her return from an interview at the Hare Krishna temple with Steve.

"Mom! Oh, Mom! They're so nice! I didn't know they would be so nice! I want to join them!"

My heart plummets. Steve lurks in the hallway, looking shame-faced.

"Oh, Mom! We had such a good time! They invited me back tomorrow, to a special lunch they're having. I'm going!" She's seventeen; she doesn't need my permission, she'll go if she wants to. What can I do? What can I say?

"I tried to talk her out of it," Steve offers with a look of concern and a helpless gesture, "but she's determined. I'm sorry."

I can't find the words I want to say—at least not the polite ones. There follows a long, painful silence.

Then they break out laughing.

The friendship of Friends is a precious gift. In future years I would stay with Friends I didn't know in England, Germany and Belgium, as well as in Canada. One always knows beforehand that one will share values and will live the same simple lifestyle in which we try to "walk softly on the earth."

I GO TO SEE DON. The Saturday afternoon visit is wonderful—the usual warm time with lots to tell each other, things to share from our separate worlds and a few dynamic, laugh-filled games of crib. I'm staying with Joanne for the weekend, as I do every time, and we always have a good time, too. So, it's a good start to the weekend, heartening and fun.

Then comes Sunday morning. I arrive excited to tell him all about what we did the night before. It's not long, though, before things go wildly off track and I stalk out in a huff before time is even over.

Those two visits stand as a microcosm of the state of the relationship itself.

I drive back to Montreal infuriated all the way, phone Janice as soon as I get home and ask her to come for supper. I don't know why I can't suffer in silence, why I'm compelled to tell at least one person my problems. If she and Joanne are having trouble in their relationships, I don't hear about it. The only complaints I hear from Janice—and lots of them—are about the system in Massachusetts. David never gets charges yet he doesn't progress either. So, Janice comes for supper and over a bottle of wine (lovely living in Quebec where you can go to the corner store at the last minute and get one), I bombard her with every detail.

It started with me telling him about the play Joanne and I had gone to the night before, Angels With Dirty Faces. He had seen the movie and that led to a lively discussion of the ins and outs of the plot, the motivation of the characters, their morals, and the big point, the ending: Did James Cagney fake the fear of execution as the priest had asked him to, or was he actually scared? A rousing, lively discussion—just like old times. When we communicate like that I feel drawn in, warm, comfortable, part of a whole; it feels so right. It's what drew me to him in the first place.

Then. . . . Oh, then. Then, the other side.

He was telling me about the young guys who get transferred in from other pens, how he's disgusted with their remarks, how they compare the facilities of one prison to those of another "as if they're comparing the Park Plaza to the Hilton."

He's really worked up about this. "It's as if they're *pleased* to be here," he says incredulously. Then, in a great burst of emotion, as if issuing a proclamation, declares, "This is *not* my *home!*"

"Well, you seem to be trying pretty hard to *make* it your home," I throw back with my characteristic lack of diplomacy. This leads to a particularly unpretty scene in which he berates me for living in a fantasy world, for thinking there will be passes and parole while in reality they're trying to send him back to Maximum and it will be years before those things happen, if ever. And so we fall into a circular, very heated argument with me trying to convince him he's his own worst enemy, that he sets himself up for defeat, and him telling me I don't know anything about the system.

"But the way he said it," I tell Janice, "the way he emphasized '*This is not my home*' with such intensity, makes me think it's a subject close to the bone.

Maybe something the psychologist or the C.O. has said to him. It had to come from somewhere."

What I wonder about more and more, and Janice and I discuss it: What does how one handles solitary confinement say about a person? Does it provide a setting that allows the Inner Self to come to the fore, the real character? Or was what I saw at that time just clever survival techniques that I can't hope to see when there are alternatives? As a gregarious person he's in his element now, no longer has a need for reading and listening to the radio. He watches television, sure, but TV lacks the intimacy and depth of radio. We used to have such fun discussing what we heard on As It Happens or Morningside and the books we read. He's still up on the news, though, never misses a thing there. Always more current than me in that department.

"I know I should give up, but it's like any marriage, isn't it?" I ask Janice rhetorically. "You remember the good times, think of the good qualities, try to be understanding, try not to expect perfection, think of all the time invested. . . . "

After Janice leaves I take out our latest photo. Both his arms around me, and I fit the space so perfectly—two parts of a puzzle that belong together. So much warmth, fun, closeness and understanding radiating from it; we're sharing what we have and we're happy. Those are not pose-for-the-picture smiles, but genuine ones that spring from that deep place. Anyone seeing this picture without knowing the background would be sure he or she was seeing the joy of a couple caught in the rush of new love. Yet, at the same time, the old-shoe comfort of two people who have been together a long time and are totally at ease with each other comes through. It's all there. And continues to hold me in spite of logic.

Dear Don,

That was a nice social. And it was so good to get outside, wander around the grounds a bit. The food was excellent too, although vegetarianism has yet to make inroads into the prison world, I see.

Now that you're at Joyceville and I'm forced to rent a car, I get a chance to catch up on what's new in the world of music (three hours of radio each way). I didn't realize I was so far behind. Heard new ones from Bob Seger and James Taylor that I didn't even know about. When I lived in North Bay, between my work and going to see you, I practically lived in my car so I had a lot of listening time. And then I was exposed to the kids' music. Now there's only Belinda and it's funny she doesn't listen to music at all. Don't know why.

On the way back they played one I hadn't heard for ages. Warmed my heart—so nostalgic—"The First Time Ever I Saw Your Face" by Roberta Flack. One of my all-time favourites. A lot of memories there.

"The first time ever I saw your face." That goes back, doesn't it? There are two "first times," though, aren't there?—the first time in court and the first time I came to see you, different in nature yet linked. And both remain vivid, like they happened yesterday. Then "the first time ever I kissed your mouth." More than three years later. Not many can say that. Not many *have to* say that. And then a long wait for the next line to happen—"The first time ever I lay with you"—six whole years more. I'm sure the person who wrote the song didn't wait nine years from the "seeing" to the "laying." ☺ *And how much longer do I have to wait to lay with you again? Or for anything, for that matter. Any kind of progress.*

Also, there was an absolutely mesmerizing half-hour interview with a psychologist who explained the neurological effects of music on the brain. He started with the beat. It's a pulse, he said, that fuses with our own pulse, taps into the primitive brain. Too bad I didn't hear it on the way there instead of on the way back; it would have been fresh to tell you. He talked about the relationship between music and emotions, said as a means of arousing feelings, music has far more power than language. I could have told him that. But for each point he had what I don't have—the results of studies in which changes in the brain were observed and measured. Of course can I remember any of the facts now? There was lots of proof of how the pleasure-seeking areas of the brain are stimulated in the same way they are by fats and sugars. Proved by increased levels of dopamine. "Similar to sex, eating and taking heroin," he said. Music as comfort food. I love it! So now there's scientific proof for why I'm so taken by music. What he didn't talk about—and what I'm wondering—is why some people seem to be so much less affected.

◆   ◆   ◆   ◆

Thanksgiving weekend Belinda and I, Pam and Jason, along with Pam's friend, Cathy, made the trip to Stowe, Vermont. Jason, at fifteen months, discovered and mastered the wonder of the guesthouse stairs—the highlight of his trip. Ours was driving up, down and around all the winding roads, taking in the fantastic views, and eating in a hilltop restaurant with a panorama of autumn colours. And a trip to Stowe would not be complete without seeing where the Von Trapp family settled after their escape from Austria. Very enjoyable. And I mentally transmitted it all to you. Did you receive? ☺

◆   ◆   ◆   ◆

Did you hear Sean was involuntarily transferred to Archie and they're trying to get him classified Supermax? The good part for me is that now Joanne can stay with me for a change. I look forward to many such weekends, although I know she wants him back in Kingston as soon as possible. How they get away with these things with no consideration for family is more than I know.

Joanne has finally had enough. She went to the media. Did you happen to catch her on a CBC TV news segment? They've really got her anger up now—to the point where she no longer cares who knows about her secret life, at work or anywhere. The fight is more important. Guess I'm not there yet. Last year when I was interviewed by CBC radio about the building of that godforsaken prison at Port Cartier, hundreds of miles from nowhere, where guys will be lucky to get one visit a year, I used an alias. The only reason for the building of that prison was that it was a make-work project in Mulroney's riding.

◆   ◆   ◆   ◆

Joanne came over on Thursday evening this time to see a lawyer Friday about getting Sean back to Millhaven. It looks hopeful. I often wonder what the guys who have no one to fight for them do. They must live without hope.

We went to a Jubilation Gospel Choir concert at the Salvation Army Citadel on Saturday night. I've seen them several times—always a rousing performance—sometimes free, and if not free, then cheap. This one was free. I don't think she was really keen to go (the name could well put one off) but in the end she thoroughly enjoyed it.

One number, which I found especially inspiring, was "The Storm is Passing Over."

"See now," I told her, "there's a message for you: 'The storm is passing over.' "

"Yeah," she quipped, "but they didn't tell us there's another one right behind."

BELINDA LEAVES for Queens University and I have to find a cheaper apartment. I settle on the one Dot—a member of the Meeting with whom I'm friendly—is leaving. It's cheap, tumble-down, well-located in the McGill Ghetto, steps from *Place-des-Arts* and a short walk to both The Main and Downtown. And with the apartment I inherit Dot's apartment mate, Jean-Pierre, a street musician who doesn't speak a word of English and is so shy that in the beginning he's no more than a fleeting shadow down the hallway. In time, however, he gets used to me and our long daily conversations give the final boost to my second language acquisition. And his harpsichord and clarinet music enliven the space.

This apartment is a five-minute walk from McGill's concert venue, Pollack Hall. Up to three evenings a week, I can be found there, usually alone but sometimes with Jean-Pierre or with Judith, a new friend who lives next door. Free, and offering a great variety of musical genres, it is another reason to love Montreal, as is Place-des-Arts where I often go to hear the Montreal Symphony Orchestra. Judith, Jean-Pierre and I took in a spellbinding performance by Anton Kuerti one night. A few nights later when I asked him if he wanted to go to a chamber music quintet with me, Jean-Pierre said he couldn't possibly go to another concert for some time, the piano concerto had touched him so deeply. I well understood. That had been my reaction to the Bob Seger concert.

DON HAD HIS SECOND PAROLE hearing. I was already in the room when he entered in a temper, snarled at me. I had no idea why. I told him again—I'd already told him several times—that he didn't need to worry about me messing things up; I would support him in any way I could, my support was in no way related to the deteriorating state of the relationship. That was easy: I knew he was through with crime and could live a good life on the street without being a problem to anyone.

The day parole was turned down again, of course, because he still hadn't passed any of the hurdles.

When the hearing was over we went downstairs and the afternoon visit had started. He didn't want to go in. He's tired, he says. I've rented a car and driven over from Montreal and he's tired. He's tired and I'm pissed.

Don,

You say I sound like a broken record, that I should hear myself, that you should tape me. Well, how many times do I have to repeat myself to get you to hear? I try every way, choose all the words I can think of, to try to make you understand. Here we are, nearly three years since the last trailer visit, and why? *You really think I'm supposed to go along with this? And it's all things "they" do to you. Never anything you've done.* And only two passes, and them so long ago. Why? *I'm bloody fed up, that's what I am.* Just when there were real signs of progress—of hope for the future—you chose to sabotage yourself. *Why you would do this is beyond me. And why you can't see what you're doing is even more beyond me.* You say I don't understand. Well, I don't. And that's the truth of it.

You say there's no way you'll be paroled before seventeen years minimum. *Why is it always seventeen? Why not sixteen—or eighteen? What is this magic number based on?* Well, you're making sure that's what happens. A self-fulfilling prophecy. The reason I let it upset me—and repeat and repeat—is that I know the dear person you are deep-down, and I know there's no sense to you being there. I've seen how you are with all kinds of people, and there are so many good people who like you and are willing to help, yet you continue to shoot yourself in the foot. I'm at a loss to understand. You remind me of the ones in *Cuckoo's Nest* who weren't committed yet *chose* to stay. And what did you have to say about them?

So, I repeat and repeat. I don't know what else to do.

WE LIMP ALONG FOR NEARLY a year in the same pattern. The affection remains strong. I never doubt his basic goodness, nor do I doubt his love for me. But the situation has become untenable; it clearly isn't working and appears unlikely to change. The stretches between visits get longer and longer. No letters pass in either direction.

February 16, 1989

Dear June,

How are you? Hope everything is going well for you.

Did you notice the postmark on the envelope? Here I am, back where it all started—North Bay—the beginning and the end of the story.

And what are you doing in North Bay, you ask? Beginning and end of what story? I *do* have a way of confusing people, don't I?

One thing at a time. I'm in North Bay because I'm working here. I'll explain that part later. More important things to tell first. After all this time— more than twelve years—it's over. Officially over, that is—it's been more or less over for some time—and I'm furious. In a rage! And not because it's over. I'm mad because *I*—the ever-thoughtful female, always thinking of others' feelings—would have ended it long ago but didn't have the heart. "How could I leave him after all that time, poor boy, with him in there like that, counting on me as my support person. . . .?" Etc. and etc. Yeah, poor him, all right. But did he give a moment's thought to *me* or *my* feelings or what I thought when *he* decided? No, he just made a unilateral decision.

"I've made a decision. . . .," he wrote in a curt note. *He* made a decision! What *he* wants is what counts. How arrogant!

That's the first thing. But what *really* enrages me is that a man—even a man in prison—even a *50 year-old man* in prison—can get a woman whenever he wants! Can you beat that? It's infuriating!

I knew there was someone on the scene, of course; he had hinted about having "visits from Toronto" two or three times. And I knew I was supposed to say, "Oh? And who might that be?" but wouldn't bite. I knew, too, that he had invited someone else to a social because I showed up the same day (and she didn't). She, however, was from Sudbury, so it's evident he was looking around for prospects, auditioning for my replacement so to speak. I know why, too; I'll get to that in a minute. Then about a month ago Joanne let me know he was mushing it up with a woman in the visit room. (Sean finally made it to Medium and was transferred to the same prison.)

The third thing I'm mad at is *her*. I'm enraged that she steps in for the easy part, at the end, when there's a future to look to, the good times to come, unescorted passes and parole, while I went through all the hard years, the years behind glass. Then I get more honest with myself and admit there were going to be no good times, would be no easy part. Who knows how long it will be before he ever makes it to the street, and it wasn't going to work between us anyway, and that's the truth of it. I was going to tell him how to live his life, and he wasn't going to listen. The brutal reality—what we've known from the very first—is that he wasn't going to fit into my world, and I would have no desire to enter his. A cabin in the woods for two months, that's where I wanted to live out my fantasy. Or in a glass bubble.

You were there at the beginning so I want to tell you about the end. It's ambiguous. I went to see him in early December, the first time in three months—didn't plan it, was passing through Kingston, stopped to see Belinda, and figured I might as well while I was there. When he came into the visit room and saw it was me, he lit into me with an anger I've never seen before. Told me in no uncertain terms what he thought about me—one characteristic, that is—a conclusion he had made from something that happened so long ago. All that time—three whole years!—he'd been harbouring these thoughts and feelings and had never said a word.

For quite some time now, as you know, I've been almost totally uninvolved emotionally—no longer cared what happened one way or another, given his overall attitude, his unwillingness to follow the rules in order to advance. And so, given that there really was no longer a functioning relationship, this tirade didn't even upset me. I just sat back and listened, and when he was finished I calmly explained my side. Well, that changed everything. It was as if calendar pages flipped back years in an instant. The old warm connection fell into place, we held hands across the table (chairs are fixed—can't get any closer) and had a lovely, easy time the rest of the visit.

When time was up he walked me to the visitors' exit where we clung to each other in a kind of desperation, madly, while the rest of the guys stood lined up at their door. They wait, the guard is waiting, the whole room is waiting. Time is suspended, and we're clinging to each other, unable to let go. I'll always have that image in my head—the last time I saw him—until finally the guard started toward us, slowly (reluctantly, I fancy), stood beside us without a word, and we had no choice but to part.

There was one more contact. Two weeks later he phoned. Funny how the mind works, I can remember nothing of the conversation, of the purpose of the call, or if there was one. I remember only the last words: "I love you." The last words he said to me. *The end is ambiguous. Kris stands beside her . . . and the last words he says to her are: "I love you."*

So it was with a little disappointment that I received Joanne's news but not a lot because deep down I know it wasn't going to work. As Van Gogh once said, "It's a study that didn't come off." In the end I think there are two things that are true: we still loved each other when we parted but each of us had let the other down.

There was a time when I thought it might work on the street—when he made it to Medium, when Classification Officers and psychologists were so positive, and it looked like he was going to advance. There was a chance, maybe. But that changed. What changed it? Time? Institutionalization? Things in my own attitude? There's no one answer, but I do know (or think I know) what triggered the end.

He called me at the office one day and said something about parole plans and living with me. Well, diplomacy is not my suit. "We'll talk about that later," is what a thoughtful person would have said, or—even better—I should have just pointed out he'd have to live in a Halfway House before he could do anything. But no, Ms Impetuous blurts out with, "The way we've been getting along lately, there's no way you can live with me." I don't know what's wrong with me sometimes. But it was the truth.

From then on I noticed a change. I think that got him to thinking that if he couldn't count on me, he'd better look elsewhere.

So, here I am—ironically—back in North Bay, back where it all started, working up at the military base. Things were getting crazy at the psychologist's office (especially him; I think *he* needs a psychologist!) and so on a Thursday in January I gave two weeks' notice. Saturday morning I sat down with a coffee and the Montreal Gazette to look for my new job. And there it was—Wanted: Teachers, Willing to Travel.

It's a temporary job, testing the spoken English of Francophone members of the armed forces. A company has contracted to do the testing on all bases across the country in a blitz over the next few months. Twelve of us had a two-week training course at a military training facility at St-Jean-sur-Richelieu, not far from Montreal, which was like living in a hotel. All but one of the others had been teaching English as a Second Language to adults, which made me think that's what I should do next.

So, here I am at the North Bay base for six weeks, on what I consider to be a paid vacation. I have a nice room, eat in the Officers' Mess, go to aquafit classes in the recreation centre, and spend time with my friends. Too bad you aren't here. So far I've seen Barb a few times, Sue, and one of my former co-workers, but I find Paula has moved to Sudbury. Ivy, you'll remember, moved to Windsor a few years ago to live with her boyfriend.

The work is far from onerous. We're only expected to interview a maximum of five people a day (many days I do only two or three), and the interview can be from twenty to forty minutes long. Plus I learn lots about the military. It's another world.

Well, dear June, that's it from here. My story. You were there, weren't you? From beginning to end. I know you'll be glad it's over. You never really understood, and I was never able to really explain. But I will say with my dying breath: "He is a good person, a sweet, loving person, who loved me in a helpful, encouraging way." And I will never regret the time I spent with him.

EPILOGUE

NEW TIMES. NEW PLACES, NEW FACES.

"Do you miss Montreal?" people asked me for years. I loved it when I lived there but didn't miss it—rarely even thought of it—after I left. Living in Thailand, devoting all your energy to untangling the mysteries of an inscrutable culture will do that for you. There I taught English as a Second Language at a Teachers' College for eight months and Literacy in a UN refugee camp for the next four. Then, because Pam now had two children—Kirsten had arrived three years after Jason, serendipitously on my birthday—I decided to go to Toronto to be near them, to be what I never had, a grandmother. There, another world opened to me—the world of ballet—when I became a House Parent in the residence of the National Ballet School.

A blessing it is, I think, that good memories linger while, over time, the not-so-good ones seem to disappear. In Toronto, the Persian Garden hung on the living room wall, a pleasant reminder, soft background music, singing of the love and devotion that went into it. Its symbolism—its many affirmations of life—enriched the ambiance. But by this time Janice was divorced from David and had no further contacts with the system, Joanne and I had fallen out of touch, and no one in my daily life knew my story. The name Don Kelly never came up.

Life moved on. After four years at the ballet school I returned to Thailand—another year and a half at the college, followed by two years at a Buddhist temple, breathing along with dying AIDS patients. That, contrary to most people's expectations, was a period of total contentment. Relationships (built, in the beginning, mostly on eye contact and touch), were of the basic essence: filled with pure love, undemanding and unjudging. Later, when my Thai became fluent, comradeship was added; we were partners in the most intimate of missions. I lived in the present, every moment vital, every day satisfying.

On to Mexico City. First, six months as a volunteer at the *Casa de los Amigos*, the Quaker Centre there, and then three years teaching English to adults. Classes were small, often individual, and mostly Conversation. Since Mexicans are endowed with an enthusiastic curiosity and a cutting skepticism, class discussions were lively, interesting and well-informed; teaching was more akin to a social life than a job. I loved life in that city, the only place I've ever lived that I truly miss. Learning the intricacies of the public transportation system is a job in itself; seeking out its more than one hundred museums, an avocation. I became functional in Spanish, travelled to many parts of the country, had friends. Don Kelly's face never passed behind my eyes.

We glide along in our experience until something stuns. Back in Toronto in 2004, retired now, June calls to tell me she and Ken have moved back to North Bay after twenty-two years in Florida. And she has news. She heard that Don was out on parole but was sick and very thin.

I'm hit as if by a thunderbolt. Fifteen years have floated by with barely a thought from one year's end to the other, and I'm struck. *If he's dead . . . if he's dead and I never see him again. . . .*

Seeing him again is a thought that had never once entered my head in all these years—I haven't even wondered where he is or what he's doing; yet in this shock I learn not seeing him is a thought I can't bear. June is bewildered by my reaction. The truth is even *I* don't understand it.

What to do about it? He could be dead by now—this news is two or three years old already—dead and I don't even know. Or dying at this very moment.

I have no idea how to verify—or discredit—the story.

"He can't be dead," says June. "If he died it would have been in the news-paper."

"Not if he was living under another name," I point out, because I knew he would be. He could die and no one around him would know who he was, he'd be just another person.

Time goes on. I don't know what to do, so do nothing. But something is missing; there's a hole in my life that needs to be filled. I begin writing my memoir.

A constant source of wonderment, it is to me, that somehow when something is needed it gets sent. When I come to write about meeting Claire, it hits me that I've never read Mick's biography on her. I get it from the library and only after finishing it do I turn to the front pages. And the breath is knocked out of me. In the Acknowledgments he thanks Joanne for doing the Index. More amazing than that—something I've never seen before—his address is published in the book.

A quick check on Canada411 and I have Mick on the line. He hasn't been in touch with Joanne for ten years, but tells me where she was living then. Another Canada411 check finds her. The voice on the answering machine is unmistakable but I don't leave a message; I want to connect in person.

The next time, she answers. I'm so excited I don't even say Hello, just start gushing about how delighted I was when I called earlier and heard her voice on the recording, how I recognized it immediately but didn't leave a message because I wanted to get her in person. Taking a breath, finally, I end with "This is a voice from the past, do you recognize it?"

"Bette!" she exclaims.

We talk and talk, and follow up with many long, long conversations, an hour and longer each time. It's cheap now. She and Sean lived together only three years after his parole, and a few years have passed since then, so she has no recent news of Don.

The following summer, 2006, I went to visit her, eighteen years since the last meeting, but real friendships don't die even if they may get off the rails for a time. Through conversation I gleaned some clues on how I might learn what had become of Don. The person I phoned told me he was not only alive, but had never been ill. And he knew how to locate him. It was a relief that caused the urgency to subside. I decided to sit on it.

February 18, 2008

Dear Don,
    You'll be surprised to hear from me after all these years. I'm old now, you know—70 already. Can you believe that? Well, I guess you can because you're not far behind—although 69 *sounds* much younger. ☺
    It's a time of life when one starts to look back, go over things. You were an important part of my life for such a long time I would hate for it to end without seeing you again.
    I'll be going to B.C. in the next few months to visit Belinda—she lives there now—as well as several friends. Could we get together for a coffee or lunch, talk about old times, catch up?
    I hope all is well with you. I'm anxious to hear your news and tell you mine.
    The Persian Garden still hangs on the wall, by the way, and everyone who sees it admires it.

"I want one more look at you."

I'M NERVOUS ON THE WAY THERE, but not nearly as nervous as I thought I would be; it feels inevitable, that I'm being carried the way I'm meant to go. The bus pulls into the terminal and there he is, waiting on the platform, still handsome, white-haired now but looking far younger than his years. Strong, too, in good shape. But then I knew he would be. Pride in appearance has its benefits.

233

In a re-enactment of the very first contact visit at Archambault Penitentiary twenty-nine years earlier, we approach each other at cross-purposes. While I try to play it cool by giving him a mock punch on the sleeve, he greets me with a hug and a kiss. In embarrassment I scramble into position.

"This is crazy! How crazy is this?" is all I could think to say. All the way to the car and even after getting in. "Isn't this the craziest thing you thought you'd never do?" I ask him. *What am I doing here?* Barbra exclaims, only after the door is closed. She knows it's crazy, but there she is. His lack of response leads me to believe maybe *he* doesn't think it's so crazy.

We go to his place, he makes coffee, asks how the kids are, what they're doing, where they're living, and that same old current has transported itself over time and space, that same band of tenderness and understanding, it's there, spanning the table, tugging from both ends. We talk effortlessly and endlessly. I stay three days. Three days of warmth, comfort and sharing—of rightness—of being with that one person in a lifetime to whom you can say anything, who will understand everything, with whom you need have no pretences.

We talk and talk. Walk by the river and talk. Sit in the park and talk. Laugh ourselves silly over game after game of crib. But now he beats me almost every game. I laugh but it's a blow to the ego. Another change is, feeling its negativity is soul-destroying, I've largely given up on following the news, while his interest remains avid. And so two or three times a day he turns on the TV for a few minutes. Then we talk some more. He does all the cooking and, because I have forgotten my rubber gloves, all the cleaning up too. I just sit there like a princess.

Over coffee the second morning, I tell him I have three questions to ask. It's then that I realize something I'd never noticed before—at least not consciously. When he senses something important is about to be said, he quickens, alerts himself to give his one hundred percent.

"It's my perception that when we parted we still loved each other but each had disappointed the other. Is that your perception?"

His eyes fill to the point of overflowing. It's evident that if he attempted to say a word, the dam would break. He nods and lowers his head to hide the tears.

Second question: "I've been trying to remember the last two years we were together, all those charges you kept getting, why we never had more trailer visits, more passes. I can't remember anything specific; it's a big blur. What was that all about?"

He says he doesn't remember either. Like me, he remembers only the good. "All I know is, after my mother died I felt so bad I just gave up, said to hell with everything. I wouldn't let her visit and then it was too late, and there were things I wanted to ask her. I used to get so angry at her, but I loved her."

For the third question I go into a long-winded preamble starting with an apology for the book on him not getting published, my analysis of what was wrong with it, what would have fixed it, the writing I'd done since, the course I'd taken, how I had planned to write my story in the form of essays on different topics but the present idea had seized me, how its pull was so strong I couldn't fight it even though it meant having to leave out so much—the years of living in Thailand and Mexico and all my travel adventures. I go on for a good two or three minutes, culminating with, "So I was wondering if it would be OK to use your name and your story or if you would want me to fictionalize it?"

"It's OK."

"But this is not like the first one, you should understand. That was a story that was public information, anyone had access to it. This is personal. This is your private life. You'll be telling people you loved me."

"It's OK," he repeats. "You should include this part, too."

And so we walk by the river again, sit on the bench and listen to the rushing water, talk and talk some more. Later, in the afternoon, I say, "If I'm overstaying my welcome, if time is getting a bit long, just say so."

"When the propane's gone, when there's no electricity, no water, when the food's all gone. . . ." He leaves it in the air.

"I'll know it's time to leave." And we laugh.

On the third morning he gives me a good-bye gift, several kinds of herbal supplements for my well-being. Then we go to his favourite restaurant for the parting lunch. We enter, are shown to our seats, pick up the menus, and we're real people.

At the bus terminal I tell him to just drop me off, there's no need to wait. Twenty minutes later, the bus arrives, I board, walk down the aisle, am just about to take a seat when—what determines these things? What causes a person to choose the left side as opposed to the right? If I had chosen the other side I wouldn't have seen him. But there he was, standing on the platform, looking up at me with that same sad look, the one I'd seen at so many long-ago partings. I ran back up the aisle, signalled to the driver to hold on a few seconds, jumped off the bus and flew into his arms for a last embrace.

Dear Don,

I could telephone or email but it seems natural to write, given the history. There's something about slipping an envelope into the mailbox, imagining its progress over the next days, wondering where it is, whether or not it has reached its destination, picturing the receiving, the unfolding, the reaction.

Thank you for the card. It arrived yesterday. Such a lovely message—the big BFF on the front (Best Friends Forever is an expression I didn't know, but I've learned already that it's a well-known one), then inside: "I hope you'll be my friend forever because that's how long I'm gonna need you." It's a touching sentiment.

Nothing new here since last we talked. Just wanted to let you know I received the card OK, and thanks again. It's sitting on the bookcase, reminding me we're to be

Friends always.

Bette

"You will never untangle the circumstances
that brought you to this moment."
- Krishna in the Bhagavad Gita

Donald William McLaren Kelly

May 14, 1938 – October 17, 2009